Etta Lemon

To Nick, Daniel and Dora

Etta Lemon

The Woman Who Saved the Birds

Tessa Boase

Aurum

First published in 2018 as *Mrs Pankhurst's Purple Feather* by Aurum Press
an imprint of The Quarto Group
The Old Brewery, 6 Blundell Street
London N7 9BH
United Kingdom

This paperback edition first published in 2021 by Aurum Press

www.QuartoKnows.com

A catalogue record for this book is available from the British Library.

ISBN 978 0 7112 6338 3
Ebook ISBN 978 1 78131 814 0

1 3 5 7 9 10 8 6 4 2
2022 2024 2025 2023 2021

Typeset in ITC Giovanni Std by SX Composing DTP, Rayleigh, Essex

Printed by CPI Group (UK) Ltd; Croydon, CR0 4YY

Contents

PROLOGUE

'One baby is a patient baby, and waits indefinitely until its mother is ready to feed it. The other baby is an impatient baby and cries lustily, screams and kicks and makes everybody unpleasant until it is fed. Well, we know perfectly well which baby is attended to first. That is the whole history of politics . . . You have to make more noise than anybody else, you have to make yourself more obtrusive than anybody else, you have to fill all the papers more than anybody else – in fact you have to be there all the time and see that they do not snow you under.'

– EMMELINE PANKHURST, 'FREEDOM OR DEATH' SPEECH,
13 NOVEMBER 1913

Prologue

In a glass cabinet at the Museum of London, in the heart of the City, lies a single, purple ostrich feather. It is not a particularly large feather, just twelve inches long, but it is full and heavily luxurious, its tip plump and lolling, its fronds still faintly curled. The colour has faded over time to a subtle shade of blackberry fool, yet it still looks ready to be plucked up and pinned to a lavish hat.

Next to the feather, also in the cabinet, is a dainty, ornately beaded shoe of black kid leather; a shoe so small that you wonder whether women really were more fragile creatures back then. It is a shoe for a dance, not a political rally. But women did things differently in 1909.

Its wearer was borne away from a fracas outside the House of Commons between two burly policemen, her decorous little feet kicking – a 50-year-old firebrand carried like a naughty child. Emmeline Pankhurst was less than five feet tall, her shoe size three-and-a-half. The feather stayed attached to the hat that was pinned to her hair, but one shoe came loose in the struggle and was seized by the police as a trophy. How they must have laughed at the Metropolitan police station that night. Cinderella's slipper! Straight from the foot of the notorious leader of the suffragettes – 'that dreadful woman', as she was commonly known.

When Mrs Pankhurst died in 1928 – the year the Equal Franchise Act was finally made law – her purple feather was saved from her lodgings and preserved by the Suffragette Fellowship. And so started an industry in (often fake, but always well-intentioned) suffragette memorabilia. The feather seemed, to these old militants, the embodiment of their revered leader. It was a potent symbol of all things Pankhurst: her essential femininity, her persistence in the face of brutality and hostility, and her political colours. As every member of the Women's Social and Political Union (WSPU) once knew, white stood for purity, green for hope and purple for dignity.

It was offered to the Museum of London in 1950 as a talismanic object, a holy relic of sorts: for Mrs Pankhurst was never without her plumage. The elaborately feathered hat was an indispensable part of her brand: a way of showing the world that she was no unnatural, mannish harridan intent on a 'petticoat government'. Yet she was also steely, autocratic and dictatorial. She liked a good fight. Like a strutting cock's extravagant tail, Emmeline Pankhurst's plumage signified power.

There is another feather – or rather collection of feathers – kept in a box at the headquarters of Britain's biggest conservation charity. They tell a different, yet equally symbolic story. These feathers are not for public display. If you make an appointment to view the archives of the Royal Society for the Protection of Birds (RSPB), and if you are lucky enough to gain entrance, this box might (or might not) be brought out to you by the librarian. The records are hard to access, stored in the attics of a Victorian lodge in Bedfordshire woodland. Hardly anybody makes such a request – and why would they? Few have heard of the extraordinary origins of the RSPB, although we're all familiar with the modern institution that it has become, the British acronym that needs no explanation. The RSPB is a behemoth – a charity with over 1.1 million members, 224 nature reserves spread over 160,000 hectares, 2,000 staff and some 12,000 volunteers. It has an annual income of over £140 million and it wields great political power. Its business today is international nature conservation, whether peregrine falcons, pygmy fruit bats or Sumatran rhinos. But its leading figures tend to be bird lovers – and the majority of these have, historically, been men. In Britain, birds tend to belong, instinctively it seems, to the boys.

It was not always so. The RSPB was founded by *women* – women with an unusually singular purpose. They were going to stamp out the fashion for feathers in hats. For half a century, from the 1870s to the 1920s, wild bird species were systematically slaughtered around the world for the millinery trade in one of the most lucrative commodity markets on earth. At its peak, the trade was worth a staggering £20 million a year to Britain – around £204 million in today's money. In 1891, as the insatiable fashion for feathers stepped up yet another gear, two exclusively women's groups – one in Croydon, one in Manchester – banded together to save the birds. They gave themselves an ambitious title – the Society for the Protection of Birds – and their determination was rewarded with a Royal Charter in 1904. As the RSPB grew in scale and stature, so the men involved attempted to take charge.

The women at its helm came largely from the upper echelons of society, but their campaign against the plumage trade would bring them into unprecedented conflict with those from the lower classes. Thousands of invisible working women were caught up within this industry's coils: feather washers, feather dressers, fancy feather workers, willowers, milliners and shop girls. A fight against the plumage trade meant, too, a fight against other, more vulnerable women. In blowing the whistle on 'murderous millinery', the RSPB would also be pitting themselves against women – sister against sister.

Lift the lid on that box at headquarters, and you will find the original essence of the RSPB. Inside are half a dozen millinery trade feathers, much like Mrs Pankhurst's – dyed, dressed and mounted on wire, each a highly worked hat ornament, all redolent of a particular time and place. Open this box, and you are transported back to the streets and drawing rooms of Victorian and Edwardian society, where every woman of every class wore a hat. In the early years of the twentieth century, when an ounce of feathers from the American snowy egret was worth twice as much as an ounce of gold, the female foot soldiers of the RSPB turned detective. They scoured the great department stores and millinery shops of Britain, cross-examining other women – milliners and saleswomen who swore blind that their hat trimmings were artificial, not made from wild bird skins – that they were manufactured from horsehair, or grass, or dyed cock's feathers. The feathers in this box comprise hard evidence, gathered in stealth and examined by experts. They are the authenticated proof of a despicable trade. The box was labelled 'contraband' and it symbolised animal cruelty. Today, each feather represents a protected species. You would no sooner wear the exquisitely soft down of a great crested grebe on your head, the tuft from a snowy egret or the cascading rust-red tail of a Raggiana bird-of-paradise, than you would a fox or a white weasel around your neck, with dangling nose and paws. How have our sensibilities been changed so completely?

One remarkable woman led the anti-plumage campaign of the RSPB – and she did so quietly and heroically for half a century, leading it to eventual victory. She campaigned so doggedly, and for so long, against what she called 'murderous millinery' that she became known as 'Mother of the Birds'. Her struggle to get the world to care about birds met with as much derision, contempt and indifference as Emmeline Pankhurst's fight for the vote. The millinery and the plumage trade demonised her as a 'frothy fanatic', a 'feather faddist'. Right up until the First World War, the idea of bird protection was as laughable to the general population as the concept of female emancipation.

She stuck to her convictions though, and she won her fight. The law was changed, plumage imports were banned and the strange female fashion for 'avian adornment' receded into the unimaginable past. Unlike Mrs Pankhurst, she is today a forgotten figure – even within the RSPB. When I began my research there was not a plaque, not a portrait at headquarters, not a mention in the canon of those women who helped shape the twentieth century. It was as if she had been completely erased from the conservation narrative. Yet she has proved, in her way, to be as deeply influential to the modern psyche as her contemporary, Mrs Pankhurst.

Her name is Etta Lemon.

At the heart of this book are two difficult, driven, heroic and compassionate women of vastly differing ambitions, personalities and methods. While Mrs Pankhurst saw herself as the saviour of women (even if few women, back then, knew they wanted saving), Mrs Lemon was the avenging angel of the birds. They were born just two years apart, but the story of Etta Lemon unfolds in these pages first. Unlike Emmeline Pankhurst, Etta did not have children and she gathered momentum earlier. The Society for the Protection of Birds preceded the suffragettes by some 12 years.

When Mrs Pankhurst hit her dazzling, dictatorial stride in the years leading up to the First World War, the two campaigns ran side by side, snapping at each others' heels. Their leaders fought over methods and members, the conservative RSPB learning to imitate the shock tactics of the suffragettes, and they ultimately found themselves in diametrically opposing camps. Their convictions clashed.

Emmeline Pankhurst transformed her weakness for fashion into a type of political armour. She exhorted her militant suffragettes to use their style to further the cause – to be the most elegant ladies in the public sphere. Pictures of suffrage rallies show hundreds of magnificently hatted, white-dressed women moving as one. Look closer, though, and a forest of pointed birds' wings and feathers is visible, sprouting and swaying above the throng. To Mrs Pankhurst, 'Votes for Women' was the only cause worth fighting for. To Mrs Lemon, this was an appalling travesty, in every sense. Etta was anti-fashion, anti-feminist – and vehemently anti-suffrage.

How and why could two such passionate women, entering the political sphere at the same moment in history, be so opposed in their aims and values? Why would Mrs Lemon's boundless compassion not include sympathy for women's rights? And why would campaigning for the vote make Mrs Pankhurst dismiss animal rights as a side distraction? Each story sheds a troubling light on the other, while each campaign illuminates the other, in unexpected ways.

Before we get to the storming of Parliament in that triumphant purple feather, we will go on a much wider journey. A series of invisible women will step out of the shadows and show us their worlds. Feather workers, factory girls, milliners, shop girls – all are women who stand to gain in the fight for equal rights. We will track the fashionable plumed hat and those who wear it – in the glittering opera house and the raucous music hall, the stately home and the slum.

In the eyes of Mrs Lemon and her Society for the Protection of Birds, Mrs Pankhurst's purple feather did *not*, in fact, represent murderous millinery. This was an ostrich plume, clipped in the Cape Colony from farmed birds: a highly lucrative trade worth, at its pre-1914 peak, £2.6 million a year to Britain's economy. But the ostrich plume had its particular commodity chain, which inflicted cruelty in subtle and ingenious ways – predominantly on women.

At the start of its journey, Mrs Pankhurst's feather was shipped in a large consignment of 'raw' plumage from the southernmost tip of Africa, north through the Suez Canal to the Port of London. Here it passed from the stevedores to the sorting room and then to the auction houses of Mincing Lane. Once under the hammer, the feather was sent to be unpacked, washed, dyed a deep purple, beaten and then trimmed in a series of fetid outhouses and backyards in the City of London.

Its gorgeous fronds were thick and long, as was the fashion. But look closer and you might see tiny knots, the fronds lengthened by small fingers – ostrich 'willowers', aged as young as five, working from home for a penny a day. Then the feather was curled; most likely by an apprentice curler aged 13, earning two shillings a week. Once 'finished', it was wrapped with mercury salts in bleached tissue paper – chemicals that lingered in the lungs of the women who produced them. The plume then passed to a millinery warehouse, where it was bought by a milliner.

Now it was wrestled onto a wire and cambric base and stitched into place, the milliner's toughened forefinger pushing and pulling the needle in and out of the velvet bandeau. And so the purple feather, now adorning a hat, made its way to a shop – perhaps one of the new department stores. Here it fell under the keen eye of Mrs Pankhurst on one of her shopping dashes down Regent Street. The colour was perfect, of course.

Serving her were two shop girls – no chair to rest on, no lunch break; sleeping in a dormitory above the store and scraping a living. One girl wrapped the hat in more bleached tissue. The other packed it in a box – made by a homeworker in Bermondsey, a woman who glued together two dozen a day for tuppence.

So while Mrs Pankhurst's feather might not be, on the face of it, 'murderous millinery', it still held in its fronds an invisible world of ruthless male commerce and exploited female labour. Mrs Pankhurst wore it as a political statement. It was how she nailed her colours to the mast. But it was also, ironically, an emblem of female abuse.

Part 1

Feathers

1

Alice Battershall

1885

On a September morning in 1885, a young woman and her mother stood in the Guildhall dock, close by St Paul's Cathedral. Alice Battershall, 23, was charged with stealing two ostrich feathers. She had concealed them about her body while working for Abraham Botibol, a prominent feather manufacturer operating from Carthusian Street, an alley just off Aldersgate Street in the City of London. The women were propelled into the ornate Justice Room by Police Constable Wackett, a 27-year-old former butcher, specialist in larceny and plain-clothes investigator. Wackett had reason, today, to feel satisfied.

It was a busy morning at the Guildhall – the busiest for some weeks. Ostler's horses waited patiently in the square outside, shadowed by St Lawrence Jewry. The late morning sun fell in a needling beam straight up King Street, touching the Guildhall's grand gothic entrance. Inside, a stream of petty criminals came, one by one, before Alderman Phineas Cowan. Their offences ranged from 'indecent pictures on matchboxes' to 'bad meat'; from a five-year-old boy found begging, to cruelty to horses. Few women came before him. Fines of ten or five shillings were the normal punishment.

The theft of ostrich feathers was a more interesting case. The ears of the *Morning Post*'s reporter pricked up as Mr Cowan asked some searching questions. Alice Battershall confessed that she had been 'put up to the theft' by her mother, Emma Battershall, 44, who in turn had passed the items on to wardrobe dealer Sarah Greenhalgh, who lived just ten doors away in Finsbury. To Mr Botibol, the feathers were worth seven shillings apiece; but Mrs Greenhalgh knew desperation when she saw it, and her fixed price for Mrs Battershall was one shilling per plume. She had, she said, bought three ostrich feathers off Emma Battershall during the past fortnight, and probably 20 more off her 'at various times'. PC Wackett had, it appeared, stumbled upon a female fencing ring.

This was not the first time such a case had come before the Court of Common Council, the City of London's adjudication system for petty crime. Mr Botibol was a regular in the Guildhall Justice Room. He had, he pointed out, lost 'a large number' of plumes recently. Yet he was also known in the courts as a hard-nosed man of commerce – a London-born, middle-aged Sephardi Jew with heavy interests in the trade and prone to exploit his largely female workforce.

On this September morning, Alderman Cowan weighed the evidence, taking into account Alice Battershall's punitively low and irregular wages of five shillings a week, and the fact that the sudden 'feather slump' of 1885 had further squeezed her earnings. Fashion was a fickle creature, and despite promises of 'Constant Employment for Ostrich and Fancy Feather Hands (Good)', Botibol's workers were laid on and off as required, making this a highly precarious living. But a crime was a crime. The magistrate pronounced that since the elder woman had 'led her daughter into this matter', she would be sentenced to six weeks' hard labour in prison. Alice was condemned to three weeks. This was an unusually harsh sentence by Guildhall standards, where punishment by hard labour typically amounted to three days. One might even suspect Botibol and Cowan of a conspiracy.

Alice Battershall was a feather washer – an unsavoury, unskilled job, and a lowly link in a now vanished trade. If you look under the letter 'F' in the *Post Office Directory* for 1885 you will find them, clustered around the City and the East End in a litany of occupations entirely lost to us today. There, among the flageolet makers, flannel factors and flag makers, the fender and fire iron makers, fibre dressers and fire bucket makers, are the highly specialised artisans of the feather trade. Here are Alice and her cohorts – feather washers, purifiers, dyers, beaters, curlers, willowers and shapers. Mrs Pankhurst's plume would have passed through every one of these stages before it reached the milliner's shop. This was a commodity with its own language and hierarchies; its gradations of skilled and unskilled, men's and women's work, particular health hazards, rates of pay, slack seasons and a known network of mostly Jewish employers between which the workers passed, were dropped and picked up again. Plumage was a legitimate Victorian trade, just like the fur, leather or taxidermy trade. It was an all-encompassing world.

Two thousand 'feather hands' were employed by London's plumage industry in the 1880s; thousands more worked in the *plumassiers* of Paris and the 'feather foundries' of New York. Alice's fingers picked over and prepared feathers that would end up on the heads of princesses and courtesans, of suffragists and debutantes, music-hall singers and parlour-maids. She was invisible then and she's invisible today. We don't have an image – just a two-inch newspaper cutting on her crime, headlined 'Police Intelligence'. Yet we can imagine her standing there in the Guildhall dock, in a squashed straw bonnet with a defiant straggle of plumage, her skirts long and full, her corset tight and her grubby bodice buttoned high at the neck.

Alice's symbolic role, in this tale, is to stand in for all the 'feather hands' employed by men like Botibol in London's lucrative plumage trade. Alice can be found washing and curling ostrich plumes in every census return – from her teens, right up to her death, in 1921. By then, her daughter, Louisa, was working in the trade alongside her.

Alice Battershall represents the hidden link between the plumage hunter and the millinery counter. She links the impoverished slums of the East End with the high glamour of courtly circles. She is not, nor ever likely to be, politically active – she is just getting by – but Alice and her exploited co-workers are a spur to those women who fought for the vote and for equal rights. She stands to gain in this story arc.

Yet she also stands to lose. The industry Alice depends on to stay afloat is the focus for Mrs Lemon's imminent bird protection agitation. She is a mute symbol of the vilified, 'repulsive' plumage trade. If Mrs Lemon wins her battle to halt the millinery juggernaut and ban the importation of feathers, Alice Battershall, and those like her, stand to lose everything.

The theft of a feather seems, today, an absurdly petty crime. But behind that swift, stealthy and almost erotic action of Alice Battershall's – her fingers pushing the plumes softly up each leg-of-mutton sleeve of her tightly buttoned jacket – lay a complex value system, the meaning of which is now entirely lost to us. These were not just feathers to the Battershall women, nor to manufacturer Mr Botibol.

Most obviously, they represented hard cash – instant cash, in the case of Alice and her mother. Botibol dealt in more abstract realities. He wasn't attached to the two feathers *per se* – it was what they represented that mattered. These ostrich feathers had come into his apprentice's hands via a highly sophisticated mercantile web serving a global fashion industry. Each stolen feather had its own intricate backstory of hunter or ostrich farmer; Jewish agents in sun-baked ports of the British Empire; bare-backed stevedores loading and unloading the holds of cargo ships with names like *Bookhara*, *Arab* and *Trojan*, ships which ended their long journeys at the Victoria and Albert Docks in East London. In 1885, Britain's imperial capital was the world's modern feather bourse. Monthly, Abraham Botibol walked a curving route to the Cutler Street and Billiter Street feather warehouses from his premises off Aldersgate Street. Nobody outside the trade was allowed in these many-floored brick buildings. Identity was checked at the door; warehouse attendants shadowed each visitor. This was a masculine environment with a highly sensual, luxury booty. Each floor, each high-ceilinged room contained unimaginable quantities of quills, exotic bird skins and plumes, laid out in their raw state for inspection. At busy times, it was said that dealers 'nearly suffocated under their wares'. The millinery trade moved from 'fancy feathers' (the plumage of wild birds) to ostrich plumes, to artificial flowers and back again, as the fashions and seasons changed.

Botibol dealt mostly in ostrich plumes: for court, ladies' fans, funerals, hats and the stage. There were plumes for every tier and wallet of society – from the most luxurious, full-bodied 'White Prime', to a diminutive ostrich 'tip'. Every woman aspired to own one. Whatever your outlay, a plume would retain its value as an investment, as well as an adornment, kept wrapped in tissue in a box, cleaned and re-curled once a year, then passed down to your daughter. Working girls saved up and clubbed together for a plume, taking it in turns to wear it on their best hat.

In the early years of the trade, each feather had come from a wild bird, hunted down and killed in the Sahara Desert. But since 'the Eclipse' egg incubator had been patented in 1864, ostrich farming in the arid Western Cape of southernmost Africa had taken off. Birds could now be raised in their hundreds and clipped or plucked every eight or so months, flooding the western market with so many plumes that it was hard to imagine there were enough heads left among women to wear them.

The Billiter Street feather warehouse was stacked with luxurious, soft bundles, freshly unpacked from their wooden cases and tissue paper wrappings. The preserving naphthalene crystals had been shaken out; the plumes measured, weighed and laid out in 'lines' according to quality and provenance, each lot separated by chalked wooden boards. There were 14 varieties of ostrich plume on sale, and countless grades within them depending on where from the bird they had been clipped – Whites (the most luxurious), were followed by Feminas, Byocks, Spadones, Boos, Blacks, Drabs and Floss. They ranged in colour from creamy white to jet-black; from the full-blown and palmy to the stunted and bedraggled. Buyers had two days in which to inspect stock before a sale. Carefully, Abraham Botibol would pick up each feather by its stalky quill and balance it in his hands. One needed, so they said in the trade, an 'ineffable feel for feathers'. What profit could be turned on each bundle? What were the cost margins? What might he stand to gain? Or – if the whimsical fashion market changed its mind – what might he lose?

As demand for 'plumiferous' fashion accessories soared from the 1870s onwards, importers, brokers, auctioneers, wholesalers and feather handlers grew by the hundred. Most were concentrated around one tight area in the City of London, bordered by Aldersgate, London Wall, Bishopsgate and Old Street. Auctions had increased from quarterly to bimonthly and now were held monthly (soon to become fortnightly). Botibol attended them all. He was buying for both British and the foreign markets. Some 80 per cent of what he routinely bid for would be exported 'in the rough' to Paris, Vienna, Berlin and New York, where it would be processed by female labour into the fancy decorations required by milliners on both sides of the Atlantic.

And so Alice Battershall's two feathers came under the hammer, a trivial part of a highly critical whole – a luxury commodity shipped in tonnes, packed in cases, bid for in bundles and weighed in pounds. Once delivered in crates by horse and wagon, the feathers would then be shuttled through a cascade of treatments by Abraham Botibol's workhands. They would be strung, dyed, washed, dyed again, dried, thrashed, trimmed, finished, parried, willowed, fashioned and curled. He might sell a single item to a millinery wholesale warehouse for seven shillings, or direct to a customer for 30 shillings. Once affixed to a ladies' hat by a milliner and displayed in a Bond Street shop window, its value could be anything up to £5 (£500 in today's money). On the black market, though, as those plumes passed from the Battershall women to wardrobe dealer Sarah Greenhalgh, their value was just one shilling.

Baldly, feathers represented cash.

2

Inspector Lakeman

1887

One shilling was actually a good return for a plume on the black market. A trawl through the newspapers of the 1880s reveals that the warren of courts and alleys between Clerkenwell and Whitechapel were thick with stolen feathers. Stuffed behind lockers, down corsets, under attic floors – feathers were secreted here and there in a nefarious trade operating brazenly alongside the manufacturers.

In 1886, Abraham Botibol was back in the courts again in pursuit of another worker, 49-year-old Mary Anne Baker. The woman was accused of having stolen five shillings-worth of ostrich feathers, subsequently discovered in her lodgings. She argued that she'd been given them in lieu of pay, which wasn't such an implausible defence since the industry was in one of its periodic slumps. During a downturn it was easier to pay workers with feathers rather than with hard cash. But Mary Anne Baker wasn't believed. She was sentenced to 21 days' hard labour: the same punishment as Alice Battershall. She had stolen to stay afloat.

There were no unions for those working in the feather trade. This was a below-the-radar world, almost invisible to the public eye, its nimble-fingered female workers acutely vulnerable to exploitation. Not *quite* invisible, though. The Victorian government's Factory and Workshop Inspectors were remarkably thorough, writing detailed, surprisingly nuanced reports. Inspectors Mr Lakeman, Major Beadon, Mr Blenkinsopp, Mr Knyvett and

Mr Henderson combed the streets of industrial Britain, making spot visits to working premises. They were looking for employer abuses.

Since the Factory and Workshop Act had been updated in 1878 to include all trades, the working day had, in theory, improved for Britain's workforce. These inspectors were searching for evidence of overcrowding, poor ventilation, inadequate safety and, in particular, overworking. The Act now stated that women were to work no more than 56 hours a week – a rule that had backfired, as it prompted women to take extra home for piecework wages. This meant you were paid by the piece, be it stitched buttonholes, boned corsets or curled ostrich feathers.

Mr Lakeman's responsibility was for the small workshops of the Central Metropolitan District, London. Unlike the textile factories of the industrial north, this was a shadowy, impenetrable world. These were rooms over stables, attics up decrepit stairs, back chambers containing dozens of slop-work tailors, umbrella pointers, glove makers and shoe heelers. Mr Lakeman despaired for central London's exploited workforce: 'poor people . . . hard working, struggling to maintain themselves and passively submitting to the exigencies of a hard lot.'

With his naphtha lamp, he walked the alleys, the courts and cul-de-sacs, combing through the capital's extraordinarily diverse artisan workforce, skilled and unskilled. 'Artificial Flowers, Artificial Leaves, Artificial Teeth,' begins this list of industries in Lakeman's annual report for 1887, '. . . Hats, Helmets, Harmoniums. Labels, Lime Juice, Lapidaries.' He peered into the workrooms which filled the backstreets of Shoreditch, Spitalfields and Whitechapel – businesses taking up one or more rooms in 'dirty, decaying and dilapidated houses.'

Out of seeming chaos and squalor, Lakeman began to spot patterns and clans. These workers weren't an amorphous mass: they had their own rituals, manners and guises. They were deeply tribal. Take the box-maker girls. 'Heavy fancy boxes' – hatboxes, for example – commanded good wages with no slack time. Earnings were around 17 to 21 shillings a week. 'The work is rough and dirty, and so are the workers', daubed as they were in animal-based glue. Small fancy box makers (for gloves, jewellery, fob watches) earned 12 shillings a week. 'The peculiarity of these girls is loud laughing and singing, jesting, a penchant for sham jewellery, silk handkerchiefs around their shoulders and ostrich-feathered hats; festered ears are not uncommon, caused by the corrosion from brass earrings.'

Further down the economic food chain, the inspector counted at least 2,500 girls making artificial flowers for hat and costume trimmings – the low season standby for those in the feather trade. 'No industry is in more fluctuation,' he noted, 'for fashion alternates between flowers, birds, feathers and velvets.' Hat fashions on the high street had an entirely different nuance when viewed through his enlightened eyes. 'It is a mystery how they live, and especially has it been so for this year, as no feathers have been worn, the fashion having given a turn to birds, wings of sea gulls, and velvets.'

He found 'little girls' of 12 and 13 working for nothing while they learned the trade, graduating then to wages of two shillings and six pence a week for the first year. He found that the full wage for artificial flower makers (older women, usually with many children to support) was not more than 12 shillings. A 'poor' household at this time was defined as a 'moderate'-sized family with five or six children living off 18 to 21 shillings a week. He noted few signs of respectability among the artificial flower makers, such as you found among seamstresses or milliners.

'Evidences of home neglect are to be seen,' Mr Lakeman recorded. 'Girls come in at 9 and 9.30 without a breakfast, they lie in bed up to the last moment. They are untidy, even slatternly, and in their food taking they do not exhibit advanced evidences of civilisation.' There was far worse than bad table manners, however. 'When slack times come these girls feel the pinch severely, for parents are labourers who can hardly provide for themselves. I am unwilling to narrate what I am told is done during periods of depression.'

The spectre of prostitution haunted those Victorian inspectors as they made their rounds. Girl after girl on starvation wages, scraping along on precarious seasonal work. How were the Alice Battershalls of Victorian

London expected to get through the year? Two thousand women might be employed in the ostrich feather trade, but only during the months of February to June and August to November. This left three months a year with no wages. Like Alice, they were left to fend for themselves.

The lust for modern plume wearing had pushed prices down, and workers' wages even more so. 'An ostrich feather is now within the reach of all who fancy such pretty decorations,' wrote Lakeman, 'therefore we have extensive workshops fitted up with every convenience where hundreds of little ones are busy at work.'

Lakeman appeared regularly in the Guildhall Court of Law, prosecuting opportunistic feather manufacturers for a multitude of abuses. If it was hard to nail them on poor wages, working environment, sanitary arrangements or overtime, there was one area where he had considerable success. The new Factory and Workshop Act had made it an offence to employ a child under ten years of age full-time. Since the Elementary Education Act of 1880, children between five and ten had to be in school, full-time. Those aged ten to 14 could be employed, but only on alternate or half days.

In 1883, a Mrs Bird, feather manufacturer of Fore Street, was forced before the magistrates for keeping child labourers away from school. Mr Lakeman had stumbled upon Minnie Mumford, a 13-year-old kept in a 'close room, not of the cleanliest' for up to 11-hour shifts, on three shillings a week. This had been going on for six months. Mrs Bird argued she was teaching her apprentice the business: 'She did not know she was doing wrong.' But it wasn't the hours, the pay or the filthy conditions that enabled Mr Lakeman to take this case to court – it was the fact that Minnie was not attending school. He was able also to prosecute Bird for not possessing a weekly school attendance certificate.

Alice Battershall and her sister workers were invisible to the eye of the consumer in the milliner's shop. Yet they represented the more visible face of the feather industry: women employed in workshops and small factories, protected (up to a point) by the new Victorian legislation.

Even poor Minnie, shut in her airless room in Fore Street for 11 hours a day, was found by Mr Lakeman's government-issue lamp. There was another side to the feather trade beyond Mr Lakeman's jurisdiction, though: the invisible labour taking place in domestic workshops. These were the homeworkers, the vast Victorian workforce engaged in 'sweated labour', doing repetitive tasks to earn extra shillings. In cramped private homes, around kitchen tables, feathers were painstakingly 'finished' and curled by female hands. Although Lakeman could take note, he was powerless to help.

To discover this twilight world, you had to press beyond the respectable thoroughfares of commerce. Here, in the courts and alleys of the East End, in 'rotten and reeking tenements', were the fur pullers, the makers of goatskin boas, the matchbox assembly lines and envelope cutters. Here, in the residential streets that fanned out from the ostrich manufacturers' realm, you would find women and daughters in ones, twos and threes, hard at work on ostrich plumes.

When ostrich feathers enjoyed a brief resurgence in 1935, Abraham Botibol's son, Cecil, hunted down all those female workers he had mothballed in the late 1920s – 'finishers' who had lost their living in the post-war plumage crash. 'It just took them about two weeks to brush up,' he told a reporter, 'and then they were as good as ever. It isn't so much a matter of practice, this ostrich feather work; it's almost instinct. Some people never learn to do it, but those that do love the work. It is almost a hobby with them, like knitting or crocheting.'

There they sit, the feather finishers, in small domestic rooms, the air thick with dust and down. First they pare the quills back with a sharpened piece of glass to make them pliable for shaping. Then they 'fortify' the quills with wire before sewing them together – up to seven plumes at a time – to give the appearance of a single, gorgeously full feather such as Mrs Pankhurst's. This is known in the trade as 'laying up'.

Next they curl the feathers with a knife, scraping delicately down each frond just as you might curl ribbon with scissors. 'A lightness of touch' was thought necessary to be an ostrich curler; a 'gentleness in drawing the knife over the feather particles one by one to produce the curl'. Just one broken fibre would 'damage the whole'. This was considered the most skilled craft of all among ostrich hands, a craft requiring a surprising three-year apprenticeship. More often than not, the feather manufacturer got his plumes curled by trainee girls of 13 on two shillings a week, rising to four shillings by their third year.

The government inspector noted in his reports that these women's noses were running, their eyes sore and that racking bouts of coughing would cause them to break off from their work. Pulmonary tuberculosis was a slow and steady killer of women in the feather trade – but how beautiful was the finished article, sent back to the manufacturer in a long twist of tissue paper.

Children also played their part. 'Willowing' an ostrich feather meant lengthening it by tying extensions onto every single flue – one, two, or even three extensions, until the feather had that bouncing, full, airy head that would set a hat off so gracefully. Tiny fingers were good at this job. An inspector for the New York Board of Health calculated that one woman and two children might labour for 'a day-and-a-third' on a single ostrich plume – whose preparation required as many as 8,613 knots – just to lengthen it throughout by one inch. In 1910, this earned them three cents, jointly: around £15 in modern money.

The feather workers were a very particular tribe, one which Lakeman struggled to penetrate or understand. There was 'a don't-care style about them, loud laughing, singing music-hall songs when at work. Their dinner consists of weak tea, bread and pickles.' Pity, then, the government inspector in his bowler hat and tailored greatcoat, leather satchel in hand, picking his fastidious way into this overwhelmingly foreign, female world. 'If you speak to them you are laughed at,' he complained, 'question them and you are intruding, follow them out when work is over and they exhibit a freedom not bounded by restraint.'

Lakeman trailed these girls home at a discreet distance: 'They dwell in courts and alleys, their surroundings are evil, their aims only daily existence, their desires promiscuously low.' To his mind, every element was connected – the desire for cheap clothing, the unfeasibly low wages, the lack of moral compass.

The inspector's reports take us some way into Alice Battershall's world, but she and her workers remain a statistic – a generalised mass of jeering girls, eating tea and pickles, belting out music-hall songs. We know the physical circumstances of their work, their pay packets, their apparel. But who were they? Where did they spring from? What were their particular circumstances that might have led to the theft of a feather? Did the idea of women's rights, or even animal rights, have any purchase in their lives?

To penetrate Alice Battershall's world further, to put a face to the faceless, we must travel into the slum.

3

97 Lever Street

I found Alice's home using the online census records; fortunately, she had an unusual surname. She and ten other Battershalls lived in the ward of St Luke's, Finsbury, at 97 Lever Street. I had an address and I also had a guide: the 'Descriptive Map of London Poverty', compiled in 1889 to accompany the philanthropist Charles Booth's *Life and Labour of the People in London*. This colour-coded map, which showed, house by house, the city's great spectrum of rich and poor, would take me from Abraham Botibol's premises on Carthusian Street right up to Alice's front door on Lever Street. What would I find? How bad would it be? In 1885, the *Pall Mall Gazette* had published a sensational survey claiming that one in four Londoners lived in abject poverty. Did this statistic include feather thief Alice Battershall?

This is a book about women and activism – but it is also about the slum. The slums of London's East End not only fed the plumage industry with female labour, they honed the social conscience of a generation of middle-class women. Those female 'slummers' of the 1880s and 1890s, early amateur social workers, were the women who were to shape life in the twentieth century. Every character in these pages who championed human or animal rights, who fought for the vote (or even opposed it) in the years leading up to the First World War, cut her teeth in the slum. Mrs Pankhurst and Mrs Lemon, meddlesome female members of the workhouse Boards of Guardians in Manchester and Redhill, had intimate experience of the slum. It was the middle-class activist's training ground.

In 1886, a wealthy English shipping businessman called Charles Booth set out to scientifically dissect the working classes – their streets, their homes and workplaces – fully intending to prove that London's poverty wasn't as bad as supposed. His ambitious project was to counterbalance the fashion for sensational slum literature with hard facts. With a team of volunteers, he wanted to coolly, dispassionately record the reality. Seventeen years and seventeen volumes later, he had to conclude that it was actually worse than originally thought.

'Each district has its character – its peculiar flavour,' he wrote. 'One seems to be conscious of it in the streets. It may be in the faces of the people, or in what they carry . . . or it may lie in the sounds one hears, or in the character of the buildings.'

I wanted to enter Alice Battershall's neighbourhood not as a sensation-seeking slum traveller, but as she herself might have done – a feather washer walking home at the end of a 10-hour day, some 130 years ago. In mapping London's poverty, Booth divided the metropolis up into 12 districts – from Hammersmith in the west, to Greenwich in the east; Hampstead in the north to Clapham in the south. Alice lived in 'District V, East Central', a 15-minute walk north from Abraham Botibol's premises, in the ward of St Luke's – between the notorious slum areas of Clerkenwell to the west and Cripplegate to the south. She lived on the borders of the land of commerce and commodity: alongside the feather dealers, furriers, leather makers and India rubber dealers of Aldersgate and City Road. St Luke's was renowned as a 'rookery' – a zone of criminality, perfectly positioned on the edge of the City.

The colour code to the 'Descriptive Map of London Poverty' runs from red to blue: the darker on the spectrum, the more intense the social deprivation. West London is rosy-hued (pale pink and red being used to signify the middle classes), while the east is the colour of gathering thunderclouds. Light and dark blue mark out the working classes and chronically impoverished. Black is for the dens of vice: 'loafers, criminals and semi criminals' living 'the life of savages', according to the map's key; people 'whose only luxury' is drink.

There is no black on Lever Street. The street was classed as purple: people who had 'a hard struggle to make ends meet', wrote Booth, 'but they are, as a body, decent steady men, paying their way and bringing up their children respectably'. But looking closely, one can see that behind the respectable facade of Lever Street the destitute were crammed into courts and back alleys. Here were knots of dark blue: desperate folk who might work three days a week if lucky. Here, too, were strips of pale blue: labourers, poorer artisans and street sellers, vulnerable to depressions in trade and victims of competition. At the far end of Alice's street, on Shepherdess Walk, stood the red-brick St Luke's Workhouse – a physical reminder of the pressing need to work, and the certain horrors of an impoverished old age.

Using the *Post Office Directory* for London in 1885, we can follow Alice home past Lever Street's parade of shops: cheesemonger Alfred Cole, surgeon James Hutton, looking-glass maker Edward Jacobs, hairdresser Frederick Green. Her neighbours were Zephaniah Budd's chandler's shop (a grocery) and Henry Luckett, umbrella maker. Opposite the Battershall's house was 'Slopers', a coffee shop where thieves were allowed food on credit (according to the local policeman who accompanied Booth's researcher) and paid the owner 'either in money or in kind'.

The astonishing number of trades plied on just one road conjures a sense of highly motivated industry, and of the minute grades of expertise available among London's poorly paid, politically unrepresented, artisanal workforce – from 'secret springer' to watch glass maker, 'hair worker' to truss maker. Each house also contained workers who did not show up in the *Post Office Directory*: mothers and daughters engaged in 'home work' or sweated labour.

Behind closed front doors, around kitchen tables, buttons were being sewn onto waistcoats; hatboxes glued by the dozen; corsets hand-stitched and ostrich feathers curled. The 1881 census shows 11 women on Lever Street working for the millinery industry as artificial flower makers, hat trimmers and feather curlers. By the 1891 census – mirroring the growing fashion for larger, more heavily decorated hats – 25 women were working on Lever Street in feathers and artificial flowers. Their names evoke a distant era: Lizzy Spitter, Nellie MacNamara, Minnie Guinibert. This was Alice's tribe.

Number 97 sat on the corner of Lever Street and Little Clarence Street, a short cul-de-sac marked dark blue on Booth's map ('very rough'). Alice lived with her parents and eight siblings aged from 21 to a few months. Sisters Jane and Rose were aged just eight and one when their mother was jailed for feather theft. The Battershalls' story is that of Victorian Britain: an agricultural past and a hard-pressed, degraded, urban present, all in the space of one generation. Alice's shoemaker father, Elias, was the son of an agricultural labourer from Newton Abbot, in Devon, who had followed his two older brothers to London. There he married Emma Peckham, daughter of a cabman, in 1859, aged 22. Daughter Emily was born four months later.

Mr Battershall might have had a distant memory of the countryside, of birds and the sounds of nature. Alice, his second born, had no such connection. The family stayed in St Luke's for the rest of her life, moving just a matter of yards backwards and forwards over the years. The idea of animal rights would have been an absurd luxury in this environment; the concept of women's rights beyond all comprehension.

4

Women Undercover

In a world where families like the Battershalls moved house just a matter of yards over four decades, changes were felt keenly. The most troubling and profoundly affecting transformation for the feather workers occurred in the early 1880s. 'Whitechapel,' declared a report of 1884, 'has never thoroughly recovered from the overcrowding that arose when, night after night, wagon-loads of poor Jews were brought up from the docks, where they had just arrived, still panic-stricken, from Russia.' The assassination of Alexander II in 1881 had unleashed a wave of anti-Jewish emotion in the Russian Empire; violent pogroms drove thousands of refugee Jews to Britain and the United States over the following years. East London was transformed.

The new arrivals soon made up a solid block that extended north from Aldgate along Commerical Street, and from Spitalfields in the west to Mile End in the east. Some 30,000 Eastern European Jews entered London, most going to Whitechapel. The feather and garment trades were flooded with cheap labour. Exploitation was rife.

Charles Booth and his investigators took a keen interest in these newcomers to the women's trades. To many, the Jews were as alien as the slum dwellers, and were subject to the same prejudice. In order to penetrate properly the unfamiliar worlds of both female workers and the Jewish community, Booth decided to send two women undercover.

Clara Collet was a graduate in political economy and an expert on working women. She was a fierce advocate of the living wage, criticising parents who let their daughters labour for 'pocket money' – thus handing a 'present' to their employers 'which may or may not be shared by the employer with the consumer'. Unlike Mr Lakeman, tut-tutting about gaudy silk handkerchiefs and inappropriate finery in his government reports, Clara was keenly sensitive to the working girl's innocent desire for adornment – and alert to the consequent dangers.

'There is hardly one thing which the Girton or Newnham girl requires in the way of food, clothing, or lodging, which is not equally desired by the City workwoman,' she wrote in her preface to 'Women's Work' for Charles Booth, published in 1889. Girton and Newnham were the two women's colleges of Cambridge, set up amid general fear and ridicule in 1869 and 1875, respectively. 'The Girton girl can resign herself the more easily to shabby dresses and hats, has no fear of caste on account of poverty, and can offer her friends weak tea and a biscuit without any dread of being considered mean and inhospitable,' wrote Collet. 'She has the happy conviction that her own personal merit is all sufficing.'

Here, then, is the 'New Woman' – educated, flat sharing, book reading, socialising. She probably rides an early bicycle, shuns boned corsets, wears shop-made clothes and smokes cigarettes. Her insouciance and bravado will come, in time, to threaten deeply the status quo. She is the suffragette in embryo – and in 20 years' time, she will become a political force that cannot be ignored.

Compare this with the insecure warehouse or factory worker earning 12 shillings a week (about £80 today). 'She seems to imagine that her whole future depends on those appearances which must be kept up,' Collet wrote. This sort of girl attaches great importance to 'outside things'. 'She starves herself first, living on tea and bread-and-butter; she stints herself in bed clothing and underclothing next, and attributes her colds and bronchitis to original weakness of constitution.' The next inevitable step, according to Collet, was to dip in and out of prostitution. 'These girls do not sell themselves for bread; that they could easily earn. They sin for the externals which they have learnt to regard as essentials.'

In other words, they sin so that they might dress with pride. During four months of hard investigative work in the East End, Collet invited women to tea in her flat and heard their stories: from forays into prostitution (Jack the Ripper was a very real threat that autumn of 1888), to 'saving clubs' for hat feathers (each girl contributed a shilling, then drew weekly lots to choose the spender). Journalists frequently mocked working women's attire, their 'three-storey hats' adorned with a 'wilderness of feathers', but it was a way of maintaining self-worth in a degrading workplace.

Into the Jewish quarter Charles Booth sent his cousin Beatrice Potter, the daughter of a businessman (and soon to marry the Fabian socialist Sidney Webb). Potter took an almost clinical interest in poverty. To get closer to her quarry, she rented squalid lodgings in the East End and applied for a number of tailoring jobs, incognito, to get first-hand knowledge of the trade. She was contemptuous of slum explorers – middle-class women ministering to the poor with their tea parties and Bible readings, all good intentions and Bond Street hats. These 'unknown saints', she thought, were 'exceedingly pathetic'. Far better to forensically investigate the life of the working classes, then put one's findings to political use.

Potter tramped the streets of Whitechapel in 1885 looking for work as a 'plain 'and' (a 'plain hand' – her cockney accent was a mixed success). Like Collet, she was highly alert to the appearance of those around her. Fashion – high, vulgar, bad or absent altogether – was the prism through which they tried to understand their subject. Fashion was the key to everything. Male social explorers didn't understand, as these Victorian women did, that every article of clothing was replete with meaning.

'Machinists and pressers, well-clothed and decorated with heavy watch-chains,' were noted by Beatrice Potter; 'Jewish girls with flashy hats, full figures, and large bustles; furtive-eyed Polish immigrants with their pallid faces and crouching forms, and here and there poverty-stricken Christian women.' It was as one of these last that she disguised herself: in buttonless boots, a 'short' (ankle-length) skirt, ill-fitting coat and a 'tumbled black bonnet' on top of 'an unkempt twist of hair'.

'Pages from a Work Girl's Diary' – a typical day spent undercover – was published in *Nineteenth Century* magazine in 1888, the year the House of Lords investigated sweated labour. On this day, after dozens of fruitless enquiries, Potter found herself in a large workroom belonging to Moses and Son, producers of 'Cheap Clothing'. The room was crowded with women and girls as 'ill-clothed' as her. 'At the head of a long table, examining finished garments, stood a hard-featured, shrewd-looking Jewess, in stamped cotton velvet and with a gold-rimmed eyeglass.' The woman – Mrs Moses – wore a heavy watch chain, a 'plentiful supply of rings' and a spotlessly clean apron.

Her married daughter was more ostentatious: 'a golden-haired young lady, beautifully gloved and bonneted, covered with jewels, but with a somewhat unseasonable tippet of sable-tails'. Mr Moses appeared when a vicious row broke out between the two machine pressers (men, earning 12 shillings a week) and the women finishing machine-stitched trousers (on five shillings a week). 'His face was heavy and sensual, his eyes sheepish, his reputation among his wife's "hands" none of the best.'

5

'Crewe Factory Girl'

1894

How did social activists like Clara Collet and Beatrice Potter hope to alter the fortunes of girls like Alice Battershall? Did the working girl even *know* she needed helping? Inarticulate, often illiterate, excluded from men's unions and intimidated by their bosses, the majority of these women didn't know how to press for change. Most were so ground down that they couldn't see beyond the next day. Collet and Potter's most urgent goal was a 'living wage', believing that immorality was the direct result of starvation wages. But who was going to plead the case of the working-class woman in parliament?

The 1884 Reform Act had been a blow to the quietly growing suffrage movement, widening the franchise for men but slamming the doors shut on votes for women (in this case around 100,000 wealthy, property-owning women – who would probably be Tory voters, and thus unpalatable to the Liberal prime minister, William Gladstone). Now even agricultural labourers had the vote, while women did not. In every sphere of work – from domestic service to the feather trade, from clerical work to teaching – women's pay was vastly inferior to men's. Pay them more, the men's argument went, and they'd neglect their rightful duties of homemaking and child-rearing. But the exploitation of women workers was beginning to rankle, and not just among suffragists and middle-class social activists.

Ada Nield was an uneducated girl of Alice Battershall's age, labouring in another exploitative women's trade in the industrial north. She went on to become a formidable public speaker, suffragist and trade unionist, but Ada first enters this story as a young factory worker who dares to speak out.

During the summer of 1894, an extraordinary series of letters was published in the *Crewe Chronicle*, Cheshire. Signed simply 'Crewe Factory Girl', they exposed the appallingly unjust working conditions for 400 girls and 100 men in a clothing factory producing uniforms for soldiers, policemen and railway workers. So eloquent were these dispatches, few believed they were real.

'I have come to the conclusion, sir,' wrote Crewe Factory Girl in her first missive, 'that so long as we are silent ourselves and apparently content with our lot, so long shall we be left in enjoyment of that lot.' She vowed to be silent no more. Her plea was for a living wage so that girls like her could actually live, rather than merely 'exist'. 'We eat, we sleep, we work, endlessly work, from Monday morning to Saturday night, without remission. Cultivation of the mind? How is it possible? . . . Certainly we have Sundays, but Sunday is to many of us after our week of slavery, a day of exhaustion.'

The factory was not named, but a vivid description was given. Crewe Factory Girl depicted the finishing department where piecework was stitched away at by hundreds of young women, who paid for sewing silk out of their own wages. They earned on average eight shillings a week for working a ten-hour day: tuppence an hour. 'A "living wage"! Ours is a lingering, dying wage!' To supplement this, women were forced to take home extra work five nights a week, at least four hours' worth a night. Many of her colleagues were single parents supporting large families. 'It will be unnecessary to point out how fearfully exhausting and tedious it is to sit boring at the same thing for 14 or 15 hours at a stretch.'

Crewe Factory Girl didn't want pity. She wanted justice. She wanted an eight-hour working day (but nine would do) and reasonable pay. 'Why, because we are weak women, without pluck and grit enough to stand up for our rights, should we be ground down to this miserable wage?' But by

25 August, 11 extraordinary letters later, she was forced to sign herself '(An Ex) Crewe Factory Girl'. Her identity had been revealed and she was sacked, along with 12 of her supporters. Ada Nield was 24 when she wrote the letters, a Cheshire yeoman's daughter. Her parting shot in the *Crewe Chronicle* was to 'beg' her fellow workers to be 'resolute in doing their part by uniting themselves, which is the only way to accomplish anything substantial'.

Unlike Alice Battershall, Ada has a voice, and it is bracing to hear it – not Charles Booth's observations of the slum, or Inspector Lakeman's note-taking, or the opinions of middle-class women investigators. Ada knew how girls like her were talked about 'with contemptuous scorn' as 'quite the lowest class of female workers': 'a noisy, cheeky, idle, ignorant, shallow class of girls'. It made the blood in her veins 'boil with indignation'. If the conditions of the factory girl's life weren't so awful, she argued, 'she herself would improve'.

It wasn't Bible classes, model dwellings or temperance groups that were needed, but unionisation for female workers. Both Alice and Ada stood to gain from women in politics – from the introduction of a minimum wage, workers' rights and improved healthcare and housing. Both were stuck in a grinding trap of sweated labour and poverty. One of these women would stay there; the other propelled herself out. Within days of being sacked, the auburn-haired Ada Nield was addressing a Labour meeting in Crewe alongside Eleanor Marx, active socialist and daughter of Karl. Ada's employers – outed as Compton Brothers – were promptly investigated by W. S. Maclaren, Liberal MP for Crewe and supporter of the Manchester National Society for Women's Suffrage. Ada had become a *cause célèbre* precisely because of her rarity value. She was working-class – and she had spoken out.

6

The Skylark

1892

Ada Nield's experiences politicised her – and there was nothing quite so authentic as experience. Middle-class activists had to content themselves with travelling into the slum and trying to raise the expectations of the working classes. But what if you tried to take women *out* of the slum to show them something of beauty and the natural world? Could you reform proletariat tastes and habits through exposure to a higher order? Was it absurd to hope that a common girl could become a nature lover?

Around the time of feather worker Alice Battershall's crime, a wealthy young woman was working as a volunteer at a philanthropic Girls' Club in central London, honing the campaigning skills for which she would later became so very famous. 'It seemed to us the world was upside down. Being young we felt very hot about it, and had an idea that we and the enlightened young people of our day could do something to set it the right way up!' So wrote Emmeline Pethick-Lawrence in her autobiography – suffragette extraordinaire, treasurer of the Women's Social and Political Union from 1906, and right-hand woman to that more famous Emmeline, Mrs Pankhurst.

This was the late 1880s and her allotted district ran from Marylebone Road south to Soho and east from Regent Street to Tottenham Court Road. Her Girls' Club members worked mostly in the clothing trade, earning around seven or eight shillings a week for an 11- or 12-hour day: a step up from the feather workers, who toiled for less, further to the east. 'They never had new clothes or new boots. They wore the bedraggled garments which in those days were the badge of the workers.' They lived with their families, often in one squalid room rented for eight shillings a week. As for their mothers: 'Most of them were so sodden with misery, and so downtrodden, that it was impossible to hope to create any happiness in their lives. We could only vow that we would put such a spirit into their daughters that they would never submit to being so brow-beaten.'

Clubs like these proliferated in Victorian cities, set up by middle-class women for the benefit of their lower-class sisters, always with a civilising agenda. One of the best known was the Girls' Friendly Society, or GFS, formed in 1875 by Mary Townsend to bolster morally vulnerable girls with literacy, Bible and sewing lessons. Most importantly, it would give each young girl a friend 'in a class above her own'. The different classes were as alien species to one another.

Emmeline Pethick-Lawrence (or 'Pethers', as she became known to the suffragettes) was there to teach, but instead she learned. She understood the vital importance of never losing one's audience. She studied the girls' 'amazing Cockney resilience', their 'vitality and eagerness for life' and their extraordinary courage. She observed the relentless 'drink, dirt, starvation and brutality' of their lives, and thought they deserved better. In June 1892, her small group of volunteers came up with 'a very daring suggestion', something that had never been done before. They decided to take a handful of girls out of the heart of the metropolis and into the countryside.

The idea of a week's holiday was unheard of. It was, in every sense, a 'really revolutionary idea'. Every employer had to be visited and made to promise that their workers would have a job to return to. With much shrieking and handkerchief waving, the band of girls boarded a steam train and departed for nearby countryside. None had left the flat streets of central London before; none had adequate walking boots. Pethers found two of them crying with exhaustion in a ditch.

Like Alice Battershall and her neighbours on Lever Street, these were young women who had never known quiet. They had never seen the stars, never picked a flower. They had never heard the cuckoo, and when it began to sing they looked about for a clock. 'It was some time before we could induce them to believe that a cuckoo was a bird.' The only skylarks they knew were the sixpenny caged version, compulsively jerking their heads upwards towards the sky. When the girls saw one hovering above its nest, they became 'agitated'. 'Here's a bird that's got a fit!' one cried. 'It can't go up and it can't come down!'

Their ignorance astonished Emmeline Pethick-Lawrence. She would never forget that trip to the countryside full of 'wonder and fear and delight'.

We don't have a photograph of the Soho girls – but an image of a similar trip to Sussex has survived. On a late summer's day in the mid-1890s, a party of women from London's East End posed in their Sunday best on the lawns of Hancox, a Tudor hall near Battle. They were there at the invitation of Milicent Ludlow, a regular volunteer at a university settlement run by women for Bethnal Green factory girls.

It is a riveting image, not least for its rarity. On the lawn, ranged in four precarious tiers, are 40 young women: waists corseted, sleeves puffed out at the shoulders and tight on the forearm, skirts heavy and long. The black-and-white image pushes them a little further away, but their outfits would have been gaudily coloured by new Victorian dyes, bright as a flock of parakeets.

What stands out most of all is their humanity: arms slung around each others' shoulders, smirking or staring uncertainly at the camera. One has the painfully thin face of the consumptive. These are girls trying very hard to look their smartest. Each outfit tells its own story of borrowing and reworking; of shillings squandered on a finishing touch; even, perhaps, of theft. The 20 teenagers are bareheaded; the other, slightly older women wear either the straw boater made fashionable by Alexandra, Princess of Wales, or broad-brimmed hats on heads held self-consciously. Ribbons, false flowers and feathers sprout from their hats; artificial nature, fussy against a background of rambling roses.

'The girls were wild and rude beyond anything one could conceive of,' wrote Milicent's friend, Alys, who had helped out. Were they capable of appreciating nature? Most educated people thought not – but then it was impossible for the urban working classes to get anywhere near it. Milicent's future husband, Norman Moore, wrote from London that the only flying thing he had seen all week was the weather vane on the steeple of St Mary-le-Bow in Cheapside – a gleaming nine-foot copper dragon. Yet Milicent kept a letter from one Eliza Winter, thanking her for 'my lovely time': 'I do feel so much better I am picture-ing the scenery all day long, and the lovely garden I shall never get out of my eyes.'

Sitting at the end of the front row in that photograph is the hostess, with the self-conscious smile of the upper middle classes. Milicent Ludlow's boater is tipped elegantly towards her forehead. Arranged on top, by professional hands, appears to be a modish collection of jaunty black wings. This one might expect from the Bethnal Green girls, whose guiding star was popular taste, but perhaps not from Milicent – gentlewoman, farmer, scholar and philanthropist.

Milicent's winged hat neatly symbolises the central irony of the era – that when a well-meaning and socially responsible woman wanted to look her best, she thought nothing of wearing a dead bird on her head.

Lever Street, home to Alice and other feather workers, had neither parks nor gardens. The nearest grass was in the graveyard of St Luke's, a ten-minute walk away. Whereas today cherry blossom borders the street, back then it was sooty terraced housing. In a story about women's vexed relationship with birds, it is worth noting the complete absence of birdlife in the feather workers' domain.

Ultimately, as I peeled back the layers surrounding feather thief Alice Battershall and her neighbourhood, it became evident why animal rights was an indulgent irrelevance in her hard-pressed world. The fight for survival took up any spare energy – and it was humans, not birds, that most needed help, according to Emmeline Pankhurst. And so in starting a campaign to save the birds, Etta Lemon faced an almost impossible struggle.

Part 2

Birds

7

Young Etta

1887

Each little flower that opens
Each little bird that sings
He made their glowing colours
He made their tiny wings . . .

As the congregation of St Margaret's Church warbled its way to the end of 'All Things Bright and Beautiful', a young woman slipped a small notebook and silver pencil from her purse. She surveyed the pews around her. Bonnets, she noted, appeared to be in decline among the fashionable ladies of Blackheath, a fast expanding suburb south of the capital. Hats, on the other hand, were becoming more and more outlandish. The riding bowler, favourite look of the Princess of Wales, had risen upwards into a flowerpot shape, its brim now jutting out over the face. As for the trimmings . . . Soaring above the congregation was an extraordinary display of nature. Once you homed in on the hats, it really became impossible to look at anything else.

In 1887, the year of Queen Victoria's Golden Jubilee, trimmings included spiders, water beetles, caterpillars, lizards and toads. The hat itself had become an irrelevance: 'simply an excuse for a feather, a pretext for a spray of flowers, the support for an aigrette, the fastening for a plume of Russian cock's feathers,' wrote the French art critic and arbiter of taste Charles Blanc. A subtle shift was occurring, away from mid-century-modesty to late-century New Woman chutzpah. The hat was becoming a provocative thing of sexuality. 'It is placed on the head, not to protect it, but that it may be seen better,' wrote Blanc. 'Its great use is to be charming.'

Miss Margaretta 'Etta' Smith wasn't one for high fashion. She noted the hats in her church with a dispassionate, forensic eye. Her interest lay in feathers – or rather, in birds. As the congregation filed down the aisle and milled out onto the crest of Belmont Hill, she opened her notebook and wrote three words at the top of the page: 'Feather Bedecked Women'. She then jotted rapidly a list of names and species. Peacock, Asian pheasant, eagle, grebe and heron. Hummingbird, swallow, robin, blue tit and chaffinch.

Whole owls' heads with staring glass eyes were all the rage that season, along with the breasts and wings of brightly coloured parrots. Native seabirds, ducks, doves and blackbirds were used to create 'Mercury wings', placed skittishily on either side of a woman's head. Birds-of-paradise were everywhere: whole, halved or simply the flame-coloured, softly cascading tail of the Raggiana species. Miss Smith had a passion for the paradise.

The 'unkempt' look was also in vogue that jubilee year. *Harper's Magazine* suggested rearranging old bird pieces in new positions – perhaps splayed on the crown of the hat, as if fallen straight out of the sky, an 'appealing expression' on its taxidermied face; or else peering over the brim as if in 'earnest incubation' on a nest. *Myra's Journal* was featuring hats 'nearly concealed by their feather ornaments', with green- or gold-coloured plumes as the favourite colour. Miss Smith's pencil noted other travesties: tiny songbirds trimming bodices, decorating 'novelty' capes or flying out of fur collars.

Once back at the large family home at 46 Lee Terrace, Blackheath, Margaretta Smith would peel off her gloves, sit down at her desk and devote the rest of the morning to her task. Each lady on her list – and it was always the same offenders – would be written a personal letter describing the horrors behind their fashion accessories. The birds they wore had in all probability been slaughtered during the mating season, she explained. This meant starvation and death for their orphaned fledglings. All but the African ostrich feather met with Miss Smith's condemnation, for ostriches did not (it was hoped) die for their plumes.

Margaretta Smith's admonitory letters fell, one by one, through polished brass letter boxes onto waxed hall floors, where parlourmaids or butlers picked them up and placed them on silver trays. They were delivered at breakfast – in bed or in dining rooms – throughout the prosperous parish of St Margaret's.

This is the only known story about the formative years of Etta Lemon, née Smith. Those letters written in her youth to 'feather bedecked women' every Sunday became (so wrote James Fisher, author of the 1966 *Shell Bird Book*, who knew her) an 'oft-repeated boast' as an adult. He believed it: Mrs Lemon was 'redoubtable'. It was clearly important, in her own narrative, to present herself as righteous rather than peculiar. She told people that this early act of mild militancy was inspired by the popular natural history writer Eliza Brightwen, whose emotive account of a heronry raided by plume hunters appeared in *Wild Nature Won by Kindness*. Brightwen's book wasn't published until 1890, when Etta had moved on from personal letter writing to more public campaigning – but it served to retrospectively condone her actions. She wanted to feel at the vanguard of a *movement*.

There were four women behind the Society for the Protection of Birds, but all the anecdotes have stuck to Mrs Lemon. She was the prime mover, 'The Dragon', the keeper of the flame. As I untangled the individual stories of the four, hers was the voice that leapt most vividly from the archives. Her Evangelical spirit seemed to fire up and characterise this society for half a century, from its fervent beginnings in 1889, to the brutal coup thought necessary to remove her from her perch in 1939. She was the Margaret Thatcher of the bird world – visionary, forthright, divisive and, in the end, out of touch.

A director of the Natural History Museum once hid down a stairwell rather than be harangued by Mrs Lemon for some bird protection failure. She was 'never much of a scientific ornithologist,' wrote James Fisher in the 1960s, 'but a woman of tremendous drive and a humorous ruthlessness and courage.'

By then, she had passed into folklore – a Victorian fanatic considered fair play for pot shots. She was unattractive, with 'a mouth like a rat trap', commented a former long-serving RSPB staff member on her portrait. She had no children because she 'might not have known how to do it'. In the official history of the RSPB, *For Love of Birds*, published for its 1989 centenary, journalist Tony Samstag called her the 'Fulminator in Chief' – 'one of those whose Christian name was once and forever "Mrs"'.

It seems hard for anyone to imagine Mrs Lemon as a young woman. Did she also inspire unkind sniggers in the 1870s and 1880s? As an adult, her 'directness of approach' and 'brusque' manner often raised eyebrows, the Reverend J. B. Phillips said at her memorial service in 1953. He added that she had 'tremendous courage', too. For a young Victorian woman to write such pointedly intrusive letters, singling out fellow women for their dress – their *identity* – was certainly courageous. One might forgive it in an 18-year-old (her age when she started the habit), but in a 27-year-old (by that jubilee year) it appeared aggressive and unwomanly. Her habit suggests an unusual insensitivity both to the feelings of others and to what people might think of her. Birds, for Etta Smith, came before humans.

Where did the brusque Miss Smith spring from? What formed her singular character? 'Nothing is known of her early years,' reads the entry for Margaretta Lemon, née Smith, in the *Oxford Dictionary of National Biography*. This was written by an RSPB insider in 2004, 60 years after her death.

Etta was born in 1860 on a stretch of the Kent coast, a place where a curving shingle beach meets the sky, not far from Dover. Brother Edward and sister Woltera Mercy followed swiftly after. Their father was Captain William Elisha Smith, former top marksman of the Royal Sherwood

Foresters, now head of the renowned School of Musketry in Hythe. Smith was a man with a past, having swapped north London for 'Moopla', a sheep farm in New South Wales, Australia, aged 17. He'd professed himself glad to get away from the heavy religious atmosphere of his childhood, boasting that he hadn't even packed a Bible. But in Australia Smith suffered a spiritual crisis. Ten years later, he gave up the sheep farm, returned home and began seeking answers.

Captain Smith 'passed from death unto life', as the Evangelicals put it, while working at Hythe. He had started to organise weekly visits from charismatic preachers, first to the family home and then to Hythe Town Hall. His wife, Louisa, their three small children and all the soldiers were required to attend. Here, in front of the assembled throng, before one exceptional preacher, Captain Smith had his moment of epiphany. He was 'brought to the Lord'. He became what we might call today a born-again Christian. Captain Smith's make-up of discipline, expert marksmanship and religious zealotry pervaded family life. Louisa was the daughter of a similarly devout army commander, one of the Barclays of Blackheath – a family renowned for its philanthropy and Evangelical zeal. The name the couple chose for their younger daughter, Woltera Mercy, meant 'military ruler'. As the girls grew up, they preferred to be known as Etta and Mercy.

Etta's early years were spent among the long, white barrack buildings at Hythe – buildings constructed to house military lunatics in 1842. The children played to an incessant background rattle of rifle fire as hundreds of soldiers passed through this musketry school. Weapons filled the buildings, the men's conversations and the detailed reports of shooting experiments filed by her father. The air blazed and crackled along the pebbled shooting range, all guns pointing out to sea, the cries of seabirds faintly audible in the pauses.

Birds were – and are – everywhere on this flat stretch of Kent coast. Grebes come to winter on the sea in diverse, floating colonies: great crested, red-necked, black-necked, Slavonian. The eider alight here from the north, along with Arctic skuas and brent geese. Etta grew up to the song of seabirds – the calls of terns and waders, purple sandpipers and turnstones, gannets and gulls – as well as the noise of the guns.

In March 1867, when Etta was seven years old and her siblings six and five, their mother died in childbirth. The baby, named William, died too. A stillborn baby, Mary, had been buried the previous year. By December 1867, their father had already remarried. His new wife, Mary Ann Woollaston, was 26 and a sugar plantation heiress. Captain Smith, 43, was now bent on a new mission.

Done with guns, he moved his family to the middle-class suburb of Blackheath, home of his late wife Louisa's family. He now offered his professional services up to the Evangelization Society, founded in 1868 to preach the gospel to those not reached by ordinary means. Captain Smith joined at the start as honorary secretary. His job was to find extraordinary preachers and send them to unusual places. 'Miracles of grace' – that is, quantifiable conversions to Evangelism – were the bottom line.

Captain Smith organised urban open-air preaching events, marquees on village greens, house-to-house visits, cottage meetings and tract distribution throughout the United Kingdom. The society's headquarters were in the heart of London, just off the Strand. Daily, Captain Smith caught the commuter train from Blackheath station, leaving his young family in the care of their new stepmother and a governess. This did not last for long. Louisa's relatives contrived to send Etta and Mercy away to boarding school – far away, to a place called Hill House in the village of Belstead in Suffolk. It was thought to be the best solution.

Etta, too, was done with guns. Her time at Hythe had filled her with a horror of the sound of rifle shot, but had stirred the beginnings of a lifelong passion for birds. Her young horizons had been filled with things on the wing. She had lost her mother at a cruelly young age, but at Hill House she found an influential replacement.

Mrs Maria Umphelby's school for girls was filled with children who needed a substitute home or family. There were children of the British Empire, children of the Raj, orphaned children, girls somehow surplus to requirements when gentleman fathers were widowed or remarried. Unlike the newer, more academic girls' schools (North London Collegiate School, Cheltenham Ladies' College), Hill House was run along an older, family-style model with no dormitories and many siblings. The 30 pupils, aged six to 16, all called Mrs Umphelby 'Maimie'. She was the closest to a mother most of them had.

Mrs Umphelby had been chosen by the Barclay relatives for her fervent religious beliefs. She was a Revivalist Evangelical; a woman of 60 who infused her curriculum with the celebration of God's glory. Countryside walks were done at a march while shouting out Revivalist hymns. 'He is fitting up my mansion/Which eternally shall stand, For my stay shall not be transient/In that holy, happy land,' the girls bellowed as they tramped the fields and forests.

Drilled in the right way, instilled with discipline and piety, it was hoped that they would go on to become indomitable women: 'a band of admirably trained daughters' who would 'go forth over the wide world'. Missionary work – at home or abroad – was the unspoken goal of their education. In choosing Mrs Umphelby's regime in preference to a governess at home, the Barclays had put down a stake in their two young granddaughters' futures. This was a school that prepared women for public life.

Etta returned to Blackheath aged 16, and was immediately sent abroad – to a finishing school in Lausanne, Switzerland. This was the conventional coda to an upper-middle-class girl's education, yet Etta was not a conventional girl. She remained impervious to the fashion manuals of the day, to the absurdly time-consuming ritual of the Victorian lady's toilette and to those fashionable, constricting costumes. She returned at 18, proficiently fluent in French, to face an uncertain future.

While brother Edward went on to read Medicine at Cambridge (styling himself 'Edward Barclay-Smith'), the Smith sisters of the Blackheath household had to do what was expected of all young women of their class in the 1880s. They occupied the long wait for a husband with social calls and charitable work.

There is a photograph of Etta Smith, taken after her return home. In it, she reclines in a chair, her hair pulled unfussily into the nape of her neck. She is uncorseted, wearing a highly worked, smocked bodice edged in dark lace in the 'artistic' or 'Aesthetic' style, and her brown eyes are lost in thought – real thought. There is a hint (in that faintly sardonic set of the mouth) of her determined character. She holds a large open book, not a posy of flowers. She is herself, and also her future self – a girl taut with promise. This is the young woman to whom the novelist Henry James would later write letters in decidedly flirtatious tones, admiring her 'noble presence and stature'. This saviour of the birds was, James enthused, 'a priestess of the genial day'.

It's equally possible, of course, that this photograph is actually a portrait of somebody consumed with frustration. An intelligent young woman with no hope of further education like her brother's, trapped with her stepmother in the social rounds of well-to-do Blackheath – hence her wry smile and haunted eyes. Yet the evidence suggests otherwise. On returning to London, Etta found that she was perfectly placed – in her time, family and location – to develop her formidable talents.

8

Young Emmeline

Emmeline Pankhurst's early years were not that dissimilar to those of Etta Smith. As one girl grew up in the far south of England, another was growing up in the north, two years apart in age. Both were eldest children of middle-class homes; both were sent to small, select girls' boarding schools run by gentlewomen; and both were expected to step aside while their brothers' further education took precedence. 'What a pity she wasn't born a lad,' said Emmeline's father, Robert Goulden, recognising his daughter's sharp mind. Both young women were drawn into the political orbit of their parents – Emmeline attending her first suffrage meeting in Manchester aged 14, Etta listening to countless Evangelical preachers.

Their stories then begin to diverge. While Etta was sent to health-giving Lausanne, Emmeline travelled to the more sophisticated city of Paris for her final years of education. She studied science and literature, attended political soirées and learned to dress like an elegant Frenchwoman in veiled hats, velvet cloaks and evening gowns. It was in Paris that Emmeline acquired the soft, ultra-feminine air that she was to wear like a suit of armour for the rest of her life.

While for Etta, self-image and how others saw her didn't matter one jot, for Emmeline it was quite the opposite. In Paris, she discovered the transformative power of fashion. She began an addictive relationship with clothing stores – shopping became and remained 'one of her favourite pastimes'. She learned that, for a woman, image is everything if you want people to listen. It was a lesson that would, in time, serve the suffragettes well.

Emmeline returned home to Manchester a different creature, outwardly transformed into a Parisian. She was now 'a graceful, elegant young lady . . . with a slender, svelte figure, raven black hair, an olive skin with a slight flush of red in the cheeks, delicately pencilled black eyebrows, beautiful expressive eyes of an unusually deep violet blue, [and] above all a magnificent carriage and a voice of remarkable melody,' wrote her daughter Sylvia in 1935, still captivated after all those years by the memory of her mother. 'More than ever she was the foremost among her brothers and sisters.'

Unlike Etta, Emmeline did not have to wait long for a husband. As the story goes, she went to hear a political meeting addressed by a Dr Richard Pankhurst in the summer of 1879. Standing with her parents on the steps outside the hall, awaiting the 'Red Doctor', Emmeline saw a 'beautiful hand' opening the door of a cab from the inside as the vehicle pulled up. The figure that followed the hand was not so beautiful, but the ideas he represented were intoxicating. Four months later, they were married: the 44-year-old, red-bearded barrister – political extremist, agnostic and rabble-rousing socialist – and the 21-year-old refined beauty, desperate to do 'some great thing' (as her daughter Christabel later put it).

By 1885, when Etta Smith was still in her parents' house in Blackheath, Emmeline Pankhurst was 27 with four children under five years old. Her husband's fledgling political career meant there was not much money and so her first, impecunious married home was in Chortlon-on-Medlock, a working-class district of Manchester. Money problems dogged Mrs Pankhurst throughout her life. She knew, in a way that Etta was never to discover, what it was to be hard up. Poverty taught her resilience, financial shrewdness and a freeing disregard for home comforts. It also made her more able to take risks.

Marriage and motherhood did not stop her, but they slowed her trajectory. 'Dr Pankhurst did not desire that I should turn myself into a household machine,' she later wrote, pointing out that she had joined the executive committee of the Women's Suffrage Society while her children were 'still in their cradles' (precisely the sort of 'un-motherly' behaviour that led to criticism of female suffragists). But she also played the conventional role of supportive wife to her husband's socialist ambitions.

And as the children continued to come, so Emmeline Pankhurst's quicksilver beginning slowed to a long burn. By 1889, she had given birth to five babies, moved to London for her husband's career and buried her four-year-old son, Frank, killed by diphtheria from poor drains at their modest house in Hampstead Road. She was exhausted. Here her story pauses, while she recovers her strength and the Pankhurst children grow. Her moment will come later, in her 40s.

By contrast, young Etta Smith had no husband or children. There were no brakes on her early development. This, in part, explains why the anti-plumage crusade pre-dated the suffragettes by some 12 years. Unwittingly, the three childless women who led the campaign on behalf of the birds – Etta Smith, Emily Williamson and Eliza Phillips – paved the way for the subsequent political activism of women like Emmeline Pankhurst. They were the first to break into the public sphere, Etta at the forefront.

9

The Train Carriage

1880s

If you cut through Etta at the age of 8 or 80, you would find Evangelism at her core. Her Christian faith gave her an unshakeable righteousness, both feared and admired by all who worked with her. It vindicated her budding political activism; it informed all that she did for the birds, and all that she achieved in a lifetime of good works. Family anecdotes recall visiting relatives living in terror of offending the Almighty – a niece ticked off for washing her stockings on a Sunday; a nephew held in silent disapproval for delaying pre-breakfast prayers (everyone on their knees, elbows propped on hard dining chairs). While Emmeline Pankhurst saw the Church as part of the establishment élite, suffocating rather than encouraging equal rights for women, for Etta it was her bedrock.

The Evangelicals ran three out of every four voluntary societies in the Victorian era – their success entirely down to the missionary zeal of men like Captain William Elisha Smith, brilliant at goading others into voluntary work. Etta watched her father grow his fledgling society from unsure beginnings, evolving into a confident and powerful 30-year reign. Captain Smith professed himself 'the happiest man in England' as he went about his work; to his daughters, he was a powerful role model for disciplined, meaningful work. Their father used Etta and Mercy to vet and report back on new speakers. They knew his five points for an effective preacher by heart, printed on a card on his office mantelpiece:

'Begin low, Proceed slow, Mount higher, Take fire, Then expire.' Captain Smith was uncompromising in his selection. 'When you can stand on a platform, and look a thousand people in the face for five minutes without speaking,' he would say to aspiring preachers, 'and then quietly begin to preach the Gospel to them, let me know.'

Women did not speak in public in the 1880s or 1890s. Those who did – mostly early suffragists, vainly trying to rouse support – were viewed as unnatural and offensive to femininity. The Evangelization Society was unusual in using a handful of women speakers, and Etta's experience of watching them in action eventually pushed her to take to the podium herself.

In 1898, aged 38, she would pick up a silver medal at the International Conference for Bird Protection in Aix-en-Provence for a speech delivered in fluent French. The following year, she spoke so brilliantly at the International Congress of Women in Westminster that a male journalist thought her 'discriminating advocacy' far superior to 'any amount of passionate and headlong declamation'. In other words, she spoke like a man.

Etta learned to speak in public, and she also learned to write. The Evangelicals grasped and exploited Victorian print culture, using an army of volunteers for their prolific publications. Captain Smith put his meticulous elder daughter to work writing tracts and journals, poems and children's stories. The work gave her journalistic discipline, an editor's eye and a flair for publicity. But it was the daily commute to her father's office in central London that was to play the greatest part in her future life; perhaps the most significant part. The journey to the office brought her into contact with a range of powerful and privileged men.

Blackheath boasted the highest number of first-class season ticket holders of any station on the line. Standing with Etta and Captain Smith on the platform were the great and the good of Victorian London – solicitors, engineers, surgeons, politicians. Among them were a young barrister and his father, who also caught the early train into London's Charing Cross station and then walked in the same direction up the

Strand as did the Smiths. All four would turn right into Surrey Street, Captain Smith and his daughter peeling off into the Evangelization Society headquarters, while William George Lemon and his son Frank rounded the corner to the Temple.

Etta began to anticipate the journey up to town. Mr Lemon senior (bald, his chin fringed with a half-moon of beard) was an interesting gentleman whose opinions chimed with hers on many matters – including the vexed issue of 'feather bedecked women'. William Lemon was passionate about many things, but particularly about God's creatures.

Had Miss Smith heard, for example, about the first imperial wildlife measure just passed in the Far East, drafted by his son Arthur? And this new 'vegetarianism' fad – was it just for socialist cranks like George Bernard Shaw, or was it enlightened to abstain from eating flesh and blood? What were her feelings about vivisection? He thought it a disgraceful racket. The Victoria Street Society was doing admirable work on that front thanks to Miss Frances Power Cobbe – the first lobbying group of its kind. It was a pity the lady persisted in wearing that muff with a bird-of-paradise sewn onto it: this gave her opponents such scope to scoff. An ivory-handled umbrella, too.

Miss Smith might, he suggested, like to join one of the Fur, Fin and Feather clubs springing up across the country; perhaps hear some of the latest debate on animal protection. He'd heard of such a one setting up in Croydon, not so far away, in the home of Mrs Eliza Phillips. William Lemon was himself campaigning to open a local branch of the Royal Society for the Prevention of Cruelty to Animals here, in Blackheath. He hoped she would be an early member. One of his first campaigns would be for a large sign on Belmont Hill: 'Please Give the Horse His Head When Going Uphill.' He'd witnessed disgraceful use of the cruel bearing rein on that hill, forcing the horses' heads uncomfortably close to their chests – and all for fashion. Those coachmen ought to know better.

William Lemon was a dazzlingly energetic self-made man, born to a stable groom in the West End. He'd been appointed headmaster of the School for Sons of Missionaries at the age of 22, before switching to a successful career as a barrister at 36. A Nonconformist Congregationalist and a fanatical Freemason, Lemon was one of the towering presences of the parish.

Like Etta's father, Captain Smith, William Lemon was the living embodiment of the Victorian sense of public duty, and his five children were also steeped in it. His son Frank had graduated from Cambridge and recently followed him into the law. Gentle-faced, with very pale blue, slightly bulging eyes and a sparse blond moustache, Frank respectfully let his father hold forth as the train rattled north into London.

So here is Etta, in the late 1880s, poised for action: passionate, alert and indignant. A woman in her late 20s, in search of a cause. While Emmeline Pankhurst's fate was sealed by a 'beautiful hand' opening a carriage door, Miss Etta Smith was not so impulsive. But the daily commute to and from Charing Cross station with Frank Lemon would come to play a decisive part in what happened next.

10

Of Bird-Wearing Age

1886–88

In February 1886, a bird-obsessed American bank clerk was carrying out an experiment. Like Miss Etta Smith, he carried a small notebook and pencil and, as he walked through uptown Manhattan late one afternoon, he jotted down what he saw on ladies' hats, coats, muffs and stoles. Frank Chapman, 22, was a man who knew his species. From Monday to Saturday, he rose before daybreak to watch birds in the countryside surrounding his home near the Hudson River, before catching the 7.30am train from West Englewood station, New Jersey. Leaving the office at 6pm, he caught the commuter train home again and headed back into the field until the light faded.

The stroll down 14th Street to Broadway offered a different sort of bird spotters' paradise. Chapman's list, published as a terse letter to *Forest and Stream*, reads like a ghastly parody of a day in the field. 'Blackpoll warbler, three. Baltimore oriole, nine. Purple grackle, five. Bluejay, five. Swallow-tailed flycatcher, one . . .'

Plumage from America's wild birds flashed past as he walked. He noted 15 snow buntings that afternoon, 21 golden-winged woodpeckers, 16 quail and 21 common terns. He saw a rare Acadian owl staring out from the top of a woman's head; a stippled, grey-brown greater yellowlegs; and a little green heron, with its glossy black cap and red chest. One sorrowful 'laughing gull' (black head, white body, grey wings) caught Chapman's eye as he stood outside Arnold & Co's marble-fronted 'palace of trade' on Broadway. New Yorkers might have noticed a bowler-hatted young man, with a sloping dark moustache, staring intently at elegant women as they descended from carriages or gazed at the plate glass window displays.

He counted 40 native species, but he was sure there were more. Most birds were so mutilated and mismatched by the hands of clever feather workers that they were impossible to identify. 'It is probable,' he wrote, 'that few if any of the women knew that they were wearing the plumage of the birds of our gardens, orchards and forests.' A paradise tail would sprout from a pheasant's breast, or an egret's nuptial plumage from a swallow's angular wingspan, the whole dyed an unnatural crimson red, mustard yellow or turquoise blue. All had been worked over by the hands of immigrant Russian Jewish and Italian women in the 'feather foundries' of the Lower East Side, where the air hung heavy with plumage particulate.

Chapman had thought he'd known, more or less, what he'd find on New York's smarter shopping streets. Still – he was shocked. In case that particular afternoon had been an aberration, he repeated the experiment the next day. In all, he counted 700 ladies in hats. Three quarters of these hats contained feathers. Here, in the microcosm of the 'Ladies' Mile', between 14th Street and Broadway, was the proof of the estimated statistic: that around *five million* birds were killed annually for the use of milliners in North America. No bird was safe.

Networks of hunters fed bird skin dealers, who fed the trade auction houses and millinery warehouses of Europe and America. It was a system of almost diabolical perfection. One professional hunting outfit, J. H. Batty and Associates, were reportedly 'taking almost anything with feathers' in Florida at this time, each hunter killing up to 150 birds per day. There were ten million women of 'bird-wearing age' in the United States. But what *was* 'bird-wearing age'? Editorial and advertisements for children's millinery in contemporary magazines featured nodding plumes, tiny songbirds, kitten-soft marabou or albatross down and impish wings. If you were old enough to wear a hat, you were old enough to wear a bird.

Chapman's walk became famous. In essence, he'd simply done exactly the same thing that young Etta Smith was doing in church in Blackheath – and at exactly the same time. But he was a bank clerk and a man – and so he had turned his bird-wearing statistics into a neat table, which he had made public. *Forest and Stream*, 'a weekly journal of the rod and gun', was widely read – not by women of fashion, but men of influence. This little letter, with its meticulous twitcher's table, ended up in Congress. Thanks to Chapman's uptown walk, a bird protection act was adopted by New York State in May 1886, but it was not enforced.

'The headgear of women is made up in as large a degree as ever before of the various parts of small birds,' reported George Bird Grinnell, the founder of America's newly formed bird protection Audubon Society. 'Thousands and millions of birds are displayed in every conceivable shape on their hats and bonnets.' The destruction of wild birds for millinery purposes had reached 'stupendous proportions'. It could not be sustained.

On Wednesday 21 March 1888, a historic plumage sale was held at the London Commercial Sales Rooms in Mincing Lane. Sales catalogues from the leading commodity broker Hale & Son were circulating well before the event. One fell into the hands of a correspondent for *The Auk* – the journal of the American Ornithologists' Union, not long established. Styling himself as a plumage dealer, he decided to pay a clandestine visit.

Those, like him, who entered to browse the displays baled, piled and pegged out on boards at the Cutler Street warehouse might have felt themselves to be walking through the most prolific taxidermist's workshop in the world. It was like a lesson in natural history, although few of these buyers had any interest in the subject. What they saw in the jewelled mounds of lifeless feathers before them was profit. *The Auk*'s correspondent calculated that here was a greater diversity of birds than all the ornithological collections known to him in the United States and the United Kingdom combined. In its sheer quantity and variety, it was a sale that broke all previous records.

Here were birds by the shipload. Whole hulls had been unpacked by gangs of dockers, clambering over vessels from the shipping routes of the British Empire – from South and Central America; Southern Asia, Nepal and India; Burma and China; the East and West Indies; New Guinea and Australia; East, West, North and South Africa. This haul made ostrich feathers seem dull. Ostrich plumes had slumped in the mid-1880s: the market was open to new ideas. And, in the world of fashion, the window of opportunity was narrow. Hunters across the globe combed swamp and forest. Gun barrels smoked. Laden ships sailed slowly towards the Port of London.

The accepted trade wisdom was that bird plumage could be worked into eight basic forms for a standard hat trimming. The plumes of ostriches, herons, birds-of-paradise, crowned pigeons, egrets and 'vultures' could be made into 'aigrettes' – the tufty spray used to give a hat height or width. Pads and bands – the essential padding of the milliner's craft – came from a number of dismembered birds including barnyard fowl, pheasants of all kinds, parrots and pigeons. Wings, breasts, 'pompons' and quills were supplied by a huge variety of species, the more brightly coloured the better. Birds could be dismembered and reassembled; a whole peacock or owl might appear to coil its flattened body around a hat. Smaller birds could be used whole.

The Dressmaker and Milliner trade quarterly used a very particular language for avian adornment: euphemistic, reassuring and lightly sentimental. Wings were 'novelties'; breasts and plumes 'trimmings'; whole birds were a 'very effective decoration'. The wearer took on the bird's winsomeness; 'dressy' trimmings with beaks and eyes were 'especially suited to young ladies'. Minutely observed descriptions of the latest Paris fashions were thus disseminated, in English and German, to wholesalers and milliners in London, New York and Berlin:

> The handsome black aigrettes of the Paradise bird, which are fluffy and curled at the top, are rivals of the straight aigrette . . . *Die prachtvollen schwarzen Aigretten des Paridiesvogels, welche oben Kraus sind, drohen den Abgang der geraden Aigrette.*

This London sale included 16,000 packages of 'osprey' (the fine nuptial plumes of the snowy egret), peacock, argus and other green-, red- and gold-coloured wild pheasants; also of various species of duck and heron. The next category was breezily unspecific: 'various bird skins'. Cravenly imprecise to *The Auk*'s undercover reporter. He 'figured up', in his quick whip round: 'between 7,000 and 8,000 parrots', shipped from Bombay, Calcutta and South America; about 1,000 Impeyan and 500 argus pheasants; and some 1,000 woodpeckers. There were 1,450 large, pitiful bird skins labelled 'Penguins': just how ignorant *were* those feather dealers? These he identified as little auks and great crested grebes (the latter were in danger of extinction, prized for their extraordinary head feathers that stuck out in a halo during the breeding season).

The list continues, and it is hard to read; harder still to envisage the sheer quantity of bright plumage, limp and scaly feet, inert beaks and shrivelled eyes. Eviscerated bird samples were heaped on tables, piled against walls, pegged out on boards and stacked up on shelves. To modern eyes, the slaughter is incomprehensible. There were 14,000 quail, grouse and partridge – a head count that would be considered a grossly excessive hunting 'bag', even for the time. (The biggest shoot in history, at Lord Burnham's Beaconsfield estate in 1913, caused King George V a moment of remorse: 'Perhaps we went a little too far today, David', he said to his son. Six guns slaughtered 4,000 pheasant.)

Moving on, *The Auk*'s reporter noted 'about 4,000 Snipes and Plovers' and some 7,000 starlings, jays and magpies. The deeper he walked into the warehouse, the brighter became the colours: over 12,000 tiny hummingbirds, walnut-sized creatures in hues of yellow, scarlet, gold and midnight blue; some 5,000 rainbow-hued tanagers; 6,000 blue creepers and 1,500 other creepers. ('Probably family Coerebidae,' he noted, fleetingly imagining the live bird in its tropical habitat – the slender, curved bill; the flash of yellow belly; the shaggy round nest with a side entrance hole.) His time was running out and the numbers had become meaningless: 'Several hundred *each* of Hawks, Owls, Gulls, Terns, Ducks, Ibises, Finches, Orioles, Larks, Toucans, Birds of Paradise, etc.'

Particularly high prices were paid for the skins of unusual birds, such as the King of Saxony bird-of-paradise, with its strange head wires, or Pesquet's parrot, with its bright red chest feathers – both from the mountains of New Guinea. Best of all would be a bird that nobody had seen before. The atmosphere in the warehouse was one of muted frenzy, as dealers sorted through bales of feathered skins searching eagerly for novelties.

Before he left Cutler Street, *The Auk*'s journalist mingled, uneasily, with these dealers. He learned from one plumage man that the trade in birds for women's hats had been 'enormous' last year. The man boasted of selling *two million* skins of small birds 'of every kind and colour'. 'What a bloody Moloch is fashion!' *The Auk* concluded its report. 'And how thoughtlessly otherwise intelligent and tender-hearted women obey her behests!' Campaigners at the time estimated that London's feather markets threatened 61 bird species around the world with extinction, from the Indian green parrot to the African marabou stork; from the South American macaw to the tropical sooty tern.

If a bird wasn't, to a British lady, remotely familiar, then it had an otherworldly, innocent, storybook quality to it. It belonged to distant parts of the British Empire, which spooled like a brightly coloured diorama through the Victorian mind. A bird-of-paradise, scarlet tanager or tiny viridian hummingbird had no real back story. It wasn't perceived as a species with mating rituals, grooming habits, a distinctive call and hatchlings to feed. It was a commodity just like any other – leather, ivory, tortoiseshell or ostrich feather.

11

The Tea Party

1889

When the origins of the RSPB are evoked today, there is always a little scoffing at the gentility of it all. Stephen Moss, the veteran birder, touched on the story in *A Bird in the Bush* (2004). 'Like many great British institutions, the Royal Society for the Protection of Birds grew from humble and somewhat unlikely beginnings,' he wrote. 'In February 1889, a group of respectable and middle-class women gathered . . .'

They gathered around teacups and saucers in suburban Croydon, of all places: in the home of Eliza Phillips, a 66-year-old vicar's widow. How tame it sounds. Mrs Phillips, one of the four 'redoubtable' women behind this society, is never mentioned today – in part because she was old, Victorian and fervently Christian. Since she was also head of publications at the early SPB and writer of trenchant pamphlets about birds and feathers, the 'Christian ornithology' slur on this early epoch in bird protection was meant for women like Mrs Phillips.

She died in 1916, before seeing the plumage ban for which she had fought so hard passed in parliament – or, indeed, before seeing any discernible decline in women's lust for feathers. She was 94. But this long campaign was just the final episode in an unusually fully lived life, for a woman. Eliza Phillips was not, it turns out, completely respectable.

Before the safe haven of her vicar, Eliza had first married rather scandalously. Robert Montgomery Martin was divorced, penniless and, at 47, twice Eliza's age. He was her 'Dr Pankhurst' figure: a formidably energetic social reformer, author and traveller; a chronicler of empire, protector of minorities, campaigner against slavery, naturalist and assistant surgeon to far-flung expeditions. What he lacked in ready money, he made up for in glamour. Eliza Barron was a well-educated Londoner and daughter of a civil servant. The two enjoyed 20 years of marriage and much exotic travel, but no children.

After her first husband's death, in 1868, Eliza had her epiphany on animal rights. She shared a cross-Channel boat with a herd of cattle and witnessed first-hand the terrified animals slamming into each other as the vessel plunged through the waves. When she married the Reverend Edward Phillips in 1874, moving to a fort-like house in Tunbridge Wells, Eliza became the prime mover at the local RSPCA branch. She now had four servants, great local influence and an upright husband penning ecclesiastical works. For many women, this would have been enough. But when Edward died a decade later, she shook things up again.

Mrs Phillips might not have lived in the centre of London but she was easy to visit, even for a lady like Miss Etta Smith, who travelled alone. Vaughan House on Morland Road was a newly built, substantial villa on a thoroughfare neatly dividing the Surrey countryside from the expanding suburb of Croydon. It looked out onto heathland, a lake, gentle woodland and a scattering of farms. Linnet and corn bunting picked over fields just a short stroll away. Vaughan House sat shoulder to shoulder with other houses not dissimilar to the Smith family residence in Blackheath, all cream stucco and imposing entrances.

As a growing suburb, Croydon had the edge on Blackheath. It was a leisure destination for Londoners and even royalty, with its own spa, landscaped gardens, handsome Theatre Royal and a slew of magnificent municipal buildings springing up off architects' plans. Three railways had opened within 30 years, and an educated middle class was highly active in dozens of societies – from the Croydon Literary and Scientific Institution, to the all-male Croydon Microscopical and Natural History Club. If you had to pick a pertinent spot and a time to launch an all-women, Fur, Fin and Feather Folk society, Croydon in 1889 would do very well.

Morland Road is now an avenue of unloved tarmac and relentless brickwork. A block of flats, fenced off for demolition, stands on the site of Vaughan House, every window broken. There is nothing to indicate that this is where something momentous was born. Nor are there any records, for no minutes were taken of Mrs Phillips' monthly meetings. These were quiet Sundays in middle-class suburbia: beyond notice, you might think.

Inside, the mahogany dining table would be laden with best silver. Fish knives, soup spoons, little gleaming salt cellars, finger bowls, napkin rings. Mrs Phillips would be checking once again that Cook had not left the head on the salmon – their special guest, Mr Hudson, hated to be reminded of cruelty when eating. No larks' tongues in aspic for the great naturalist; no song thrush vol-au-vents for the entrée. A carriage had been procured and sent to South Croydon station to await his arrival.

The Fur, Fin and Feather Folk had been meeting monthly since Sunday 17 February 1889. And before its two dozen lady members gathered for afternoon tea in the drawing room, there was a luncheon for the inner circle. Mrs Phillips provided her house, her contacts and her righteous convictions. Her good friend, Miss Catherine Hall, a Bayswater spinster of 50, donated the money. Miss Etta Smith, 29, brought the organisational skills and the zeal. The guest of honour was – when his travels permitted – the nature writer W. H. Hudson, a sharp-cheeked, pointy bearded, loquacious 48-year-old. An honorary man. A cock among hens.

The suburban tea party is so easy to knock, with its decorous rituals and its absence of alcohol, passion and, above all, men. But the tea party was the political threshing ground of the 1880s and 1890s. Women could not easily hire public spaces. They were excluded from the male preserve of the club. The professional societies were as impossible to penetrate as the universities. The Linnean Society for natural historians, the Zoological Society, the Geological Society, the British Ornithologists' Union, Thomas Huxley's scientific 'X Club' – all were men-only coteries.

'All grass roots activism starts around the kitchen table,' social historian Alison Light told me. The tea party was a quietly potent device. It might have appeared anodyne or frivolous to husbands, sons and fathers, but it had teeth. That year of 1889 there were many tea parties, increasingly political in intent.

In Hampstead, Eleanor Marx rallied middle-class socialists around porcelain teacups to support the striking East London dock workers and their families; the wives had declared a 'rent strike' and children were going without food. In Fitzrovia, her friend and ally, Clementina Black, was launching the Women's Trade Union Association, making powerful speeches over Earl Grey tea and Madeira cake. In Osnaburgh Street, near Regent's Park, social investigator Beatrice Potter (soon to become Mrs Webb) took her first, tentative tea with the Fabian Society and discussed the exploitation of workers; strikes had doubled since the match girls' stand in 1888.

In Bristol, Quaker sisters Anna Maria and Mary Priestman galvanised their social circle to set up soup kitchens to feed the striking cotton workers. In Southwark, Octavia Hill threw fundraising tea parties with immense determination, finally securing enough to buy Parliament Hill Fields, in Highgate, for public use. And, in Kensington, the popular novelist Mrs Humphry Ward felt that enough was enough and, through an assiduous schedule of 'At Homes', enlisted a large group of well-connected friends to sign her petition *against* giving women the vote.

'A Solemn Protest Against Women's Suffrage' appeared in the *Nineteenth Century* magazine, signed by 104 society ladies including Mrs Leslie Stephen (Virginia Woolf's mother), Mrs Herbert Asquith (Helen, first wife of the man who would become a Liberal prime minister) and Beatrice Potter (who later regretted adding her name).

Mrs Humphry Ward – founder of Somerville College, Oxford, in 1879 – argued that the physical weakness of women placed limits on the rights they could legitimately demand. Active 'female citizenship' – using womanly thought, conscience and moral influence to serve a community – was already a reality. And, wrote Mrs Ward, it was because women like her were 'keenly alive to the enormous value of their special contribution to the community' that they opposed 'what seems to us likely to endanger that contribution': 'We are convinced that the pursuit of a mere outward equality with men is for women not only vain, but leads to a total misconception of women's true dignity and special mission.'

In truth, many of these educated ladies were uncomfortable at the thought that women outside their social circle, women less intelligent than themselves, could be enfranchised. If women of all classes got the vote – well, this would change British society irretrievably. Published in June 1889, the 'Solemn Protest Against Women's Suffrage' gathered 2,000 more signatures.

Mrs Emmeline Pankhurst took tea, too. At 8 Russell Square, the new Bloomsbury family home of the Pankhursts, the 'Solemn Protest' was met with scornful derision. Mrs Humphry Ward's reactionary appeal against suffrage was such a provocation! Like a call to arms, it prompted the suffragists to forget their many differences and to rally together. Two weeks after Emmeline had given birth to Harry, her fifth and final child, the Women's Franchise League was founded over teacups in her double-length salon on 23 July 1889.

The league saw itself as the voice of radical suffragism. Civil inequality was going to be overturned. *All* married women would have the vote. Its treasurer, Mrs Alice Scatcherd, was a wealthy Yorkshirewoman who rejected the middle-class dress code of wedding ring and veil as 'badges of slavery' (which meant she had great difficulty checking into hotels with her husband). Mrs Pankhurst, who personally never went out without a veil, was described at this time by a female admirer as 'a living flame, active as a bit of quicksilver, as glistening, as enticing. She was very beautiful and looked like the model of Burne-Jones' pictures – slender, willowy, and with exquisite features.'

The atmosphere of 8 Russell Square, with its Aesthetic-style décor (all Japanese blinds, yellow walls, scarlet lampshades and William Morris drapes), could not have been further removed from the atmosphere at 22 Morland Road, Croydon. Here, instead, were aspidistras, pouffes, curtain valances and antimacassars. Christian tracts lined the walls. Had Mrs Pankhurst been aware of them or cared, no doubt the earnest ladies of the Fur, Fin and Feather Folk would have been derided in much the same way that the old, constitutional suffragist movement of the 1870s was ridiculed by Pankhurst's circle for its staid and fusty membership. The 'Spinster Suffrage Party', they called it.

Yet the Croydon Folk *were* radical, in their way. Each member had journeyed, alone, by public transport in order to attend. They wore clothes that marked them out as 'considered', rather than restricted (no boned corsets, no absurd bustles and certainly no feathers). Each lady was nailing her colours to the mast – and perhaps these were different colours to the values instilled at home. They were women of different ages, and of marginally different classes. One member, Hannah Poland, was the 15-year-old daughter of a fish merchant from Paddington.

Etta Smith had found her tribe. Here was a group of women who felt as passionately as she did about the rights of God's creatures – and about birds, in particular. For one afternoon a month, she was absenting herself from her father's driving mission to save Christian souls.

It was an all-female group, yet they gave pride of place to a man. During their discussions, they deferred absolutely to him. W. H. Hudson was embroiled from the start – but rather than working as their leader, he was, more accurately, their figurehead. To bend the public ear, they needed a man on board, and he became their ventriloquist. The prolific writings of all concerned make it possible to reimagine how conversation might have flowed.

But first luncheon, at which wine would be downed, so that by the time tea was served Mr Hudson's tongue was well oiled and his thoughts had a habit of running in dozens of different directions. Such as teagles. Just now he had a thing about teagles. 'I swear that *cannibals* had more respect for God-given creatures than our Ruskin-reading, civilised persons of the Nineteenth century!'

A thump on the side table, a rattle of porcelain cups on saucers. The assembled ladies leaned in. Walking in the West Country just this last week, he told them, he'd come across dozens of dead and wounded birds who'd swallowed baited hooks – 'teagles' – and, because of their meagre size, been rejected by the trapper and left to die in agony. 'And the local squires will do nothing – nothing! – to interfere with these so-called old customs of the people.'

Etta Smith had her own stories to contribute and frustrations to air. The male-dominated Greenwich Natural History Society was said to have compiled an extraordinarily diverse list of local birds, from sparrowhawks to stonechats, nightingales to merlins. Only when shot could a species be added to the list – such as the parrot crossbill recently taken at Eltham. Etta abhorred the masculine need to provide proof by removing eggs, and the 'taking' – killing – of birds. Too often, clergymen were among the worst offenders. How could they condemn the uneducated bird trapper, when the very organisations intended to promote ornithology contributed to the birds' demise?

And here lay the nub of it. Men shot, examined, indexed, stuffed and then displayed their birds behind glass. It was the only way of studying birdlife, so they claimed. Binoculars were little better than opera glasses; photography was in its infancy. Mr Hudson was, most unusually, not that sort of naturalist. He was born in the lawless Argentinian countryside to settler parents, and had spent his youth studying the local flora and fauna. He was happiest barefoot in the bush. A prolific writer, his style was florid, emotive and accessible – particularly so to women.

Mrs Phillips had discovered Mr Hudson and drawn him into her orbit. She admired his ability to seize, with passionate directness, the heart of an issue. Most polite tea party conversation focused on the weather and the servants. Here at Vaughan House, anecdotes revolved around animal cruelty – and there was no shortage of horrible stories. In February 1889, a rural teacher had been prosecuted by the RSPCA for sending his boys into the village to pick up a cat, and then chloroforming it in their presence and dissecting it. Mrs Phillips had read about it in the *Surrey Advertiser*. Teagling, shooting, poisoning, clubbing, caging, skinning, noosing, maiming . . . So great was the onslaught, it was hard to know where to start. How to help? How could one make a difference? They were, after all, just a handful of ladies. And their interests ran in such diffuse directions – from live-bait fishing to caged birds; from the cat fur trade to the cruel use of dog carts.

Bravely, Etta Smith ventured an opinion that the Fur, Fin and Feather Folk needed to sharpen their focus. If they were to pick just *one* outrage against nature, then they might hope to change public opinion. There was the scandal of caged birds, for example, sold by the thousand at Petticoat Lane market. Or the cruel pole trap, designed to catch a bird by the legs just as a gin snares a rabbit, leaving it to die a slow and lingering death. Or there was the question of feathered hats.

Published that year, a widely read new book, *The Evolution of Sex*, characterised women as having evolved 'a larger and habitual share of the altruistic emotions'. Women, claimed the male authors, excelled 'in constancy of affection and sympathy'. Every member of the Fur, Fin and Feather Folk gathered there today was living proof of this theory – and yet every lady adorned with feathers also gave it the lie.

'It is our vanity – *women's* vanity – that stimulates the greed of commerce,' pronounced Mrs Phillips, her pitch rising. There was said to be something masculine about Mrs Phillips at full throttle, a pulpit trick learned from her late husband. 'It is our money – *women's* money,' she continued, looking fiercely around the room, 'that tempts bird-slaughterers to continue their cruel work at home and abroad.'

Mr Hudson dropped his voice conspiratorially to tell the Fur, Fin and Feather Folk about his recent visit to a plumage warehouse in Cutler Street, London, where he walked ankle deep – 'literally waded, ladies' – through bright-plumaged bird skins, piled shoulder high on each side of him. Did women of fashion have *any* idea where their adornments came from, he wondered?

Mrs Phillips rose again, teacup in one hand, saucer in the other. 'All women who speak in public with their heads bedecked with stuffed birds are surely belittling their messages. I am thinking of certain ladies who speak on religious, philanthropic or aesthetic subjects. These hats make me think of a keeper's gibbet.' A pause while the ladies savoured this striking comparison. She would come to use this phrase again – and again. She could go on, but –

'My own belief,' said Mr Hudson, tamping down his pipe, 'is that the humming-bird exceeds all creatures in loveliness. Not dead in the hand, when it has only a scientific value and interest; nor a dead humming-bird worn in a lady's hat, which to my mind is a thing hateful to look at.' (Murmurs of assent.) 'I wonder if any lady who had once seen this *vivid* little airy fairy creature alive and sparkling among the flowers could wear it as an ornament – dead and dusty and crushed out of shape, all its glory gone! I wonder if its small red heart – round and ruby red, like a small ruby worn on a finger-ring – ' (here, he snatched up the slim, ringless hand of Etta Smith and held it out to the seated ladies) ' – a little while ago swiftly pulsating with the intense joyous energy of life – I wonder if this heart of a humming-bird were to be placed in any lady's palm …! But this is to digress.'

There was always a lot of talk, Etta reflected, once her blushes had subsided. But what was being *done*?

12

Emily Williamson

1889

The Society for the Protection of Birds, like so many radical ideas of the time, came from Manchester. This great city in the north-west of England was the nineteenth-century centre of radical, intellectual life. Anti-slavery, pacifism, freethinking, republicanism, nonconformism, vegetarianism, women's suffrage – all were threshed out first in the city's drawing rooms, town halls and men's clubs. Emmeline Pankhurst was a typical product of Manchester – but Manchester's bird protection movement sprang from a rather different social milieu.

While Mrs Eliza Phillips could be found pouring tea for her ladies some 200 miles away in Croydon, Surrey, a Mrs Emily Williamson was opening *her* front door to a very similar gathering of polite animal activists at The Croft, a substantial house in the prosperous Manchester suburb of Didsbury. Here we find her, dispensing tea and fruit cake with the help of housemaid Annie, in a large drawing room in the city's leafy Victorian borders. This is the popular image promoted by the RSPB today: hers is the name most often linked with this society's start – and yet, perversely, she is the least visible of the joint founders. While Etta and Eliza come vividly to life through their writing and speeches, Emily appears all but mute. She is also, historically, faceless, although her house is still standing.

The Croft sits at the edge of what is today Fletcher Moss Park, an alpine garden created by Emily and her husband in the 1880s, on acquiring the house and its four-hectare grounds. Robert Williamson was the son of an eminent naturalist; a successful solicitor with a passion for the flora of the Alps. He had amassed a large quantity of plants during several geological mountain expeditions, his wife at his side, and they built a miniature mountainside cascading away from the foot of their new house. There were conifers, gentians, rockrose, edelweiss, aubrieta and alyssum. And there were birds. The whole garden hummed and twittered with birdlife, as Mediterranean seedpods grew fat and cracked in the sun. It was, in part, distraction therapy. The couple had been married for seven years and still there were no children.

Hearteningly, this alpine garden survives today thanks to a team of volunteers. It's a lush, surprising, otherworldly space, seemingly far from England's north with its spiky palms and giant, fleshy plants. Bird feeders hang from every spare bough, blue tits and robins darting rapidly back and forth. At the foot of the garden is a small pond where a heron can often be found, standing so still it looks like a statue.

In 1989, the RSPB chose The Croft as the spot to mark the charity's centenary, and if you look very hard you will find a square metal board bearing the charity's logo: 'Action For Birds – 100 years.' Yet the name on the plaque is not Emily Williamson's. 'The unveiling was performed by the Society's President Magnus Magnusson on 17th February 1989 at The Croft where the Society was founded one hundred years ago,' it reads.

The *Manchester Evening News* covered the unveiling of this plaque, and described Emily Williamson as a 'stout Victorian woman'. In 1889, she would have been 34. Where did this information come from? The RSPB had assured me there were no surviving photographs, the charity's old London headquarters having been bombed during the Blitz. As with the young Etta Smith, it seems that nobody has really tried to find out.

Emily's great-nephew is, according to ancestry.com, the eminent Cambridge zoology professor Sir Patrick Bateson, FRS. He had no idea, until I contacted him, that his maternal great-aunt was co-founder of the RSPB. His daughter, Melissa Bateson, Professor of Ethology at Newcastle University (and author of a thesis on the behaviour of foraging starlings), was equally surprised to learn about her great-great-aunt.

Professor Bateson was eventually able to track down a photograph of Emily Williamson, a picture that rebuffs that 'stout Victorian woman' cliché comprehensively. This is the first time her image has been reproduced. Now we can admire the dark eyes and full lips of the young Emily. She looks gentle, compassionate – and sensual.

We know that she was also imaginative, spirited and driven. I found her obituary from *The Times* in Manchester Central Library (this was all that they had on her), a three-inch column that made more of her dedicated social work than it did of her connection with the RSPB. Emily would often catch the train into Manchester with Robert to pursue her various interests, while only five miles to the north, Emmeline Pankhurst was busying herself with the Manchester National Society for Women's Suffrage. Did the paths of these two women cross? Were they aware of each other? What did women's rights mean to Mrs Williamson of Didsbury? We simply do not know.

Emily founded the Society for the Protection of Birds (SPB) in February 1889 because she was angry at being barred from the all-male British Ornithologists' Union (BOU). A fervent bird lover, she was increasingly distressed by the use of grebe feathers and head frills in women's fashions. The soft underpelt of the great crested grebe was everywhere – on collars, muffs, hats, even on children's coat trimmings – while its head frills were in particular demand by the millinery trade to decorate hats. She did not know how to begin to protest, but the BOU seemed like a good place to start.

When the men turned their backs on her, Emily retaliated by banning them from her own group. The SPB started as an informal gathering of female friends, with no constitution or committee and just two pennies required for a membership card. Women signed a pledge to wear no feathers, the ostrich and game birds excepted (since plumes were obtained without killing the ostrich, and game birds were shot for their meat, not for their feathers). Numbers grew and Emily began to advertise the society by letters to the press, which intrigued male editors.

Punch received Mrs Williamson's letter from Didsbury in October 1889, the same week that Royal Academician Henry Stacy Marks spoke out in the magazine against feathered fashion: 'I always say that people like birds for three reasons,' he said. 'To shoot. – To eat. – To wear.' An exhibition of Marks' bird paintings, from the artist's own life studies at London Zoo, was about to open at the Fine Art Society on New Bond Street. The coincidence of Emily's letter and Marks' exhibition looked, to *Punch*, like a trend. The magazine took up the cudgels, hectoring in verse those who 'Lessen, as by annual inches,/Our supplies of tits and finches'; who 'Cause the stork, the crane, the gannet/To skedaddle from our planet'.

Under the headline 'Birds and Bonnets', *Punch* endorsed this new society, formed (in the words of the SPB) 'to discourage the enormous sacrifice of bird-life at present exacted by the milliners' – and, as the editor pointed out mischievously, 'acquiesced in by the matrons and maidens the milliners cater for'. How hard would it be for women to give up feathers, after all? 'Not a *very* severe self-denying ordinance that, Ladies?'

On the night of 25 November 1890, a bitterly cold frost crept across Britain from the south-east. People woke to find their windows iced over with spiralling, fern-like patterns and hedgerows furred in hoar frost. The freeze deepened and snow began to fall. Blanketed in thick fog, London did not glimpse the sun for the entire month of December. The Thames was covered in ice floes, 'a moving mass of white crests'; the Dee, near Chester, was frozen solid for five-and-a-half miles. Temperatures as low as -17 degrees Celsius held the country in a vice for eight weeks. Birds perished in their thousands.

That winter marked a shift in attitudes towards nature: a moment when the stream of letters from 'sentimental' bird lovers began to be heeded. Highlighted starkly against the frost and snow, birdlife edged its way into the nation's consciousness. 'Bessy heard the birds pecking at the food in the walk in the night,' wrote Emma Darwin, the naturalist's wife, in her diary on 7 January 1891. 'I will have some put out late as well as early. Such a mass of starlings in the field and the rails trimmed with them.'

Previously the hobby of benevolent ladies, bird feeding was soon taken up across the classes. Mr Hudson noted hundreds of working men congregating on London's bridges and embankments during their lunch hour, throwing leftover scraps of food to the birds. A tentative relationship with nature had been established. On 9 March 1891, just when it seemed that an exceptionally mild spring had arrived, a freak snowstorm blew again into southern England and Wales. It buried trains and uprooted trees; snowdrifts covered entire London houses. The blizzard raged for four days – and this time, people remembered the birds.

The Royal Society for the Prevention of Cruelty to Animals (RSPCA) felt that the moment was right for some focused agitation on the cruel fashion for avian adornment. As soon as the snow melted, the society brokered a meeting between the Manchester Society for the Protection of Birds and the Fur, Fin and Feather Folk of Croydon, inviting their respective leaders to its headquarters at Jermyn Street, Piccadilly. This was a politically expedient move, for the RSPCA couldn't itself become embroiled in the demands of extremists, being, by nature, a moderate pressure group. Instead, it encouraged enthusiasts to form their own societies for more specific ends. An army of smaller agencies – homes for dogs and horses, anti-hunting groups, societies for the suppression of vivisection, pit pony charities – were given support, advice and the free use of meeting rooms, while the RSPCA retained its neutrality.

An invitation from such a weighty institution to leave the feminine sphere of the drawing room felt like a mark of unusual respect. The ladies prepared, cautiously, for business. Mrs Emily Williamson, 36, put the finishing touches to her *tailleur*, the made-to-measure walking suit of the 1890s woman, fastened her feather-free hat with a lengthy hatpin and boarded the London steam train at Didsbury station. Mrs Eliza Phillips, 68, caught the train from East Croydon to Victoria. Miss Etta Smith, 31, travelled from Blackheath to Charing Cross. All walked, hesitantly, towards 105 Jermyn Street.

13

A Very Ambitious Title

1891

It was always instructive coming up to town, and especially so in the cluster of streets around Piccadilly. Here was the heart of fashionable London: a bewildering, ceaseless throng of shoppers, omnibuses, coaches and horse riders advancing noisily from every direction. Long traffic jams beset Regent Street as each carriage tried to park outside the shops. The aristocracy made straight for the cloistered calm of Old Bond Street, where no buses were allowed – the gleaming, crested carriages parked in rows attended by dapper 'tigers' in cockaded top hats, rug over arm, awaiting their mistresses.

Etta Smith walked slowly along the grand curve of Regent Street, stopping to examine the shop windows. You never knew what facts you might learn about the latest 'novelties' direct from Paris. She passed Messrs Lewis and Allenby, its windows festooned with cascading watered silks of exquisite, rainbow shades. Past Jay's, the high-class specialists in mourning costumes – deep mourning, half-mourning, quarter-mourning; the heavily draped fabrics rich with jet-beaded embroidery. Here was a display of feathered bonnets for the bereaved, soft with bird-of-paradise tails and snowy heron plumes, all dyed an unnatural, lustrous black. She paused outside the International Fur Store at 163 and 165 Regent Street, a business enjoying a brisk season thanks to the extended big freeze. Here you could find pelts and 'small furs' to suit every pocket, the 'cash only, no credit system' sign in the window hinting at keen prices. White ermine was back in vogue this year; silver fox, mink, beaver, bear, sable from Russia and Alaska, chinchilla and Tibetan goat. From a distance the window display resembled a pack of animals on the loose – not so very different to that of 'The Jungle' on 167 Piccadilly, premises of celebrated taxidermist Roland Ward.

Stepping closer, items came into focus. There was a full-length 'vigogne cashmere' cloak made from South American llama fur, lined with squirrel and trimmed with opossum; an 'Alert Fur Tie' consisting of a squirrel with its tail in its mouth; and a 'Magicienne' fur bag muff, with three glossy heads of mink, stoat and weasel dangling from it, their little glass eyes glinting.

Etta Smith noted the luxurious black capes made of astrakhan, the tightly whorled fleece of unborn karakul lambs from the high mountains of Central Asia. For the pelt to be harvested, both lamb and ewe had to die two weeks before birth. Sealskin coats, too, filled the International Fur Store's glass windows – the favoured look of the 1890s woman about town. 'She wears a sealskin coat; its grace and shape I note . . . She wears a little bonnet; a bird that's perched upon it; to fly seems ready,' went the words to a Valentine's ditty. The waspish English novelist Maria Louise Ramé, who went by the pen name of Ouida, was contemptuous of the hypocritical 'New Woman' and her double standards, dabbling in philanthropy, elbowing her way into public life 'in her sealskin coat with the dead hummingbird on her hat'. The sealskin jacket and the feathered hat went together. They were a look. One might call them a brand.

Etta walked on. These women were everywhere on Regent Street. Society milliner Helene & Co had a dazzling display of colour: acid-green parrot wings, the carmine of scarlet tanagers, the turquoise and gold sheen of peacock. The colours of spring 1891 were decreed to be green, maize yellow and light purple: 'The effectiveness of the combination is well displayed in hats of fancy purple straw.' A wide-brimmed hat decked entirely with jewelled hummingbirds sat on a pedestal, trailing silk ribbons. Weeks had been lost to bad weather, so there was no time to waste before this season's fashion gave way to the next. Ladies, huddled in furs, strolled in pairs, stopping at the windows, intent on the latest novelties. Etta took out her little notebook and pencil.

In 1891, there were 548 milliners selling from establishments in central London. Ninety of these alone operated from the West End, fanning out west from Piccadilly towards Kensington. Regent Street was home to 14 millinery stores, from the exclusive Jay & Co ('by special appointment to the Queen') to the more contemporary Louise & Co (two double shop frontages at the top and bottom of Regent Street; another shop on the Brompton Road). French names signalled the latest fashions (Mademoiselle Emelie Rhoda, Madame Adelaide Purrier); English names (Miss Jane Davis, Mrs Millie Carter, Perrin & Co) spoke to the more conservative.

Crossing Piccadilly Circus, Etta dodged carriages and omnibuses, skirts lifted slightly out of the mire, and turned right into Jermyn Street. Where better to target feathered fashion?

'R. S. P. C. A.' was spelled out in large letters across the facade of number 105, headquarters of the society now for 22 years. Between the classical columns stood a concierge in liveried uniform and peaked cap, ushering visitors in through enormous front doors. There was a constant to and fro of foot traffic; a shuffling bustle of purpose. The ladies were not the only item on the agenda for the day. It was a large building – two joined together – with a wide, creaking staircase and a clanging Victorian lift, hauling visitors up to the maze of smaller staircases and corridors that forked their way through the interior. It smelled of polished wood, dust and age, and was crammed with offices.

The women were greeted and shown into a larger room. We do not know what was said at the meeting – but it was a significant one for the RSPCA, a society that permitted an offshoot ladies' committee, but would not let women sit on its general council until 1896. True to the founding spirit of these two different groups from Croydon and Manchester, it appears that the session was informal, collaborative and focused on practicalities rather than personalities. No one woman pushed herself forward.

Emily Williamson caught the train back to Didsbury and to her husband. What was her state of mind? Perhaps Robert had cautioned her not to relinquish control. Perhaps his legal brain had foreseen what gentlewomen are inclined to do to when striking bargains: allow good manners to prevail. But his wife returned home having given full permission for her Society for the Protection of Birds to amalgamate with the Fur, Fin and Feather Folk of Croydon, conceding that a serious organisation for bird protection needed a wider range of tactics and a more formal structure. She had also bequeathed her society's name, with her blessing, as it was felt that something less twee was needed. Robert was forced to agree: you might get away with 'Fur, Fin and Feather Folk' in Surrey, but certainly not in Manchester.

In May 1891, Emily formally relinquished her status as secretary to young Hannah Poland, now 17, and accepted the offer of a vice presidency (the first of many such, for people of influence). She knew that this was a nominal title – attending annual meetings rather than campaigning on the front line. From this point on, Mrs Williamson turned her attention to social work in Manchester, where she was remembered for her 'quiet dignity' and 'lovable disposition', along with her formidable organisational powers. She remained an entirely supportive and amiable local secretary for the (R)SPB until her death, running the original branch in the relative obscurity of Didsbury, then later another in Brook, Surrey, and finally one in Kensington. In the 45 years that she was vice president, she spoke only once at a meeting – about the society's origins.

If the Manchester group provided the name, the London group supplied the energy, and Etta Smith was at the forefront of manoeuvrings. When a lawyer was needed to draw up the constitution of the merged organisation, she suggested a young barrister of her acquaintance, Frank Lemon. It is possible that Frank's father, William, was instrumental in the deal, pulling strings at the RSPCA to formalise that desk in the corner. But it was Frank who did the paperwork, and Frank who willingly became entangled with the society, and the woman at its heart, for the rest of his life.

The resulting constitution ruled thus:

1. That members shall discourage the wanton destruction of Birds, and interest themselves generally in their protection.
2. That Lady Members shall refrain from wearing the feathers of any bird not killed for the purposes of food, the ostrich excepted.
3. That each Local Secretary shall subscribe one shilling a year, and each Ordinary Member pay two-pence (postage free) for Card of Membership.

From these small beginnings, something extraordinary was to grow.

14

Flight

1891

Not everybody was so delighted by the birth of this new society.
The news of its ambitious aims attracted 'smiles of amusement',
wrote Etta, much later. Their first report, with its balance sheet showing
an income of £7 13s 8d, was described derisively in one of the London
weeklies as 'a sparrow's housekeeping book'. The journal *Nature Notes*
reported on the SPB under the title 'Birds and Bonnets', reproducing a
short letter by Hannah Poland, originally printed in the *Yorkshire Post*.
The editor followed this with a letter from the Reverend Francis Orpen
Morris, the 82-year-old author of *A History of British Birds*. Natural
historian, anti-Darwinian and anti-feminist, he could barely restrain
his anger.

'One is always glad to hear or read of any such right minded
endeavours, and especially so in the case of a society formed for the
furtherance of the object of them,' he began with elaborate civility. But
then he let rip – for they had stolen his idea! 'I did my best in that
direction some years ago in a letter I wrote to *The Times* at the request of
Lord and Lady Mount-Temple, and headed it "The Plumage League".'
It transpired that the Reverend Morris had tried to whip up opposition
to avian adornment in 1885, six years before these upstart ladies came
along and claimed the moral high ground for themselves.

He boasted of the blue-blooded backing of this original 'Plumage
League', 'mostly – indeed almost exclusively – from the higher and

highest circles, from the late Duchess of Sutherland downwards'. He blamed the league's supporters for not taking his idea further – 'I have heard nothing of it recently' – and bemoaned the lack of a '"head centre" of operations'. Above all, he mourned the waste of his brilliant title – 'I do not think a better can readily be suggested than that I have mentioned above, "THE PLUMAGE LEAGUE".'

The Reverend Morris suggested, somewhat patronisingly, that these SPB ladies could perhaps be co-opted into the original movement, which could well use their time and enthusiasm. 'I hope not a few of your readers will communicate with the lady, the writer of the above-given letter, and encourage her righteous effort in any way they can.'

Nature Notes was the magazine of the Selborne Society, a naturalists' club with the broad, if fuzzy, aim of preserving birds, wildflowers, forests 'and places of popular resort'. Formed in 1885, in memory of eighteenth-century naturalist Gilbert White, the society's members were mostly male, luxuriantly whiskered and deeply proprietorial about nature. When the Honourable Mrs Cavendish-Boyle and Lady Mount-Temple founded The Plumage League in that same year, it was swiftly absorbed into the Selborne Society to lend it heft and rechristened the 'Plumage Section'. Each member of the Selborne Society was urged to form a branch, and these branches were rooted in prosperous Hampshire and Surrey. The secretary of the Croydon branch, conservationist Edward Alfred Martin, helped advise Eliza Phillips on setting up her Fur, Fin and Feather Folk in 1889. He consequently looked possessively on the SPB as his 'own fledgling'.

At the foot of the Reverend Morris's letter, editor James Britten (a bespectacled British Museum botanist) added a belittling note: 'As to the name of such a society, that suggested by Mr Morris is immeasurably the better. To assume such a very ambitious title as "The Society for the Protection of Birds" for a band of ladies who do nothing but abstain from personal iniquity in the matter of bonnets, may give occasion for the unrighteous to scoff.'

*

Britten was proved wrong. Within six months, Eliza Phillips, Etta Smith and young Hannah Poland had grown this little 'bird and bonnet' society from 1,000 to 5,000 members; by 1893, the membership had almost reached 10,000, most of them women. Their names are redolent of female mettle: Evangeline Hake of Leamington, Winifred Kimmins of Stonehouse in Gloucestershire, Miss Buttress of the Rectory in Retford, Miss Edith Elliot of Walsall.

The SPB might not have had the high-profile patronage of the Selborne Society's Plumage Section (headed by Queen Victoria's daughter, Princess Christian of Schleswig-Holstein), but its leaders possessed formidable organisational skills. 'Revived and admirably reorganised', noted the RSPCA of the SPB in its annual report. Using pre-existing women's and animal rights networks, the women grew their society laterally, like a branching taproot.

Unlike the Selborne Society, with its male egos and luxuriant whiskers posturing in the public eye, the strength of the SPB lay invisible and underground. Its foot soldiers were its local secretaries. By the end of the society's first year, there were over 50 of them scattered throughout the British Isles – from Dorchester to Dublin, Edinburgh to Esher. It was undoubtedly middle class, but not 'like a list from Debrett's', as the RSPB's historians have suggested. Many did not need to work for a living: the wives of clergymen, academics and military men. Others did: from music teachers and nurses to a young London librarian who lived in a hostel. One woman was a hatter's daughter; another a boot and shoe dealer. Just one had a title: Lady Brownrigg of Maidenhead, married to a baronet.

These women were required to actively spread the word and sign up new members. With every local branch secretary stepping up to take on the voluntary work, another network was tapped into and conscripted. The SPB was a model of devolved leadership: all branch secretaries working to an unashamedly populist common goal. They were going to stamp out the fashion for feathers in hats.

The idea of a pledge of abstinence was key to the society's success. A personal commitment was required – just as with the temperance movement, or the women's suffrage movement. A membership card might cost just two pennies, but this was an emotional contract. The gushing, sentimentalising, sensitive sort of woman repellent to the male ornithologists, with her talk of 'feathered friends', 'songsters' and 'dicky birds', was precisely the sort that signed up in their hundreds.

Penny by penny, the funds rolled in. Some made lavish contributions: a Mrs Bagnell gave £10 (around £4,500 today) right at the start. The anti-vivisectionist and suffragist Frances Power Cobbe renounced her paradise hat (but kept her furs) and gave £5. Heiress Florence Horatia Suckling (later to write a book on the saints and their 'animal friends') gave a guinea. Most women, though, spent just the minimum tuppence on membership (rising to one shilling in 1893) – a price 'to suit every class of sympathiser'. Not *quite* every class. The SPB was beyond the reach and ken of working girls like Alice Battershall, stealing for shillings in order to eat. It presupposed a basic level of comfort, and of aspiration.

Five months after the move to Jermyn Street, this 'band of ladies' had outstripped the Selborne Society in membership. Unlike other similar organisations, the great appeal of the SPB lay in its brilliant clarity of focus. It was going to halt the mighty plumage trade.

15

Impracticable Dreamers

1892

Could Etta, Eliza and Emily really make a difference? Did women like them really have the capacity to wade into the masculine sphere and tangle with commerce and politics? The men, on the whole, thought not. The eminent Victorian philosopher and sociologist Herbert Spencer had written reams on women's biological inferiority. He held that women did not progress side by side with men intellectually, but occupied a position 'about midway between the civilized man of our era and the pure savage'.

The politician Mr Samuel Smith was one of many who agreed with this view, particularly when it came to the vote. Minority groups (such as women) represented 'small coteries of faddists who threaten to cast their vote on some petty issue dear to themselves'. They were irrational, emotional and a menace to politicians. The Liberal MP for Flintshire, Smith was a 50-something man with a rippling, chest-length, forked beard, and an abhorrence of the idea of women's suffrage. He felt that ladies had no cause to complain now that the 1882 Married Women's Property Act *and* the Guardianship of Infants Act from 1886 gave them 'reasonable control' over their lives.

Women had greater freedom and equality than ever before, he argued in 1891, in a self-published pamphlet. They now had access to higher education, to university lectures, to medical training. They edited journals; they even addressed public meetings! Old 'injustices' had been remedied. Let women – even a small proportion of women – have the vote and it would represent the thin end of the wedge. Statesmen would, in time, be replaced with 'impracticable dreamers' pushing through social reforms 'more utopian than the world has ever known'.

What *was* Mr Smith so terrified about, the new suffragist leader Millicent Fawcett wanted to know. In 1890, Mrs Fawcett had replaced the veteran suffragist campaigner Lydia Becker, bringing fresh momentum and energy to a cause that was beginning, slowly, to be taken seriously at Westminster. Her cool riposte to Smith was published the following year by the National Society for Women's Suffrage, written with her trademark blend of clarity and asperity. She professed herself amused by his hysterical image of 'wives and mothers neglecting their babies and their husbands' suppers, to attend clubs and political meetings' and destroying 'the health of unborn generations' with their 'febrile' political excitement.

What sort of women did Mr Smith consort with, Mrs Fawcett wondered? He appeared to believe that female voters would be 'animated by a practically unanimous desire to destroy the commerce, the credit, the empire and the greatness of England'. What is more, the MP for Flintshire had got his maths wrong. Against this 'horde of eleven million malignant women', he was claiming that 'the fortress of the Constitution' would be defended by just ten million men.

Who said that universal suffrage was the goal, anyway? Not Millicent Fawcett – a clear-browed, handsome 44-year-old, widow of a Liberal politician and co-founder of Newnham College, Cambridge. She wasn't proposing anything so radical as universal suffrage. Not yet. The bill about to be debated in parliament, proposed by the portly Conservative Sir Albert Rollit, MP for Islington South, was to enfranchise fewer than one million widows and spinsters. Women, that is, who were property owners, ratepayers and heads of households.

On this basis, of the characters we have met in this story so far, only Eliza Phillips would be qualified to vote. Not Etta Smith, who lived with her father and stepmother; not Emily Williamson, who was married; not Mrs Pankhurst; and certainly not feather thief Alice Battershall or her mother Emma, who rented their rooms in the rough streets neighbouring Rollit's constituency.

It was a tentative – and, to more radical suffragists – divisive measure. Yet it was enough to seriously rattle the establishment. Just before the bill's first reading on 27 April 1892, William Gladstone – who, at 82, would embark upon his fourth and final stint as Liberal Prime Minister to Queen Victoria that August – felt compelled to publish *his* response to Samuel Smith in yet another pamphlet. More measured, more deeply thoughtful, Gladstone wrote that women could not be offered the vote because he felt that there wasn't enough agitation for it. Rather, there was a 'widespread indifference' to so 'largely strange a subject'. It was too soon. The public mind was 'immature'.

True, women had made gains in the public sphere, but they were small. 'We have done nothing that plunges the woman as such into the turmoil of masculine life.' Most importantly, wrote Gladstone, if women sat in the House of Commons they would be expected to fulfil their role on equal terms with men – and this would, of course, be impossible. 'The Maker' had created two 'subtly and profoundly different' sexes. Female MPs would be physically unequal to male MPs, and therefore 'stamped with disability'.

The Spectator swiftly congratulated Gladstone on being 'large-minded' enough to speak so frankly despite a looming election. He had 'ended the question for this generation', thought the editor. There would be no votes for women, not even 'a century hence', because of their fundamental physical difference with men. Votes for women would be 'a monstrous inversion of the natural order of things'. It belonged among 'such speculative projects as the dream of universal peace'. And yet there was quiet support for Sir Albert Rollit's bill. At its second hearing on Friday 13 May, it lost by just 23 votes.

Where, in all this, was Emmeline Pankhurst? The Women's Franchise League, started with such enthusiasm in her drawing room just three years previously, was imploding. From its idealistic beginnings, attracting suffragists dissatisfied with the 'half a loaf is better than none' approach of veteran campaigner Lydia Becker and her successor Millicent Fawcett, it had now degenerated into chaotic confusion. Ironically, it was Richard Pankhurst who dominated the league, not Emmeline, and it was heavily populated by men. Up-and-coming Liberal politicians R. B. Haldane and Sir Edward Grey were members – men who might further Richard's political career. While Emmeline herself would introduce a star speaker or second a resolution, she did not thrust herself forward and she did no public speaking. The league became an opportunity to promote her husband and his causes. Richard Pankhurst had many hobby horses – co-education, marriage law reform, the plight of oppressed races in the empire, the abolition of the House of Lords – and they began to be co-opted onto the league's agenda.

Not everyone was happy about this. Many of the women felt this watered down their original aim, or that the league had set its sights too high with all these other ideals and was demanding the unachievable. Haldane, seeking excuses for not pressing their cause in parliament, said that their bill was nothing more than a declaration of principle, upon which no legislative action could be expected for years. 'Thereby,' wrote Sylvia Pankhurst many years later, 'he lighted a smouldering fire of indignation' within her mother.

By 1893, the league was extinct. Mrs Pankhurst had moved back to Manchester for her own and her family's health. Richard had stomach ulcers and Emmeline had four children aged four to 13 to care for. She was at a low ebb – 'so languid that she felt herself scarcely able to take a short stroll down Lord Street to see the shops.' This, for a compulsive shopper, was grave indeed. She turned her energies to her husband and her children and, for now, bided her time.

The women behind the Society for the Protection of Birds were not, by instinct, supporters of either Mrs Pankhurst or Mrs Fawcett, although many of their members were. The leaders held the Church's view that woman was created as Adam's helpmate, and that 'separate spheres' for the sexes was the natural ideal. Yet, in attempting to sway public opinion against the muscular plumage trade, they were plunging 'into the turmoil' (as Gladstone put it) of masculine life. Feathered hats might seem a ludicrously lightweight target to those who belittled their efforts, but their campaign dragged them, perforce, into politics.

Willingly, they waded in. 'A good wife and mother cannot leave her home to attend clubs and public meetings,' Samuel Smith MP had warned; 'and if she does she will soon cease to be a good wife and mother.' It was no coincidence that Etta Smith, Emily Williamson and Eliza Phillips were single, childless or widowed. Would they have risked family censure to become so embroiled, otherwise? Would their husbands have let them?

In the months after drawing up their constitution, young barrister Frank Lemon looked on with a kind of awe. The society was a storm of activity. While Etta Smith lobbied and wrote to the press, Eliza Phillips, now vice president and publications editor, wrote a series of trenchant, polemicising pamphlets on birds and the plumage trade to raise money. The more the team agitated and campaigned, the louder became the simultaneous public debate on femininity and a woman's rightful place in the world. Contradictory images of women were held up relentlessly in the press – and the fashion for feathered hats provided an excellent symbol of women's stupidity.

Bird-brained women, in thrall to 'cannibalistic' haute couture. Feather-headed women. Twittering women. 'Can you imagine anything more ridiculous than a young woman sporting an entire Herring Gull on her head?' asked one male journalist. Refined ladies should leave plumage to 'women of little education and possibly depraved minds', wrote Sir Harold Johnston (president of the all-male Royal Society), comparing feather wearers to 'baboons' or 'magpies'. The persistent scapegoating of women wasn't, in truth, so much about their vanity as about their new political visibility. The defiantly feathered woman had come to represent those who were seeking the franchise, university education, legal rights and greater social freedom. The American plumage campaigner Harriet Hemenway bemoaned the fact that as well as killing birds, the fashion for avian adornment was also killing women's chances of getting the vote and being listened to. For who, as she put it, would listen to a woman with a dead bird on her head?

Yet those insulting bird metaphors – twittering, tweeting, ruffling feathers – could also be flipped to women's advantage. An insatiable capacity for networking lay behind the swift and impressive growth of the Society for the Protection of Birds. Nobody instructed Etta Smith or Eliza Phillips how to go about it; they worked by intuition, showing an instinctive ability to make personal connections. If human and animal natures *were* related, then Darwin's latest ideas on the 'feminine' qualities of altruism, cooperation and empathy in *The Descent of Man* (1871) might explain their success. Far from shrinking from contact with the outside world, these women seemed to be rather good at plunging, collaboratively, into the turmoil.

The founders of the SPB have been historically dismissed as elderly and out of touch – but, in 1892, Etta Smith was in her prime. Her intense, dark eyes burned with purpose. She would willingly do all the legwork for this society; all the front-line campaigning, too. It was to become her entire world.

On 25 May of that year, Frank Edward Lemon married Margaretta Louisa Smith at Christ Church chapel in Blackheath. They were not an especially glamorous bride and groom – she was a little angular, with sallow skin; he was slightly bug-eyed, with a soft moustache. But together the Lemons made a splendid and – in time – formidable couple. Marriage was the making of each of them. And finally, at 31 years of age, Etta could step out from her father's controlling shadow and spread her wings.

16

Courting the Men

1892–3

I t had started as a women-only movement – but very quickly it became
clear that this wasn't going to work. The most influential names in
ornithology and nature conservation were male. The plumage trade
was run by men. The strings of the fashion industry were manipulated
by men. Men financed the millinery trade magazines and the feather
warehouses. The majority of well-heeled, female consumers were
subsidised and encouraged by husbands and fathers. To take on these
women, they had to engage with the men. To take on the plumage trade,
they had to infiltrate it by any means possible. Men were duly welcomed
into the Society for the Protection of Birds as 'honorary co-workers'
– and willingly relieved of their money.

Revered ornithologist Professor Alfred Newton was the first man to
become a 'Life Associate', with the donation of one guinea. This was
flamboyantly topped by a £10 gift (around £4,500 today) by Lord Lilford,
president of the British Ornithologists' Union and owner of some truly
extraordinary stuffed *and* live birds at Lilford Hall, Northamptonshire.
These included shaggy South American rheas, Indian pink-headed ducks
– now extinct – and a pair of bearded vultures from North Africa that flew
free on the estate. Lilford's donation proved an irresistible provocation to
John Alexander Harvie-Brown, the celebrated Scottish ornithologist and
another compulsive collector of birds' eggs and skins: he, too, gave £10.
And so it went on.

The collecting mania of male ornithologists did not remotely chime with the SPB ladies' sensibilities; egg collecting in particular became a deepening source of embarrassment for the charity, with so many 'secret' oologists as members. But just as the tactical and pragmatic Mrs Pankhurst would come to woo the wealthy upper classes, so, too, the bird ladies would need to seek as many establishment friends as was humanly possible.

Etta Lemon and Eliza Phillips then turned to lobbying the Church of England. As a vicar's widow, Mrs Phillips was adept at this, writing articles which 'may perhaps reach the eyes of clergymen, and induce some of them to speak a few words, which . . . might save many birds' lives'. Church was, effectively, a millinery catwalk – and most vicars timidly refused to ruffle feathers. 'It ought not to be left to lay-men,' she wrote pointedly, 'not even to such a one as John Ruskin, to teach us "not to kill or hurt any living creature needlessly".'

They chose their targets with acuity. The Bishop of Durham – Bishop Westcott, president of the Christian Social Union – was signed up. Bishop Welldon was converted: headmaster of Harrow, honorary chaplain to Queen Victoria, soon to become Bishop of Calcutta, where he would put his considerable weight behind India's beleaguered birds. Canon Jessopp of Norfolk was picked for his power as a rural life journalist for the influential *Nineteenth Century* magazine.

Politicians were enlisted, too. The pro-suffrage Sir Edward Grey, young and dashing statesman in the new Liberal government, was an avid ornithologist. Mr Sydney Buxton, Under-Secretary of State for the Colonies and a keen fly fisherman, was perfectly placed to agitate on a plumage importation ban. Lord Wolseley was simply a towering force, one of Britain's most admired generals. His name alone would pull in dozens more.

They also persuaded illustrators and artists to join the campaign. Edward Linley Sambourne, cartoonist for *Punch* magazine, sharpened his pencil and set to work. 'A Bird of Prey' shows a female harpy dressed in full Victorian feather regalia closing in on a small songbird, talons at the ready. She wears a long feathered boa with a life of its own, and on her head is a fashionable hat sprouting plumes, wings and bills. It was published in *Punch* in May 1892 – but it didn't deter Sambourne's daughter, society beauty Maud Messel, from amassing a prolific wardrobe of feathers.

George Frederic Watts – elderly and revered Royal Academician, considered, by many, the greatest artist of his day – produced a large, emotive oil known as *The Shuddering Angel*, dedicated 'to all those who love the beautiful and mourn over the senseless and cruel destruction of bird life and beauty'. Iridescent, lifeless plumage lies in a heap on a tombstone, over which an angel weeps, head in hands. The painting was exhibited in London's New Gallery in 1899 and caused an immediate sensation – warranting a leader in *The Times*.

'It is a little startling to read so severe a sermon, and from such a quarter, over an offence which well-meaning people commit in all unconsciousness,' wrote the editor. 'Ladies who wear feathers in their hats do not take their act so seriously as Mr Watts does.'

In the first year of campaigning, the SPB was deluged with publicity. These ladies had great novelty value. Sixty publications carried their story, from *Country Gentleman* to *Princess* magazine; *Animal World* to *The Vegetarian*; *Girl's Own Paper* to the *Pall Mall Gazette*. Leader writers at *The Times* and *Punch* adopted the fight against feathered women as a special cause. It turned out that Etta and Eliza were surprisingly good at getting people's attention.

The Selborne Society fraternity was left looking sour on the sidelines. While the Reverend Morris fretted about the 'sentimentality' of his society's followers and its Plumage Section's 'embarrassing accretions' (that is, emotional lady members), he was made to look ridiculous by the single-minded progress of these SPB women. He sniped at them, in part, because he felt possessive. Birds belonged to rational, educated, scientifically minded men like him.

Yet Victorian women were inclined (infuriatingly!) to co-opt the birds as their special friends. They might be excluded from the ornithological societies, and prevented by their impractical dress, time constraints and decorum from studying it in the field, but women could still achieve daily contact with birdlife. Anybody could feed the birds. Anybody, no matter how circumscribed (and the 'caged bird' metaphor was highly pertinent in this patriarchal society), could watch the birds from a bedroom window or a back door.

The Scottish artist Jemima Blackburn became expert in depicting bird behaviour, simply by close and prolonged observation. It was she who made the startling discovery that the cuckoo fledgling kicked all other eggs or hatchlings out of its borrowed nest. This Blackburn sketched and described in 1871 – not in a scientific journal, but in *The Pipits*, a book for children. Charles Darwin quickly included her observations in the sixth edition of his *Origin of Species* the following year.

Women approached birds differently. Few were interested in the baggage that went with science-based ornithology: the list-keeping, the hours spent debating abstruse points of identification and taxonomy, the shotgun, the taxidermist and the display cabinets. The Victorian nature writer Eliza Brightwen, Mrs Lemon's early inspiration on bird matters, used her sentiment to great effect when writing about birds, especially mother egrets before a plumage hunter closes in: 'The little tender, loving mothers cannot bear to leave their young and hover close around them.'

A moral stance towards the treatment of animals was an attitude peculiarly linked to women – and it was a position emphatically rejected by naturalists such as the Reverend Morris. His strange hostility (given his extraordinary devotion to birds; the entry on sparrows alone in *A History of British Birds* ran to 18 pages) echoed the response of many men. Women's emotional relationship with birds was seen as backward, non-scientific and unserious. They had no business muscling in on his patch.

There was nothing sentimental about the newly married Mrs Lemon, however. Her tone was different to that of Eliza Brightwen: more forthright, harsher. The facts themselves were glaring enough. Mrs Lemon became expert in facts, and exploited them for their emotional shock value.

She had no shortage of hard evidence at her disposal. In the SPB's first annual report, she tore into the millinery trade with panache. Quoting Dr Bowdler Sharpe of the Natural History Museum on feather wearing ('a custom long banished among men excepting those of the savage tribes'), she described in surgical detail a piece of evidence before her. It was no use talking of tonnes of plumage imported. If you wanted to capture the imagination, you had to focus on the detail. Her evangelising father had taught her this much.

'Certainly nothing can well be more savage in design than a bonnet-trimming bought a few weeks ago for three shillings.' The bonnet in question was made in Paris, sold in London, and numbered for future orders. 'The chief feature is the lovely little head of some insect-eating bird, split in two,' she wrote – adding that each half of the head was 'stuck aloft on thin skewers'. It got worse. The bird's tail sat in the middle of the bifurcated head, the wings on either side, while a tuft of the buff plumes of the squacco heron (a small, short-necked, toffee-coloured bird from southern Europe) completed the 'monstrosity'. Her description of the bonnet springs vividly, grotesquely, off the page.

After just a few months, the SPB's campaign appeared, incredibly, to be making an impact. Feathered fashions seemed to be on the wane. True, you could still see stuffed goldfinches hanging in strings in small drapers' windows for a few pence apiece. There were still Saturday evening markets in London where one could find trays of brightly coloured tropical birds – tanagers, orioles, kingfishers, long-tailed scarlet trogons, tiny hummingbirds in every hue – selling from tuppence per bird. 'So cheap that even the ragged girl from the neighbouring slums could decorate her battered hat, like any fine lady, with some bright-winged bird of the tropics,' as W. H. Hudson observed in *The Times*.

They were still for sale, but the drop in prices was taken as a sign that bird wearing was declining. By the autumn of 1892, many of the smarter West End millinery establishments had ceased supplying birds altogether. A professional wildfowler complained to *The Times* of the effect the society was having. He was accustomed to hunting kittiwake gulls (known as kitty or sea swallow) by the thousand for their black-tipped wings; a single order from a plumage dealer might demand 8,000 at a time. 'This year I have not shot one sea swallow,' he said. 'This ladies' association has stopped the demand.'

But was this really the case? The SPB kept a close eye on the plumage sales. Once a fortnight, Mrs Lemon would quietly procure an auction catalogue from the feather warehouses on Billiter Street and Cutler Street in the City of London. In 1892, she was able to confirm the killing of 30,000 partridges within a few days in one area of Italy, and a single shipment of 32,000 hummingbirds, 80,000 waterbirds and 800,000 pairs of wings imported by a London dealer. Far from changing heart, it transpired that fashion had merely paused for a season, turning restlessly to other novelties. By autumn 1893, feathers were, once again, all the rage.

This time the demand was unprecedented. *Punch* carried a cartoon that October titled 'A Large Order', in which a fat, vulgar, well-dressed woman enters a shop. 'What can I have the pleasure of serving you with, Madam?' asks the male shop assistant obsequiously. The lady replies with a single word: 'Wings.'

17

Winifred, Duchess of
Portland

There was a fourth 'redoubtable' woman behind the SPB: Winifred Cavendish-Bentinck, Duchess of Portland, president from 1891 to her death, aged 91, in 1954. She was initially cajoled by the RSPCA, of which she was a vice president, to lend her name to this little bird endeavour. A title was essential for opening establishment doors and raising public awareness, and the Duchess came from the very social milieu most likely to wear lavish plumes.

A handwritten letter in the RSPB archives brings the Duchess vividly to life. Here was a very particular and patrician voice, autocratic and confident. Here, too, was a relationship.

> Dear Mrs Lemon – excuse a feeble pencil note! I caught influenza that day & have been in bed ever since – alas – I am <u>indignant</u> at the osprey – I have never possessed one in my <u>life</u> – nor had the slightest desire to do so. I personally have always thought them <u>very</u> uninteresting & ugly in a hat. You might contradict it with the fullest confidence – who is my double, I wonder. I <u>have</u> a double in height & <u>general</u> appearance – Mrs Laurence Drummond – who <u>always</u> wears one (bright green generally) so it might be her. Perhaps literature would do her good on the subject! So will you send her some – <u>by my express desire</u>! – to

18 Eaton Place. <u>Will</u> you kindly write this man Mr Smith a nice note saying I <u>have asked you to do so being ill with influenza</u> & tell him I am so glad he is interested <u>etc</u>! W.P.

In 1903 – the date of this letter – the 'osprey' had a very different meaning, the *only* meaning to the bird protection society. Rather than a fish eagle, the osprey meant the upright, tufty millinery ornament made from the fine nuptial feathers of the snowy and great egret of North and South America. It was the cruellest feather to harvest, killing the parent birds and leaving their nestlings to starve to death, and it was to become the most potent emblem for the campaign against feathered hats.

This letter gives a vignette of how things worked at the society back then. 'W.P.' – Winifred Portland: charming, faintly bullying, good at the personal touch but rarely in the office. A gossip columnist had apparently spotted her wearing the so-called 'osprey' tuft of egret feathers in her hair. Mrs Lemon, a one-woman newspaper cuttings service, had immediately sent Her Grace a copy. And it was Mrs Lemon who had to deal with the correspondence, posting one of Mrs Phillips' educational pamphlets to the imperious, beetle-browed Katherine Drummond, wife of a major-general.

The Duchess of Portland – 'Winnie' to her intimates – was, at the start, 28 years old to Etta Lemon's 31 and a ravishing clothes horse. Tall and slender with a dreamy, longish face, Winnie exuded British good breeding. She was dismissed as staid and toothless by the young men who eventually took over the RSPB in the 1930s, but in 1891 the Duchess was a force of energy. Winnie was teetotal and vegetarian. She played darts rather well, enjoyed fly fishing and had tremendous stamina, once standing still for three hours while being sewn into an antique lace dress before a ball.

When she took on the presidency of the SPB she was already deeply embroiled in a raft of other humanitarian causes – patron of the Red Cross, the Waifs and Strays Society, Our Dumb Friends League (she had a weakness for adopting pit ponies and maltreated donkeys). Winnie campaigned on behalf of young working women, setting up 'hygiene and housewifery' courses in Worksop, near the family seat at Welbeck Abbey in Nottinghamshire. She campaigned, too, on behalf of crippled miners. The dukes of Portland had benefited over the centuries from the rich coal seams of Nottinghamshire, and since her marriage to the 6th Duke in 1889, Winifred Portland had started to redistribute deftly some of this wealth.

Her largesse was as legendary as her peremptory manner. Travelling by road to Leeds on her way to address the RSPCA, she once passed a drover viciously beating his herd of cattle. She stopped her carriage, clambered down and gave the man 'a piece of her mind'. She then set a policeman on his trail to make sure he didn't do it again. All this, combined with great persuasive charm, made the Duchess of Portland close to unstoppable. Married to a man who was Master of the Horse, parent to a baby daughter who had Queen Victoria as a godmother, Winnie was ideally placed to lobby the aristocracy on the SPB's cause.

At first, she moved tactically. Rather than berate her own peer group – debutantes settling into marriage and motherhood on thousand-acre estates – she started with the dowagers. Here lay real power. The beaky-nosed Elizabeth, Dowager Duchess of Wellington was, at the grand age of 71, a ringleader of social protocol; her brother, the 9th Marquess of Tweeddale, was a past president of the Zoological Society and an expert on the birds of South East Asia (with an extraordinary private collection of stuffed birds, insects, reptiles and mammals). Where Elizabeth led, lured by the bait of a vice presidency, other *grandes dames* would follow. Eleanor, Dowager Duchess of Northumberland was another widowed 71-year-old, with no children and a sentimental spot for 'feathered songsters'. A generation younger, Susan, Duchess of Somerset was an obvious candidate: Scottish, keen on nature, a writer of a philanthropic bent. Again, she had no children.

With these three vice presidents in the bag, Winnie searched for another key player. Lady Paget was a former lady-in-waiting to Queen

Victoria; a passionate vegetarian who abhorred cruelty to animals; and an influential writer. She was held to be responsible for matchmaking the Prince of Wales with Princess Alexandra of Denmark in 1863, and she had great influence over the Queen.

It was crucial to enlist the aristocracy. Other, lesser women would then slavishly follow their lead. These were the people who set the tone. Their court appearances, their arrivals and departures in town, their country seats and the minute detail of their wardrobes were written up breathlessly, endlessly, by newspapers and magazines. It's hard to appreciate today the power and influence held by this small pool of upper-class women, perhaps 5,000 in number. But aspirational society on both sides of the Atlantic was in thrall to them. Their glamour was unquestioned, as was the wish of less privileged people to attain it.

The Duchess of Portland had a delicate battle on her hands. Not only was she expected to take up cudgels against her own kind, but against her own sex – for hers was, most particularly, a battle against women. While Mrs Lemon tackled parliament and the plumage trade, and Mrs Phillips roused conservationists and the clergy, Winifred Portland was expected to bring her persuasive powers to bear on her noble sisters. 'This is beyond doubt a woman's question,' Eliza Phillips was fond of pointing out. It was women's vanity and women's money that stimulated the plumage trade. The aristocracy led the fray.

There was just one problem – and this surfaced most awkwardly at the SPB's sixth annual general meeting on the last Friday in March, 1896. Here was a quiet but determined dissident voice; a lowly member of the society who dared to ask the obvious question. Her name was Miss Julia Andrews and she wanted to know *how* they could call themselves a bird protection society if they *killed birds*?

I was triumphant to find Miss Andrews in the AGM report, for I had been asking myself the same question: how did the aristocracy's love of field sports sit with the founding members' love of birds? Let us eavesdrop for a moment on this meeting at the Westminster Palace Hotel, a grandiose, wedge-shaped building opposite Westminster Abbey, its steps guarded by sentries in red coats and bearskin busbies. This was a favourite meeting place of politicians; a venue that lent weight to any small organisation wanting to be taken seriously.

The SPB had, miraculously, gone from strength to strength. By 1896, it boasted 15,000 members, with local secretaries as far afield as Australia and India. Honorary Secretary Mrs Lemon was in the process of finding a new, larger office on High Holborn, having outgrown the RSPCA's desk in Jermyn Street.

The AGM was a moment in which to take stock; to congratulate prime movers and loyal supporters. But it was also a time to plan new battles. The year 1896 was not a good one in the history of bird protection, and the mood of the 20-strong committee was somewhat downcast. So many new members, so much excellent publicity in the press – and yet the public appetite for feathered millinery seemed more voracious than ever.

Mrs Lemon had clipped out a page from the latest *Journal des Modes*, which reported: 'As autumn *chapeaux* were laden with blossoms, so the spring hats will be bountifully adorned with plumage, birds, wings, quills, aigrettes and three-quarter plumes.'

The annual onslaught was about to begin. *Harper's Bazaar* described a series of small bonnets each with 'blackbirds poised in pairs, with beaks meeting lovingly'; larger hats had as many as four birds perched on top. And yet in the very same issue of the American magazine, an editorial described the slaughter of mother birds by a plumage hunter, asking women to show a little more *intelligence* in their shopping choices.

'It is just possible that the advance of common sense may bring with it more equality between the sexes,' wrote *Harper's* progressive editor, Louise Booth, mischievously. If women could get their pretty heads round the basic economics of supply and demand, 'by their joint efforts they may at least develop a little independence *and* save the birds'.

The members proceeded in ones and twos through the foyer and up the wide, red-carpeted staircase of the Westminster Palace Hotel. All the ladies wore hats, of course – but none sported 'murderous millinery'.

It had been amazingly hard to keep supporters on message, and the press was greedy for news of a slip-up, such as the unfortunate occasion last year when the young Duchess of York had worn an osprey at an RSPCA prize-giving. Confections of tulle, velvet and artificial flowers swayed at a dignified pace up the stairs. There was a quantity of fur wrapped around high lace necklines – this was, regrettably, inevitable – and plenty of softly prancing ostrich plumes adding height and a certain regality. The hats of 1896 resembled small dinner platters bearing a forest of vertical trims, mixed and matched in improbable combinations and wired to exuberant heights.

There was also a high count of black top hats. Over the past five years, men had made great incursions into the SPB. Just over *half* those invited today were male, including two bishops, three canons, four MPs – and, thanks to Winifred Portland's efforts, three baronets, two earls and a lord. The society had become ultra-establishment in tone, and its increasingly staid gatherings reflected this. Its members and associates were, on the whole, not in their first flush. Each AGM began with an announcement of death, and today was no exception. Lord Lilford, joint founder and president of the British Ornithologists' Union, had died in the summer at 63. A great loss to the society, said chairman Montagu Sharpe; they would not see his like again.

More hearteningly, membership was increasing monthly, donations had been generous, and a successful *conversazione* had been held at the Royal Institute of Painters in Water Colours in Piccadilly, where Her Grace the Duchess of Portland received guests. The fashion for stuffed birds was waning, Mr Sharpe observed, but the appetite for the osprey or aigrette held firm. This, he suggested, was where the society should focus its energies.

Eliza Phillips, now aged 73, rose to her feet and looked beadily around the ornate meeting room. Intelligent ladies should be leading society in this particular battle, she said – but they were all too often seen in the opera boxes wearing hair ornaments 'exactly like the sort of brush servants use to clean lamp-chimneys'.

Three duchesses shifted uneasily on their chairs. Montagu Sharpe, whose job it was to ensure that no fanatic – founding members included – got too much air space, quickly made the tactful announcement of a new bird preservation society in America. Two Boston ladies, Harriet Hemenway and Minna Hall, had read about the snowy egret's plight in the Florida Everglades and, this February, had invited eminent Bostonians to join in creating a society just like the SPB. They were calling it the Massachusetts Audubon Society, and Mrs Lemon had already written to offer congratulations and support. There was an 'Audubon hat' being promoted in Boston, trimmed with ribbons and feathers – from non-protected birds, of course.

During the murmur of approval and interest now running around the room, Miss Julia Andrews rose nervously to her feet. The local secretary for Teddington, a 58-year-old spinster with connections in the tea trade, was slightly pink in the face. She would like to raise again the issue, she began, of shooting birds for pleasure. Game birds. Pheasant, partridge, snipe, woodcock, pigeon – what difference did it make? It was an act of cruelty, and a society vowing to protect birds should not mince its words or be half-hearted.

An awkward silence ensued. Miss Andrews stumbled on. Most of the ladies and gentlemen here knew that she had voiced her concerns at every AGM for the past three years, she said, and her members in the Teddington group were anxious to know what the society proposed to do. They would like to see a change in clause two in the SPB's charter: the clause stating that lady members 'should refrain from wearing the feathers of any bird not killed for the purposes of food, the ostrich excepted'.

Miss Andrews was not at all convinced that the ostrich did not suffer when relieved of its plumes. She had read a most distressing article in *The Times* about this barbaric business: how the birds' heads were cruelly hooded; how the stumps of quill turned quickly septic in the birds' body if not pulled out by Kaffirs with their teeth. Their teeth! She had read of birds being plucked so negligently that they died of exposure. Miss Julia Andrews proposed that SPB women should not be allowed to wear the feathers of *any* bird, the ostrich included. Were they a bird protection society or not?

The soft plumes spilling from vice presidents' heads quivered slightly as the room exhaled. Mr Hudson muttered something into the hairy ear of old Professor Newton, their heads wreathed in pipe smoke. Maybe Mrs Lemon thought of her father and the shooting range at Hythe; of the noise of those incessant guns pointing out to sea. What difference *was* there really between slaughtering thousands of pheasants and the wanton cruelty being practised on Flamborough Head in Yorkshire, where colonies of seabirds were being destroyed just for fun?

Mr Montagu Sharpe got to his feet, the consummate chairman, expert in moderation. The aim of the SPB had been from the first to seek out facts. It had investigated the facts concerning the ostrich feather, he said, and come to the conclusion that although cruelty might be practised, it was not necessarily involved in the procuring of the plumes – and that the business stood on a 'wholly different plane' to the business of killing countless wild birds.

Was it really cruel to the ostrich, interjected the bowler-hatted Liberal MP Sir Sydney Buxton? As Under-Secretary of State for the Colonies, he knew for a fact that farmed ostriches were treated with the greatest kindness, the harvesting of plumes being 'as painless as cutting human hair or trimming one's fingernails'. What's more, ostrich farms provided the Cape Colony with a vital export commodity.

Grunts of agreement came from various quarters, and Mr Sharpe moved on to Miss Andrews' objections to game birds. This was, they all knew, a difficult question for the public at large to understand. But a game bird was shot for the pot and, if they objected to this, then they would have to object to the slaughter of barnyard fowls, too; of Christmas turkeys and chickens for pies. They were not a vegetarian society, nor were they the anti-field sports Humanitarian League, which had been accused of 'spoiling other people's pleasure'. Their strength, he might hazard, lay in their narrowness of focus. They must not lose sight of their goal by going down side alleys.

Miss Andrews blushed fiercely under her unfashionable bonnet and formally withdrew her proposal. The Duchess of Portland ventured a glance at the ranks of ladies and gentlemen in her circle, and read complacent relief on their faces. They had been saved. The truth, as Montagu Sharpe well knew, was that this society could not afford to alienate its constituency. Half the people in the room were landed gentry, with estates of many thousands of acres between them. They saw nothing incongruous about supporting the efforts of the RSPCA and the SPB, while allowing themselves to be photographed, gun in hand, behind ramparts of shining bird corpses. Shooting, to these people, was a way of life. A right.

What happened to the brave Miss Andrews? Her name was removed from the list of committee members later that year – and clause two of the constitution was subtly changed: 'To discourage the wanton destruction of birds and the wearing of feathers of any bird not killed for the purposes of food, other than the ostrich, *but to take no part in the question of killing game birds and legitimate sport of that character.*' The annual report for 1896 tactfully reminded members: 'As misapprehensions have arisen, it is thought well to state that the attitude of the Society is *strictly neutral* on the question of the killing of game birds.'

This put the lid on the matter. The landed gentry could not be their target. They influenced high fashion; their husbands ran the country. The Duchess of Portland shared poor Miss Andrews' discomfort, but she had to conceal it – not only at each AGM, but at home on the Welbeck estate, and on their Scotland estates, too.

Her Grace hated shooting.

18

The Crème de la Crème

The marriage of William Cavendish-Bentinck, the 6th Duke of Portland, to his duchess was widely held to be 'an ideally happy union', despite her aversion to all that made his blood sing. *Fifty Years and More of Sport in Scotland* is the title of one of his field sports memoirs: 'Deerstalking, Salmon Fishing, Grouse Shooting and Other Pleasant Memories, 1880–1932'. His wife was at his side for most of these moments.

Watching the upper classes at play, via the shooting party memoirs and albums of the era, shows us just what a difficult task Winnie had on her hands. There was an absolute disconnection, in the minds of her circle, between the monumental slaughter of game birds bred for the purpose, and the harvesting of plumes for the millinery trade. The Duchess of Portland was forced to play the gracious country house hostess to regular shooting parties at Welbeck Abbey, making small talk with noblewomen bundled in tweeds, fox furs slung over shoulders, as they tramped after the men towards the obligatory outdoor luncheon.

The women might not have seemed important to the ritual – but they were. Their presence was crucial not only to the aristocratic sports of adultery and bridge, but also to politics. Because it took place in the feminine space of the home, the house party was non-partisan and inclusive. Conservatives sat next to Liberals whose views they might abhor (the Irish Home Rule question; the prosecution of Oscar Wilde;

women's suffrage), but once gathered round the dining table of an elegant hostess differences were set aside.

Increasingly, women were not such passive spectators. Queen Victoria detested the sporting ritual – 'it is not ladylike to kill animals & go out shooting . . . *only fast* ladies do such things' – but the 1890s woman was increasingly 'fast'. She smoked, cycled, wrote articles for the press; she travelled independently. The restrictive manners and dress of an earlier generation were being sloughed off. 'She hunts the hare and shoots the pheasant, she drives and rides with more brutal recklessness than men; she watches with delight the struggles of the dying salmon, of the gralloched deer,' wrote Ouida in her critical 'New Woman' essay of 1894.

Mary Russell, the Duchess of Bedford, was one such woman. A keen shot and even keener suffragist, she felt it was 'impossible for a woman to do a long day's walking in comfort over the moors or in turnips in a skirt which is longer than eight inches below the knee'. Mary was also an avid ornithologist, collector of birds and member of the SPB. She saw no contradiction in any of this, and her clutching after liberating male activities such as shooting (and, later, aviation – she was to become known as 'the Flying Duchess') simply sharpened her hunger for women's rights.

Winifred Portland did not shoot, but she had a certain masculine quality, too. By 1896, she had two children under three years old – but with four full-time nursemaids at Welbeck Abbey, this did not, in any way, cramp her style. She travelled widely between the Portland estates, London and Paris; she poked her nose into parliament, visited sick miners in their homes, wrote tartly worded letters to the press and learned to drive her own automobile. No doubt she also smoked. But she was conscientiously dutiful to the social circumstances of her birth and marriage. She did what was expected of her.

All her life, Winnie made a point of wearing Welbeck game feathers in her hats like a tribal flourish. She supported the SPB – but she also supported her kind. To those not in the know, her hats bore a confusing message.

*

On 4 November 1896, a record 3,113 pheasants were killed on the Prince of Wales's 6,000-acre estate at Sandringham – the third highest 'bag' shot thus far in Britain. Since the Prince's game larder was capable of holding 7,000 birds, there was room to spare. But did industrial slaughter on this scale really count as sport? By the 1890s, the *battue* pheasant shoot had reached obscene levels of destruction.

To the art critic and environmentalist John Ruskin, the mentality was incomprehensible. 'Very earnestly I ask you,' he wrote, 'have English gentlemen, as a class, any other real object in their whole existence than killing birds?' Cruelty to animals breeds cruelty to humans, preached the RSPCA. And yet the target for moralising and finger-wagging was, more commonly, the working classes. It was thought that they were unable to feel compassion towards animals because they were so like animals themselves, therefore it was the duty of all enlightened people to train and discipline them 'as though they were dogs that had never known a collar or a command'.

Rather than bite the hand that fed it, the SPB ignored the sporting pursuits of the aristocracy and turned with zealous censure on the working classes. Etta Lemon tracked the bird abuse prosecutions made by RSPCA officers and reported them in crisp detail to society members. 'In the Courts' became a regular column in the SPB's magazine, *Bird Notes and News*, from 1903. John Sly of Dorset, for example, was fined ten shillings for taking goldfinches and ten shillings for possessing two linnet decoys.

Bird catchers were 'rough-looking' men; the 'idle loafers' you would 'instinctively avoid on country lanes and commons', wrote Mrs Lemon. They set to work with their 'miserable little decoys': the linnets with bleeding legs, the yellowhammer with a broken back. Using nets and lime they caught birds by the hundred, wringing the necks of the females, 'the cocks thrust into cages or boxes' and despatched by rail to some 'foul' Paradise Court or Petticoat Lane seller, to be bought by other members of the working class. ('It's kinder to give 'em small cages; they'd beat themselves to death in bigger ones,' advised one dealer.)

The skylark, the linnet and the chaffinch were popular as family pets or for singing competitions; owners would poke out the birds' eyes with a hot needle to make them sing louder. Even to the enlightened social investigators in the East End of London, a birdcage in the window was a sign of decency and aspiration. Other British bird species were snapped up by the fancy feather industry. Domestic servants, who couldn't afford to deck themselves out in bird-of-paradise plumes, could wear Sussex sparrows' wings dyed yellow, blue and red. 'Starlings' wings wanted,' read a newspaper advertisement, 'free from moth and in good condition, sixpence per dozen pairs, any quantity up to 500 pairs.'

On the morning of Wednesday 22 June 1897, Queen Victoria was helped slowly up a green baize ramp into her open state landau for the 8-mile Diamond Jubilee procession through London. The day was overcast and humid, but as she settled back in the carriage the sun broke through the low cloud. A white parasol was raised. The Queen, a hunched figure in silver-embroidered black silk, was 78 years old.

Ten years earlier, at her Golden Jubilee, the Queen had worn a black tulle bonnet dressed with antique lace, topped with four white ostrich tips and a spray of fine snowy egret feathers – the contested 'osprey'. Today, this headpiece rests in a glass case at the Museum of London, and it is very much a record of its time. Possibly bowing to pressure from her daughter-in-law, the Princess of Wales (intimate of the Duchess of Portland), Queen Victoria – who *was* sensitive to cruelty – now wore a little black bonnet, very plain. Her jowly face was exposed for all to see. She was, in her way, making a distinct statement – because for all other aristocratic women, the close-fitting 'toque', decorated with the osprey, was the 'advocated headwear' for the jubilee, a look promoted hard in the fashion magazines. Two years hence, in 1899, Queen Victoria would forbid the wearing of the osprey on Royal Artillery helmets; it would be replaced with ostrich.

As the procession of 17 carriages crawled towards St Paul's Cathedral, the crowd's cheering was deafening. The build-up in the press had gone on for months, creating a national mood of exhilaration tinged with hysteria. Women could be seen weeping, men shouting themselves hoarse. Tears streamed down Victoria's face; she was a remote figure who had barely clapped eyes on her people these past ten years. 'No one . . . has ever met with such an ovation as was given to me,' she wrote in her journal that night. 'I was much moved and gratified.'

The climax of the jubilee season was a fancy dress ball given at Devonshire House by Louise, Duchess of Devonshire (a stout 65-year-old, known for her brown wig and gash of red lipstick). When word went out that she was planning a ball, no other society hostesses dared to compete. Instead, they invested all their efforts into making sure they were on the guest list. Seven hundred invitations were sent out just one month in advance, and they were very specific. Guests were to dress in allegorical or historical costume, pre-1815 – that is, before the Battle of Waterloo defeated Napoleon.

A rush of aristocratic women headed for the London museums, to be found (so said the press) studying portraits and engravings of ladies 'robed for coronation or beheading'. Then the battle ensued. Women – men, too – fought for the time of the best dressmakers, wigmakers, milliners and theatrical costumiers. This, added to the general rush of costume orders for the usual balls and weddings of the summer season, made the Queen's Diamond Jubilee a memorable year for the thousands of women who laboured away in gaslight, stitching, beading and embroidering, or dyeing, willowing and curling, day in, day out. The Parisian couturier Jean Worth recorded a spike in 'freak orders' for hand-sewn jewelled dresses; one piece costing 5,000 francs kept 'several girls busy for almost a month'. In almost all cases, the costumes were never worn again.

'For the kingdom of Great Britain, the year 1897 has been one of jubilation,' wrote Mrs Lemon; 'but for the bird kingdom a record year of pillage, devastation and unmerciful destruction.' The feather workers knew about the Devonshire ball, too, for the press was insatiable in its lust for detail.

'A sermon on the iniquity of spending so much money on clothes was duly preached in a fashionable church,' wrote the droll Lady Violet Greville for *The Graphic*. 'Dressmakers and costumiers were for weeks before nearly driven off their head with work and anxiety.' Some of the costumes, she revealed, cost £1,000; the jewels 'several millions'.

There were a lot of feathers. Cleopatras had to have their fans; Boadiceas their plumed helmets. Dressed as the wife of Alexander the Great, Lady Alexandra Colebrook wore an aigrette so large it might have been furnished by an entire heronry – yet it was rivalled in size by that of Princess Henry of Pless who came as the Queen of Sheba. The red-headed beauty and society pin-up Sybil, Duchess of Westmorland, came dressed as Hebe, goddess of youth. She carried a gold cup and, strapped to her shoulders, an enormous stuffed grey eagle, inspired by a painting by Joshua Reynolds.

Society photographer James Lafayette was invited to pitch a tent in the landscaped gardens of Devonshire House (the grounds stretched from Piccadilly all the way back to Berkeley Square). There, among the potted palms and Venetian lanterns winking from mature trees, the 'crème de la crème of Society, from Royalty downwards' queued in a braying crush to be commemorated. Lafayette worked like a dog from half past midnight until five in the morning, his assistants changing plate glass negatives in a clattering frenzy. He gave each sitter just one and a half minutes – but still he managed to photograph only 200 of the 700 guests.

The Duchess of Portland was too high up the pecking order not to be photographed. Lafayette's portrait shows a glowing, gentle-faced young woman with exquisite bone structure, tightly laced into a corset as the pearl-encrusted, seventeenth-century Duchess Anna d'Este. Winnie's alleged lookalike, the imperious Katherine Drummond – she of the bright green osprey – also worked her way to the front of the queue. There she is, with heavy lidded eyes, disdainful mouth and ostrich fan, dressed as a Restoration beauty in the album that was published two years later.

The Devonshire ball was a tipping point; a swansong for the great London houses. Devonshire House was demolished in 1924; today offices and the entrance to Green Park tube station stand on the spot. If there was a whisper of disquiet that night, it wasn't uttered by many. Consuelo, Duchess of Marlborough, the 20-year-old American heiress propping up Blenheim Palace, walked home through Green Park at dawn in her 'billowing dress' and was dismayed to find the 'dregs of humanity' lying on the grass. 'Human beings too dispirited or sunk to find work or favour, they sprawled in sodden stupor, pitiful representatives of the submerged tenth.'

W. H. Hudson was revolted by a different sight as he walked in Hyde Park that summer, a spectacle 'ghastly and repulsive in the extreme': elderly ladies 'in appearance so bent and discoloured and wasted with age and many infirmities as to remind one of a corpse'. The nature writer noted that they invariably sported on their silver heads 'a bonnet surmounted by an osprey of feathers torn from birds slaughtered when feeding their young'. He bashed out on his typewriter an argument that 'women who are no longer young' – wives, mothers, grandmothers – looked grotesque when dressing youthfully, and especially so when wearing birds' mating plumage. His Christmas day tirade in *The Times* set off a heated debate.

Were women really so helplessly in thrall to fashion – this 'arbitrary and incalculable authority' – asked a *Times* leader writer? The prominent illustrator Eleanor Vere Boyle wrote wearily to the editor that she had been campaigning against feather wearing since the 1870s and had given up the battle. 'I have been forced to the conclusion that, where fashion is concerned, the world of women are utterly and entirely callous and blind to every consideration excepting their own selfish vanity.' *The Times* agreed that the wearer, not the hunter, was 'the root of the evil'. Women were to blame.

'A Mother of a Daughter', stung by these comments, wrote immediately to say that the paper was being 'a little hard on the ladies', who were only wearing what was provided for them by the shopkeepers. They didn't slaughter the birds, after all, and would willingly buy something else –

but (so went her disingenuous argument) women were 'helpless when surrounded with feather and fur trimmed hats and bonnets, great difficulties always being thrown in the way of any alteration'. She knew, she said, from personal experience in executing orders, how difficult it is 'to get what one wishes done'.

These women gave orders; they were not told what to do. They set the tempo. They controlled their servants, their daughters and, obliquely, their husbands. They presented too hard a nut to crack. And so the SPB turned its attention to an easier target. Rather than pursue the wearers, Mrs Phillips and Mrs Lemon chose now to focus on the makers – the milliners who supplied the tempting spoils.

PART 3

Hats

19

Dying to Get Out

To see a privileged Englishwoman in all her monumental glory, one had to be in Old Bond Street between the hours of two and six in the afternoon. Here you could watch an extraordinary, ritualised promenade – the glittering equipages, sleek horses, liveried servants, exquisitely outfitted women, and that very particular air the aristocracy gave to every place they chose to frequent. The shop windows here were discreet, but worked very hard at tempting those who *had* everything in the world to covet something more. Old Bond Street was not to be confused with the less exclusive New Bond Street, to the north of Burlington Gardens, where 'animal-like' scenes erupted at the summer sales. On Old Bond Street, omnibuses were banned and an atmosphere of cloistered calm prevailed. Here, the intricate dance of wealth, power and sexuality had centre stage.

What sights had swayed up and down its length in these last years of the nineteenth century! Fashion was engaged in a restless rewriting of the female form: in expansion and contraction, lengthening and curbing, with every year. In the 1880s, the bustle was the thing, growing ever larger until it stuck out aggressively and waggled with each step. When the bustle began to shrink, the sleeve began to swell, ballooning by the early 1890s to exaggerated proportions so that women had to walk sideways through narrow doors. These enormous upper arms gave the illusion of a tiny waist, pulled in by a broad ribbon belt with silver clasp.

Trains shortened, hemlines climbed infinitesimally, hips narrowed, silhouettes morphed into a forward-tilting S-shape.

Hats, too, kept pace – up, down, in, out. The Gainsborough, large with the side turned up; the postilion, high like a flowerpot with narrow brim; the high crowned toque with banded brim; the wide-brimmed hat worn tilted sideways; the witch-like crowned hat; the gypsy hat. And the trimmings . . . 'Fashionable hats all resemble walking gardens,' declared *Women's World* in the spring of 1896. One season later, it was predicted that autumn hats would be 'bountifully adorned with plumage, birds, wings, quills, aigrettes and three-quarter plumes'. The 1890s favoured one, single, high ornament – an aigrette, a soaring cock's feather, one or two ostrich plumes. Now, at the end of the century, a rising mood of confidence was finding expression on top of women's heads. Hats were getting bigger, brasher and even more eye grabbing.

Yet it was one thing to read, in the fashion magazines of the time, the descriptions of these extraordinary feathered creations. It was quite another thing to make them. Whose fingers were assembling the murderous millinery?

Opening a hat shop remained a persistent fantasy for the impecunious gentlewoman – a fantasy that was mercilessly exposed in Edith Wharton's 1905 novel *The House of Mirth*. 'I shall look hideous in dowdy clothes, but I can trim my own hats,' declares the exquisite Miss Lily Bart, whose fortunes fall so low at the precarious age of 30 that she is forced to find work in a New York milliner's. 'Here was, after all, something that her charming listless hands could really do; she had no doubt of their capacity for knotting a ribbon or placing a flower to advantage.' As for the real work – 'subordinate fingers, blunt, grey, needle-pricked fingers' would make the actual hats and stitch the linings. In her imagination, Lily presides over a 'charming little shop front' where her finished creations are displayed – 'hats, wreaths, aigrettes and the rest, perched on their stands like birds just poising for flight.' Wharton evokes brilliantly the slow hell of the hat industry: 20 women with 'fagged profiles' and 'exaggerated hair', bowed over their work in the harsh north light, engaged in the 'creation of ever-varied setting for the face of fortunate womanhood'.

This 'dainty' occupation was, in effect, no better than the sweatshops of feather workers in New York's Lower East Side or in London's East End. The pay might be higher, but the profession drained the life out of its workers – had always done so. It was said that by the age of 30 or 40, milliners and tailoresses were 'in constitution at least ten years older than domestic servants'.

Each hat in production had its own table, and each table its own team of workers. At the head sat the 'trimmer' or designer, a woman in charge of a cluster of girls working under her watchful eye. In the busy seasons a half-dozen such tables might be at work, each group self-sufficient, each hat a unique creation from lining to trimming. It was the trimmers' artistic hands that bent the wired feathers this way and that, that splayed the parrots' wings, teased the kitten-soft grebe down and coaxed the artificial roses into bloom. The trimmer's job was to improve upon nature. The head milliner acted as the whip-cracking forewoman.

In the summer of 1884, a young milliner wrote an anonymous letter to *The Times* in response to the ongoing debate about appalling working conditions in the fashion trade. She worked, she said, from eight in the morning until half past ten or eleven at night. 'That may not seem very much, I daresay, when you hear it told,' she wrote, 'but it is bad enough when you have to do it.' She sat with 20 other girls around three oblong tables in a small, one-windowed room. 'There we sit, all through the morning, afternoon, and evening, stitching and trimming away, with the sun pouring in on us, and the room getting closer and closer until you feel you can hardly bear it any longer; and then, when eight o'clock comes and you are dying to get out and have a mouthful of fresh air, you are told that you will have to stop for an hour longer, or perhaps two or three hours.'

Some of the younger girls would put their heads down and cry quietly at this point. 'I have felt like crying myself,' wrote the girl, 'if it was any use.'

And yet her employer was a sought-after millinery establishment in the West End, and the anonymous letter writer the envy of her peers, possessor of a respectable and 'genteel' trade. Millinery was also held to be a 'safe' trade: once trained, you could get work anywhere. The profession most often attracted educated females from the precarious lower middle classes who needed to earn a living. With a costly three-year apprenticeship, it was not something you went into lightly.

In the London Metropolitan Archives in Clerkenwell is a stiffly folded, long sheet of paper, stamped and sealed with three blobs of red wax on 1 November 1886. This unnerving document is a deed of ownership between an apprentice milliner and her master. George John Green, a bootmaker of Middle Street in the City of London, was handing over his youngest daughter, Mary Ann, 'of her own free will and accord', to Leonard William Cubitt of nearby Fore Street, in order to learn the trade of Infants' Millinery. Her juvenile signature was carefully inked at the bottom of this stiff indenture document, along with her father and Cubitt's. For three years, Mary Ann Green – 13 years old – was to be effectively enslaved.

Len Cubitt was a 43-year-old manufacturer of frilly accessories, from collars and cuffs to bonnets and lace caps. He had started small in 1870, but now employed over 50 female hands in a warehouse. The standard document states that Mary Ann Green would faithfully serve him, 'his secrets keep, and his lawful commands obey'. She would not damage, waste, lend or sell his goods, 'nor absent herself from her said Master's service day or night unlawfully'. Her new master was based a ten-minute walk from the Green family home, but she would now need permission to see her four siblings and parents. Her three-year apprenticeship, at a cost of £20 (around £2,300 today), was paid for by a local charity.

For his part of the contract, Cubitt pledged that he would 'by the best means in his power' teach and instruct Mary Ann, paying her three shillings a week during the first year, five shillings during the second and seven shillings for the third and final year. Millinery was certainly a step up from being a feather worker, and Mary Ann Green would have expected to progress from apprentice (running errands, sewing bandeaux and linings) to working as an improver (shirring chiffon, sewing in linings), then a preparer (similar but more expert) and thence to a maker (constructing and covering the frames). Looking far ahead, Mary Ann's goal would be the top job of trimmer: the woman who put the decorative flourishes on hats. Perhaps in seven years.

An indenture was a contract ripe for exploitation. Bosses commonly paid their apprentices next to nothing for five years and then laid them off. Perhaps you taught the girls, perhaps you didn't – but you owned them. They slept in your house, ate your food and did your behest. Using online archives to spy into her future, I discovered that Len Cubitt died suddenly in 1889 aged 46, when Mary Ann was in her final year. Where would this have left his apprentice?

20

The Millinery Detectives

A cross the Atlantic, a minister's daughter and social reformer was deeply curious about the invisible industries on her doorstep. Mary Van Kleeck was a young woman with a dour, if sympathetic face, and an absolute disregard for fashion. She had cut her teeth in the slums of New York, studying female factory workers and child labourers. In 1913, aged 29, she had made a forensic study of artificial flower makers, the sister occupation to feather working. In 1917, she moved on to hats and the women who made them.

We are jumping ahead in time here, but the truth was that very little changed in the millinery and feather worker trade for 20 years in either Britain or America. Employment conditions were just as poor and living conditions were possibly worse, since costs had soared but wages remained stuck at 1880s levels. At this time in London, a milliner might earn 8 to 9 shillings a week – less than half of what male hatters were paid. By 1915, it was estimated that you needed 17 to 18 shillings a week to survive.

Mary Van Kleeck demonstrated the surprising truth that, far from being a safe trade, this was a highly precarious and fickle profession. Nobody had truly investigated the industry before. She went about it thoroughly, scientifically, yet with a woman's eye for telling detail.

'Unemployment is *the* most important fact in the occupation of being a milliner,' Van Kleeck discovered. 'Twice a year more than half the workers are laid off because the season is over' – in June and July, and then again in November and December. Because there was no certainty of returning in the autumn to the same spring job, many milliners were forced to hunt for jobs *four times a year*, 'twice in millinery and twice in other occupations'.

A 20-year-old girl listed the jobs that had got her through the low season – making handkerchiefs, paper boxes, ladies' shirts and babies' hats, buttonholing sweaters, stock work in a leather goods factory, canvassing for a music school, taking charge of her brother's cleaning and dyeing store, selling hats in a millinery shop on the Lower East Side, working in a grocer's store and doing embroidery. 'Between seasons I take anything,' she told her interviewer. 'The work doesn't pay much, but it's better than nothing.'

Even in the good times, their incomes were pitiful. Emily, aged 22, told Van Kleeck that she had never been able to afford a hot-water bottle for her bed or a bus fare to work – and this was after seven years in the trade. Another young woman, Bertha, couldn't afford spectacles for her failing eyesight, nor any dental or medical care. She made all her own clothes, and these had to look smart – it was a 'genteel' profession, after all. Bertha was living on $230 a year (around $5,000 in today's money). She reckoned she needed $410 – $8 a week. She listed her only luxuries as earrings, writing paper and pictures of herself ($2). Exposure to high fashion made milliners highly dress-conscious. They craved fine things for themselves, and would do anything to afford them. The link between millinery and prostitution was an open secret.

Van Kleeck could see that these women desperately needed a union, but the industry was too diffuse and too unpredictable to form one. 'You might as well try to direct the wind as to organise milliners,' one woman told her. Seasons were short, unemployment was high, turnover was rapid. The workers tended to be young and their social backgrounds as diverse as their nationalities. Milliners were 'a chance collection of individuals', she concluded, 'rather than a group of fellow employees with common aims'.

Fact gatherers like Mary Van Kleeck were instrumental in bringing these women's stories to light and, ultimately, in changing legislation on wages and working hours in America. In England, at around the same time, another woman was making a forensic study of female labour that was to have a similar impact.

Published in 1915, *Married Women's Work* by Clementina Black was the result of two years of painstaking interviews: trailing women home, knocking on their doors and talking to them. It wasn't just the work and the wages that interested its formidable author (trade unionist, industrial reformer, passionate suffragist and novelist). Black wanted to know about their health, their homes and their relationships with husbands and children. Millinery was just one of the 117 trades she and her Women's Industrial Council team investigated across Britain in the years leading up to the First World War. Black had a nose for detail, and she sat at countless kitchen tables jotting down phrases and vignettes, her stern oval glasses directed at her interviewees. These milliners did piecework for shillings: bandeaux linings for four pence per dozen, chiffon chirring at ten shillings a week, straw shapes at five pence a week. 'A bright, pleasant woman,' wrote Black, 'devoted to child (weak two-year-old), somewhat embittered by her husband's love of gambling. Thinks trade is healthy.' She found on one 'nice clean street' a dwelling of two rooms where a 'shrewd, kindly old lady, very intelligent' lived, in the millinery trade from the age of seven. She was supporting both her elderly husband and a married daughter with three children (in flight from a violent husband) on nine shillings a week.

Behind each front door was a story. There was the maker of sun bonnets, who earned an unusually high wage – but the trade was a seasonal one.

> She could earn, being a very quick hand, £1 to 30/- a week; and since she had seven dependent children and a husband who, although he earned 30/-, handed but 20/- to his wife, her earnings were absolutely needed. The remaining 10/- seems to have been devoted to the pleasure of the husband who, to use his wife's expression, 'likes a bit of life'. 'But', she added, 'he doesn't treat me badly on the whole.'

Did any of the workers think about the source of the feathered trimmings they worked with? Did they even see them as birds? And if they did, would they have cared? There was no evidence to suggest that they did. Life was a matter of getting through the day, the next week and the year ahead. In such a precarious profession, principles were a luxury. 'They never discharge you,' one pieceworker told Van Kleeck; 'you just stay until you are starved out.'

Van Kleeck's report was illustrated with a series of photographs that show, in grainy detail, the dusty and dishevelled state of millinery workrooms. Feathers and fluff lie in soft clumps on the floorboards. Materials are strewn over crowded tables and stuffed into pigeonholes. The rooms are poorly lit and heads are bent. Women (pale faces, hot hands) are picking over dead birds (limp claws, inert beaks). There is something poignantly apt in this confluence of bird skins and husks of womanhood. In the words of one American taxidermist, 'What's the birds for, if they aint to be used?'

21

Queen Alix

1901

When the news of Queen Victoria's death reached the journalists waiting at the gates of Osborne House, a mad crowd in carriages and on bicycles raced down the hill to the Isle of Wight post office, whooping, 'Queen dead!' Victoria's death coincided with the first day of the 'White Sales' – a day in which every shop window was snowy with household linen. Overnight, in one of the biggest transformations ever witnessed in the history of the drapery trade, all window displays were turned to black. 'Everything that could be dyed was used to meet the colossal demand,' remembered a draper at Dickins & Jones.

And so, on 22 January 1901, the Edwardian age officially began – but it had already reigned in spirit for some years. Britain felt more modern: there were telephones, electricity, indoor plumbing, motor cars. Morals were changing; bed-hopping at the louche 'Saturday-to-Monday' house party had become an upper-class sport among the Prince of Wales's fast set. Women were becoming ever more vocal – even Daisy, Countess of Warwick, former lover of the Prince, had started speaking in public about women's rights and the vote. 'Why on earth do you want women to be like men and copy their pursuits?' huffed Bertie to her in 1899. 'God put you into the world to be different from us but you don't seem to see it!'

The accession of the new king, an overweight 59-year-old philanderer, was greeted with caution. The most that could be said for him, wrote the anti-imperialist Wilfrid Blunt in his diary, was that 'he has certain good qualities of amiability and of philistine tolerance of other people's sins and vulgarities which endear him to rich and poor, to the Stock Exchange Jews, to the Turf Bookmakers and to the Man in the Street.'

After a long and frustrating wait for power, Edward VII set about redecorating Buckingham Palace with enthusiasm. He had electric lights installed, furniture moved, pictures rehung. He purged his mother's fusty and secretive court of loyal old retainers, male and female. Bertie, as he was known to friends and family, was a lover of ceremony, of protocol and sartorial correctness. Under his ambitious eye, the monarchy was reinvented and reinvigorated.

Alexandra of Denmark, Bertie's queen ('Alix'), was left somewhat in limbo. Her husband was everywhere – handing out honours and titles, choosing new wallpaper, involving himself in domestic politics. He even took on her cherished relationship with the Red Cross, insisting on handing out prizes himself when it had been her role for years. It was 64 years since England had had a king and no one could remember what his queen should do. 'Aunt Alix is quite ready to do what is right,' wrote her daughter-in-law, Princess Mary, 'if only she is told, but just at present everyone is quite at sea.'

Queen Alexandra was beautiful: petite, gaunt-cheeked, with large, expressive eyes. Her waist was tiny and her highly personal sense of style unerring. She did not wear large hats, having rather a small head, but managed to make the riding bowler and the straw boater look very sexy. The courtier Lord Esher thought her intelligence greatly underestimated, partly because of her growing deafness. 'In point of fact,' he wrote in his journal, 'she says more original things, and has more unexpected ideas than any of the family.' But on Bertie's accession, Alix found herself marginalised. Her role was to provide the stable family background for Bertie's public life, and to look extravagantly regal at state occasions. When the courtiers tried to advise her on what to wear at the coronation, she replied: 'I know better than all the milliners and antiquaries. I shall wear exactly what I like, and so shall all my ladies – *Basta!*'

When the day finally came – after a six-week postponement due to

Bertie's stomach operation – Alix crossed the threshold into Westminster Abbey in a dress of golden Indian gauze with a purple train. At the Queen's left shoulder, holding aloft one corner of the heavy golden canopy with a slim brass standard, stood Winifred, Duchess of Portland. She stood very tall, very elegant, in a conspicuously large diamond coronet – a woman one year short of her 40th birthday, at the very heart of the new royal court.

The Society for the Protection of Birds was elated. Winnie, their president, was poised to make the most important conversion of them all. Here was a new queen in search of a role, marginalised by her king, renowned for her sentimentality. Alix was neither ambitious nor remotely feminist, but decorous, generous and light-hearted. She projected her personality through her dress. The Queen did own accessories embellished with hummingbirds, yet she was unlikely to have dwelt long on the birds' provenance. Bertie (who in 1902 spent £90 on a Panama hat in Old Bond Street) privately despised his beautiful wife as bird-brained, though he respected his daughter-in-law, Princess Mary, for her intelligence, and appreciated the political advice of his astute mistress, Alice Keppel. Yet Queen Alexandra had an unparalleled influence among the nation's women. Where she led, thousands would follow.

The prime movers at the SPB knew this, and they were confident that the Duchess of Portland was their way in to the royal conscience. But the Duchess would not compromise her relationship with the new queen, who had already turned down an invitation to become their patron in 1895. It was a delicate situation. Winnie could not push Alix – and the SPB ladies certainly could not push someone as grand as the Duchess, despite her being their president. At successive annual general meetings following the coronation, excuses were made. 'Etiquette prevents people bringing the matter plainly before the Queen personally,' soothed Council member Captain Tailby with polished diplomacy. Therefore, 'the only way is by means of a public protest, which cannot be burked' – *smothered* – 'and must reach her'.

A plan was made for a petition, encouraged by the recent headline-grabbing 'monster petition' presented to Lord Salisbury's coalition government by the women of Lancaster. The North of England Society for Women's Suffrage had gathered 29,359 signatures on hundreds of sheets of paper pasted onto a vast roll of linen: a roll that took three hours to unroll from one spool to another. On 18 March 1901, 15 Lancashire cotton workers had taken the petition down to London – a petition so large, according to the *Englishwoman's Review*, it 'looked like a garden roller in dimensions'.

Why should the Society for the Protection of Birds not do something similar? And yet a petition to ban plumage in hats was, in the face of current women's fashion, a little like sprinkling rosewater before the plague. Birds, wings, bird-of-paradise plumes and ospreys were horribly conspicuous in the millinery of 1902. The rare huia bird of New Zealand was now feared extinct, following the visit of the fashionable Yorks in 1901. When Prince George had placed the bird's ceremonial long, black tail feather with its characteristic white band in his hat, civilised society the world over had gone wild for the huia. One Maori hunting party collected 646 in a month – and now this bird, with its elegantly curved yellow bill, orange wattles and metallic green-black plumage, could no longer be found.

The plight of the world's exotic birds was critical – but the 1902 AGM rumbled urbanely on. Lady Theodora Guest had held a reception; Mrs Suckling had arranged a musical programme; Madame Antoinette Sterling had sung cantatas. Mrs Lemon had – once again – travelled to Paris to speak (in French) on behalf of the society at the International Conference on the Protection of Animals. Their successful Christmas card sales had earned them £34 10s 8d.

Sitting on a small gilt chair in the overheated hotel ballroom, W. H. Hudson found his mind wandering. The AGM was, he later wrote to his spirited friend Margaret, Lady Brooke, the Ranee of Sarawak, 'somewhat tame and insipid, compared with other years'. (Hudson looked after her pet African grey parrot, Tootles, when the Ranee was away from Ascot. 'Tootles seems happy enough in his dull way,' he would inform her by post.) He wished she had been present at the meeting. 'The Duchess of Portland has not much to say when on her legs,' he continued, ' – if it be allowable to mention that part of the human anatomy in this connection – and our poet Alfred Austin was most disappointing.'

Austin, the Poet Laureate, with his luxuriant white moustaches and spotted bow tie, could be relied upon for his utterly anodyne rhapsodies on rural England. Mr Hudson favoured more full-blooded stuff. His eye alighted on the new SPB secretary Miss Linda Gardiner, a handsome young woman and a forceful writer, too. He'd been surprised to learn that a hefty £121 was now spent annually on the secretary's salary and other clerical assistance. The new office at 3 Hanover Square, leased from the London Zoological Society, was full of competent women.

Was the SPB slowing down, after its giddy first decade? By 1901, membership seemed to be levelling at around 20,000. Income was falling, with the interminable Boer War draining the country's pockets since 1899. The society's focus had become more diffuse, branching into other urgent areas of bird protection – liming, pole trapping, egging, caging. A team of 'watchers' had just been set up at six vulnerable breeding spots around the country, from the Shetland isle of Hascosay to Breydon Water on the Norfolk Broads, Britain's first embryonic wildlife reserves were taking shape. But the SPB's original mandate – to stamp out the fashion for feathers in hats – had frankly made very little impact. You had only to walk down Old Bond Street, or indeed any high street in any town in Britain. India might have just passed a law banning the export of bird skins, but this had failed to 'touch any responsive chord in the minds of women'.

'The millinery question' remained 'the most discouraging part of the society's work', affirmed Honorary Secretary Etta Lemon, surveying the assembled group of grandees, naturalists and middle-aged local secretaries sitting before her. Her husband, Frank, sat in the front row, emanating support. There were, she noted privately, a lot of men in this room: 26 male vice presidents to 13 women. The balance was tipping – but the women still did all the work. Capable women, energetic women, intelligent women. Why was their message so hard to get across to their sisters? Was it, she asked her audience, because women were *too stupid* to read anything other than a fashion paper? 'The emancipation of women,' Mrs Lemon noted acidly, 'has not yet freed her from slavery to so-called "fashion," nor has a higher education enabled her to grasp this simple question of ethics and aesthetics.'

The society's local secretaries had been instructed this year to take their message onto the streets. Bravely, pamphlets in hand, they had stood on pavements in fashionable shopping areas, trying to engage feathered women in conversation. And there had been conversions. Mrs Lemon read out a letter sent in to Hanover Square:

> Dear Madam – One of your pamphlets was given to me today in Tottenham Court Road. I was then wearing a hat with a large white bird in it. When I purchased it I had never thought of the bird or of the cruelty at all, but your leaflet has shown me what I did not know or heed, and in future I shall purchase no millinery with birds or wings. I write this to show that the leaflet has in this instance done good.

This somehow had the whiff of invention about it, but nobody here was going to quibble. It was Eliza Phillips' turn to speak, rising slowly to her feet with the aid of a stick. Pamphleting stunts were all very well she said, but they were impersonal, and she doubted their power.

'– Ninety nine out of every hundred women of all ranks do not read leaflets or newspapers,' interjected the clipped voice of Captain Tailby.

'Twenty years of experience,' Mrs Phillips reminded him of her pedigree; 'twenty years of experience has led me to the conclusion that the direct method is the only effective one.' Life, she said, was too short 'to beat about the bush'. She was now 79 years old. The time for cantatas and *conversazione* was over. Women had changed – and the society, too, must change its methods or it risked being left behind in the Victorian age.

However disagreeable it might be, urged Mrs Phillips, the 'frontal attack' had to be made.

22

'Egret' Bennett

David Bennett of San Diego – 'probably the most experienced and systematic hunter of wild egret or heron on this continent, if not in the world' – was known throughout California as 'Egret' Bennett. For two decades, he and his gun had ruled supreme in the egret and heron colonies on the west coast of Mexico, where he would disappear for weeks at a time during the long nesting season, slipping back into civilisation to dispose of his stock. A male reporter from the New York *Sun* tracked him down in coastal Pomona in June 1896, when Bennett had just shifted $2,600-worth of feathers to wholesale plumage buyers in New York and Philadelphia. This would be worth around $70,000 or £50,000 in today's money.

'The handsome property and the bank stock he owns in Los Angeles and San Diego' were, *The Sun* reported, 'proofs of the profit he has found in hunting egrets and herons each spring and summer for about 22 years.' The half-page feature read like a celebrity interview: plume hunting was a legitimate, macho, glamorous trade. There was glamour in its potential riches, glamour in its high-fashion destiny and glamour in its danger. 'I tell you it is hard, exacting and patient work to hunt egrets,' Bennett told the journalist. His huge profits had earned him much jealousy, but usually when he described the privations, the fiendish climate and the unbearable mosquitoes, 'most hunters think egret hunting isn't profitable *enough* to engage their time'.

Rather than keep his methods close to his chest, 'Egret' Bennett was happy to enlighten readers of *The Sun* – for who was going to follow him into the alligator swamps off the coast of Mexico? Perhaps, egged on by the reporter, he exaggerated its horrors. 'You want to hear about how we hunt egrets and herons? It is the hardest sort of life, and no one, however robust, could keep at it for more than a few months at a time. The miasma of the water and the poisonous atmosphere all about us at night, soon fills one's blood with rheumatism and fevers . . .'

Accounts by horrified naturalists of bloody slaughters at remote heron and egret colonies were becoming quite a genre in newspapers and journals. The descriptions tended to follow the same pattern: 'the delicate snow-white plumes from the backs of the egrets straying out bewitchingly in the breeze', the volley of gunshots, the carnage on the ground as the birds were picked off one by one, as easy as picking apples, and the festering piles of carcasses left to the red ants.

'I wish that the ladies who encourage this cruel trade could have seen the pitiable sight of those mangled little bodies lying in a loathsome heap, to the number of several hundreds,' wrote one eye witness in 1902, 'while the vultures lurked in the trees close by, ready to resume their horrid meal.' It was held by the SPB that 'three hundred may be killed in an afternoon by two or three men'. Plume hunters were characterised as oafish, dangerous, after a fast buck.

Bennett told it differently. 'An egret hunter must be the foxiest kind of hunter,' he said. 'These birds are the most cautious and wary I have ever heard or known of . . . fussy and nervous creatures . . . as watchful as weasels.'

His work demanded the utmost stealth. Working with three or four Mexican hired hands, he would go out in a flotilla of small boats, pushing slowly through swampy marshland and tangled undergrowth, keeping a watchful eye out for alligators. Shoots lasted a fortnight or maybe a month, and for that period of time they would not leave their boats, 'even for an hour'. They became amphibious creatures. The egrets nested in lagoon reeds far from the shore, while the herons preferred high spots, building their twiggy nests in trees. Bennett waited until the parent birds had flown off to find food, then would manoeuvre the boats into position, camouflaging them with reeds and foliage. There they would lie in silence, unmoving, barrels ready.

At around five or six o'clock in the evening, they would hear the distant *rah rah rah* rasping cry as egrets and herons returned to their nests – kinked necks, dagger bills, yellow feet trailing behind, long wings curved in an 'm'-shape. Quickly the hunters would shoot – one, two, three, four blasts of their rifles at the birds before they were 'out of range'. They were so 'easily frightened' that they were 'powerless of flight for a moment and make good targets of themselves'.

The colony deserted of all but nestlings, Bennett and his men would paddle back and forth collecting what they needed from the dozen or so white corpses on the ground – just a handful of fine, hair-like nuptial plumes which grew from the bird's back and drooped gracefully over the tail. You could get three times as many feathers off a heron, but these were worth half the price of the prized fine, white egret feathers. The hunters were systematic, patient and tenacious. They had to be. 'After we have got our birds and picked the few feathers we want from each,' Bennett told the reporter, 'we plan another onslaught in another locality.'

Each bird might yield a quarter of an ounce of feathers. A good season's 'harvest' for Bennett was 55 ounces, gathered on a spree between February and September – a cull of around 220 birds. The nestlings that starved to death accounted for many hundreds more. An ounce in 1896 was worth \$28 – but how long could this fabulous rate of return be sustained? Bennett admitted that he had contributed to the near annihilation of egrets in his 20-year career. He had already 'cleared out' Central America with his team of shooters, moving on to the Gulf of California and now the Pacific Ocean side of Mexico, where he hoped there were just enough birds to keep him going until retirement in a few years' time. He had heard stories of devastation from hunters in Peru, Columbia and Ecuador, where the great Parisian *plumassiers* once bought their stock to satiate the global demand for the osprey or aigrette.

'I am sure that in a dozen years more,' said Bennett, 'if the fashion for feathers in women's millinery prevails as now, there will be very few egrets left on the west coast of the whole western continent.' It all rested with the Parisian milliners, 'who rule the ornamental feather market of the world, make and unmake all the fashions, and create demands in our line of business'.

What would he do, asked the reporter, when all the egrets were gone? Bennett wasn't sure. 'I have never found any occupation so profitable.'

The wire-like fine feathers of the snowy egret seemed almost to levitate from a headpiece, giving the wearer the illusion of balletic grace and height. Used in their pure, unadulterated form, they could create an aureole as if the head was backlit by the sun. Dyed black, they were lustrous, sophisticated, scintillating. They also came in every other colour in-between, from Edwardian hostess Maud Messel's pale pink collection, to the lime green exclamation mark of Major Drummond's wife. Bunched together as a long tuft, they were known as the 'osprey'.

By the turn of the century, every woman of every class had to own one. No hat or head ornament was complete without. 'The only thing that can be urged on behalf of osprey wearing is that it is nowadays so thoroughly democratic,' wrote Mrs Lemon witheringly in *Bird Notes and News*. 'It proves that Mrs Gamp and Mrs Prig, with "ospreys" sticking up in their bonnets, can be just as stylish as Lady Araminta with a huge brush nodding in her hair, and that Lady Araminta knows no more and thinks no more on matters of taste and humanity than Sarah Gamp and Betsy Prig.'

In 1903, an ounce of egret feathers could fetch $32 – almost twice as much as an ounce of gold. To the SPB, this was a watershed moment. The cult of the osprey was to become their battleground.

One hundred and fifty four branch secretaries across England, Wales, Scotland and Ireland were duly briefed and mobilised for action. They were to infiltrate the stores, surprise the shoppers, question the shop girls, cross-examine the head milliners and lecture the shop managers. From Miss Ethel Magee of Belfast to Miss Lily Trotter of Eastbourne, from Lady

Brownrigg in Maidenhead to Miss Conyers in Ilkley, the foot soldiers of the SPB prepared, gingerly, for the 'frontal attack'.

Ladies of fashion did not like to be caught 'red-handed', Miss Conyers had already pointed out. Approaching the wearers of plumes was, she had found, 'a matter requiring much tact'. But her objections had been batted away by Mrs Lemon and Mrs Phillips at last year's AGM. Red-handed these women must be caught. Like 'Egret' Bennett, the branch secretaries were to become the foxiest kind of hunter. When confronted, their quarry would be cautious and wary, ready to take flight. It might well become fussy and nervous. But they must hold steady.

The original Operation Osprey was the first of its kind: a women's guerrilla marketing campaign that drew on the ingenuity, energy and indignation of a small group of activists. These were conservative women, many of them elderly. They were rectors' wives, schoolmistresses, Honourables and spinsters. Each woman was armed with a righteous pamphlet, the most trenchant yet published by the society. It was a desperate stab at shocking consumers into consciousness. Titled *The Biography of a Lie*, it began with an attack on the consumers:

> Fifty years hence, when the egret has been practically exterminated, or its plumes are no longer considered fit wear for civilised women, our descendants will read with amazement that, at a period when woman was loudly claiming to be intellectual, and rational, and cultured, she became possessed of a passion for ornamenting her headgear with a certain tuft of plumes; that to procure this she had distant lands ransacked and beautiful harmless birds ruthlessly slaughtered in their breeding time, and nestlings by the hundreds and thousands starved to death.

But what did *The Biography of a Lie* mean? Who was lying about what? Since the SPB had stepped up its campaign against the osprey, egret and heron plumes were now being peddled by the fashion industry as clever fakes. Women with a conscience were buying these clever 'fakes' as an ethical substitute, just as you might buy an imitation fur coat today. Of *course* they weren't real, ran brisk editorials in the *Millinery Record*. The trade magazine claimed to have gone 'thoroughly into the matter' and seen the 'substances employed' in manufacturing an aigrette – 'certain acids' that destroyed the flue of barnyard feathers, leaving 'perfect skeletons' that could be curled or dressed in any form. 'For every real osprey worn there are a thousand clever imitations of it.'

The same edition of the *Millinery Record* showed photographs (the first) of various society beauties crested with egret feathers – such as Miss Maud Hobson, 'a Gaiety Theatre favourite', wearing a 'becoming hat' made of bouffant white chiffon, white ostrich feather and 'sweeping plumes of curved white osprey', very much the real thing.

Other trade magazines were less sure. Don't blame the milliner, urged the *Draper's Record*: it is 'absurd' to level the charge of cruelty at those who 'simply supply a public demand, and cannot be expected to know anything of the ornithological facts, if such they be, which are from time to time paraded before the public'.

The debate grew louder, provoking publications into taking a stance and airing the broader question of avian adornment. Women's magazines began to carry disclaimers in their fashion editorials. 'Wings and feather ornaments can be so cleverly made from the feathers of birds used for domestic purposes,' wrote *Home Chat*'s fashion columnist to her budget-conscious readers. 'It is to these *made* wings that we refer when describing such adornments.'

'The Biography of a Lie' pamphlet could be bought by the SPB local branch secretaries for one shilling and nine pence per 100. It was ammunition in a crusade that would be taken out onto the streets, into shops and department stores; a crusade that would grasp the attention of the British woman in a personal and memorable manner. Today's pamphleteers might resort to stunts like fancy dress for maximum impact – but in 1903 the SPB branch secretaries were required, like the militant suffragists of the near future, to appear beyond reproach. They must not excite panic or suspicion. To fit in, they must camouflage themselves as ladies of fashion. As soon as the spring millinery appeared in shop windows, 154 women fanned out through the country, watchful as weasels.

23

Deeds Not Words

1903

In a red-brick terraced house in Manchester, another guerrilla campaign got under way that year – a campaign that, in a startlingly short time, would eclipse the bird protection movement and become the most attention grabbing of them all. This was 62 Nelson Street, the new home of Emmeline Pankhurst. By 1903, her children were not so small and needy: Harry, the youngest, was 13. She was now 45, and it was time for her moment in history to begin.

Emmeline's life had changed drastically since her spell as an elegant political hostess in Russell Square. In 1898, aged 40, she had been abruptly widowed. Richard, her inspirational partner in life and in politics, had died of a stress-induced gastric ulcer. The children at this time were aged between eight and 18; Emmeline was now sole breadwinner for a family of four. Eldest daughter Christabel remembered her mother's face changing at this time, taking on its stoical, tragic expression. It was a look she was to wear for the rest of her life. Richard Pankhurst's death devastated Emmeline, but it had the effect of propelling her forward, out of his orbit.

A new house had to be found that was small and cheap to rent. Nelson Street branched off the busy main thoroughfare into Manchester, close to the Royal Infirmary and the Whitworth Institute and Park, where the city's inhabitants were now encouraged to seek solace in art, flowers and birds.

Today, Emmeline's home sits in splendid isolation like a red toy house, surrounded by glass and steel hospital buildings and a multi-storey car park. It was saved from demolition in 1979 by a women's squatting campaign and, unlike the house of SPB founder Emily Williamson, just three miles due south in leafy Didsbury, it has long born a blue heritage plaque as the birthplace of the Suffragette movement. But it is shabby and unloved all the same, with peeling paint and crumbling plasterwork. The house at 62 Nelson Street now operates as a women's community centre and a shrine to the Pankhurst family. Inside there are photographs of extravagantly hatted protests, glass cases of memorabilia (coat pins, board games, postcards) and a recreation of that elegant, if cramped parlour, where it all began on 10 October 1903.

Mrs Pankhurst was now working full-time as Chorlton's Registrar for Births and Deaths in south Manchester, while her daughters reluctantly minded her 'artistic' furnishings store, Emerson's. It was a job that helped her forget her own misery, and re-focused her mind on politics. Registering the births of illegitimate babies to girls as young as 13, all too often victims of abuse, fired Emmeline's compassion and indignation. Without the vote, she was convinced, there would be no social reform. Without the vote, women were never going to have a fairer deal in society.

By the summer of 1903, Mrs Pankhurst's eldest daughter, Christabel, now a strikingly attractive 22-year-old, was speaking on women's suffrage in Lancashire, Yorkshire and as far afield as Glasgow, while also studying law. Adela, daughter number three, was training to be a teacher. Emmeline's middle daughter, Sylvia, a talented painter at the Manchester School of Art, was commissioned to decorate the Dr Pankhurst Memorial Hall in Salford with her murals.

Sylvia was astonished to learn, however, that women were not to be allowed to use it, since the hall was a social club for men attached to the Independent Labour Party. This was the final straw for her mother. 'We must have an independent women's movement!' Mrs Pankhurst told her friends. 'Come to my house tomorrow and we will arrange it!' Within a week of the hall opening in October 1903, the Women's Social and Political Union (WSPU) was formed.

Pronounced 'wis*poo*', the WSPU was destined to give its founder a place in history. The group, small at first, was ambitious, frustrated and publicity hungry. In time, it would outgrow its Manchester roots and become the hissing acronym on every New Woman's lips. Its founders were not like Mrs Fawcett and her so-called 'spinster suffrage party', patiently pursuing reform by constitutional means. The WSPU had the bracing, faintly pugilistic slogan 'Deeds Not Words'. It would soon graduate to militancy, mass demonstrations and violence.

Outwardly so very different, the WSPU and the SPB shared just one letter – 'S' for Social, or Society. Each was a collective, and each was trying to break the status quo. Both groups required brave, antisocial deeds from their members, asking them to swim against the current – a current that forcefully swept all Edwardian women up before it. Both groups courted controversy and earned contempt. The SPB women were jeered at as 'Plumage Cranks', 'Feather Faddists' and 'Frothy Fanatics'. The suffragettes were the 'shrieking sisterhood'. 'Go home and do your washing!' was a common taunt, or 'You ought to be tarred and feathered!'.

To Emmeline Pankhurst and the WSPU, this was grist to their mill. She was used to being pelted with rotten tomatoes from her days as a political candidate's wife. Women suffrage speakers had been booed by crowds for 30-odd years. You could not launch a 'sensational campaign' without outraging the majority. 'We threw away all our conventional notions of what was "ladylike" and "good form",' wrote Mrs Pankhurst, 'and we applied to our methods the one test question, Will it help?'

The genteel bird protection ladies were being asked, essentially, to do the same. Up until this point, they had hidden behind magic lantern slide shows, nature writing prizes and letters to *The Times*. Now, they were forced to step into the public sphere for 'the frontal attack', with the excruciating mandate to penetrate the special intimacy of the ladies' fashion store.

For both groups, the battle was about to commence. The next ten years would see a refinement and purloining of tactics, a creative friction between the two societies, and a boiling up of frustration. But it is worth noting that the antisocial activism of the staid and fusty SPB pre-dated the WSPU's militarism by some four years. Mrs Lemon and her women paved the way.

24

The Frontal Attack

1903

O ut they fanned across the country. In they walked. Scottish SPB branch secretary Mrs Murray pushed through the mahogany revolving door of Fraser & Davidson, a prosperous department store on Inverness high street advertising a clearance sale of 'Trimmed & untrimmed hats, Feathers, Ribbons & Ornaments'. Into Frederick Carder & Son of Ipswich went Miss Barne, an apparently innocent shopper entering a 'Milliners & Ladies' Outfitters'. In Plymouth, the bell jangled at F. W. Parkyn's, small scale draper and hosier of Exeter Street, announcing the entrance of Mrs Hermor. She was, she told the girl behind the counter, looking to buy hat trimmings.

It was springtime, 1903: hat-buying season. Each SPB branch secretary carried in her bag a small wad of printed society pamphlets. The more brave or brazen of them also carried a magnifying glass – and why not? When a trade feather buyer made a purchase, he would use a large magnifying glass for scrutiny, 'with all the nicety of a bird examining a flower', as 'Egret' Bennett had put it. The ladies were looking for hard evidence. Mrs Lemon had asked for osprey samples to be sent in to the head office at 3 Hanover Square; samples were to be analysed by Dr Bowdler Sharpe (curator of the bird collection at the British Museum and founder of the British Ornithologists' Club) and Professor Ray Lankester (director of the Natural History Museum). So far, every single 'fake' osprey that the two had forensically examined had proven to be the real thing – not horsehair, not whalebone, not bleached grasses or ivorine, as variously claimed.

The Society for the Protection of Birds was frequently lampooned as a hotbed of highly strung women incapable of scientific thought, guided by impulse rather than reason. Very well, went Etta Lemon's thinking. If it took science to be taken seriously, then they would give them science. But first, a little female craftiness and dissembling were required.

It is possible to eavesdrop at the millinery counter thanks to a scene reported in the SPB magazine, *Bird Notes and News*, that year. We don't know the name of the department store or which branch secretary was involved – but we do know how it happened, and in detail. No man would have written up the incident in this way, in the manner of a theatrical sketch. The piece's tone (righteous, incredulous, yet also slightly playful) is highly reminiscent of Mrs Eliza Phillips' voice. Could this have been *her* much vaunted 'frontal attack'?

The scene takes place, we are told, in a 'leading haberdashery store' in the capital. Our undercover investigator enters innocently, greets the forewoman at the counter, and tells her she has selected this store for her purchases because there are fewer ospreys than usual in the window displays.

The forewoman swiftly grasps what her enquiry might be about. 'I suppose, madam, you are one of the ladies who have conscientious objections to wearing them? We have heard a good deal about that from some society – the Society for the Protection of Birds I think it is called.' 'But,' she continues confidently, 'it is entirely a mistake. The ospreys are not real; they are all manufactured.'

'Are they, indeed?' replies the shopper, unperturbed. 'That is very interesting. I am greatly interested in manufactures, and like to encourage the wearing of manufactured articles. What are they made of?'

'Simply quills, madam,' replies the forewoman smoothly. She opens a drawer in a cabinet, takes out a white goose feather and a penknife and begins to pare away at the quill. 'In this way, you see.'

'Yes, that is all very well,' interrupts our woman, reining in her irritation; 'but you may go on with that for ever, and you will never make anything like an osprey out of it.'

'Oh, I assure you, madam, that is the method,' replies the forewoman crisply. 'We make them ourselves on the premises.'

'Really! That is still more interesting,' says the shopper. 'I suppose you would not object to allowing me to see them being made?'

'Oh – er – certainly not. Miss Jones!'

Miss Jones, who has been watching this demonstration from a discreet distance, is despatched to the manager to ask if a lady might be allowed to see the 'manufacture' of the osprey. Minutes tick by. The customer takes a small notebook from her purse and jots fast with a slender pencil. Miss Jones returns, her eyes nervous.

'The manager's compliments, but he thinks the forewoman has made a little mistake. The ospreys are not made *on the premises*.'

'My compliments to the manager,' retorts the lady with the utmost civility, 'and will he kindly tell me where they *are* made, because I will go to any part of the world to see it done!'

'The manager's compliments,' pants Miss Jones, scurrying back, 'and he really does not know.'

'No, he does *not* know,' says the customer, turning her glare on the forewoman. 'And *you* do not know, and *I* do not know; because there is no such place, and you are as well aware of that as I am. So why in the world do you go on telling that story?'

The same scene, more or less, was playing out all over the country that spring. Servile, tight-lipped forewomen and shop assistants handed over osprey samples to SPB branch secretaries – plumes that were being sold as artificial at prices ranging wildly from 5d to 18s 11d. 'In every case they were supplied without question or demur,' reported Mrs Lemon in *Bird Notes and News*, 'showing the demand is a familiar one, and the answering lie given is the ordinary way of business.' Under intense cross-examination two West End saleswomen crumpled, admitting that the plumes were real egret plumes, that no such things as artificial ones were to be had, and that 'imitation' was 'merely a trade name'.

The SPB's focus was not just on the smarter streets and boutiques. Birds were now conspicuous by their absence in the best Bond Street shops. The Duchess of Portland's influence in courtly circles seemed to be making an impact – though perhaps this was just the inevitable pendulum swing of fashion. Of the 2,000 paradise birds on offer at the London Commercial Sale Rooms in January 1903, just 100 were sold to the usual leading feather manufacturers. Parrots, too, 'excited scant attention'. A humming-bird could be had for a farthing – the smallest coin in the realm.

The dip in fashion for exotic plumage made it more affordable to the rest of womanhood. 'While these foreign birds are to be had at such ridiculous prices,' wrote Mrs Lemon to London's *The Globe*, 'that class of the community which rejoices in gaudy headgear is not likely to forgo its passion.' Her branch secretaries were instructed to focus in particular on 'suburban and inferior class shops', where 'made up' birds (fantasy birds created from a patchwork of skins) were commonly displayed 'which besides being in egregiously bad taste, commonly introduce forbidden plumage.' The novelty that spring, to be found in numerous shop windows, was hats trimmed with a wreath of stuffed bullfinches.

What was really under attack here? Bird wearing – or the rampant consumerism of the lower-class woman? Class anxiety keeps bubbling up in SPB literature – an anxiety absolutely of its time and true to its conservative members. The society's inability to reach common women was a tacit failing. The suffrage movement managed to rally thousands of mill girls and factory girls; even Mrs Pankhurst's WSPU, at its ultra-fashionable height, recruited its share of working-class women. The anti-plumage campaign had the unfortunate appearance of being anti-fun and anti-joy: another negative, finger-wagging exercise from the likes of the Temperance Society. The implication was that lower-class feather wearers were not only cruel, but socially presumptuous.

Mrs Lemon began to take a masochistic pleasure in being told the lie at each shop she investigated. It seemed to confirm all instincts she had about these base servants of consumerism. Every girl she confronted had 'some glib story ready to hand almost before the question was asked' – 'Nearly *all* artificial, Madam,' they would tell her; 'we use hardly any real ones.' Lying through their teeth, Etta noted with scornful satisfaction. 'The headgear in their show-rooms and windows bristled with ospreys whose genuineness was patent.'

25

Mrs Pattinson

Type 'milliner' into the National Archives database and you will find, for this period, just two names worthy of close scrutiny – turn-of-the-century businesswomen whose account books and orders just happen to have survived. Yet, by serendipity, they provide two fascinating stories. Both ran their own shops: one in the provincial north of England; one in the fashionable heart of the capital. Both dealt in 'murderous millinery'. And both profited from the Edwardian woman's imperative to change her look seasonally.

Let us go first to the north of England, to a ladies' outfitters in a market town in the Lake District. It is a tiny L-shaped shop, two-storey, in a prime position facing the main shopping street. 'Mrs Pattinson, Milliner' is the name on the storefront; 'Ribbons, Laces, Feathers & Flowers. Ladies' & Children's Underclothing.' Upstairs is a workroom, downstairs a long counter. Two women – one middle-aged, one very young – stand behind it.

Elizabeth Pattinson was an independent milliner and dressmaker working in the Furness Peninsula town of Ulverston – just the kind of woman to come under the scrutiny of Mrs Lemon and her branch secretaries. Her margins were tight. She knew her customers and gave them what they wanted – an affordable, anglicised, wearable version of those outfits they had spotted in the fashion plates of ladies' magazines.

How did a woman like Elizabeth Pattinson run her business? What plumes did she stock? Did she supply the snowy egret feathers? Her papers are kept at the Cumbria Archive Centre in Barrow-in-Furness: two large cardboard boxes containing a daunting number of brittle, yellowing receipts and faded order forms bound together with string. It looks as if nobody has untied these dirty bundles since Mrs Pattinson deposited them in the attic of her Ulverston home, 8 Upper Brook Street, some time before the First World War. There they had lain undisturbed until discovered by builders in 1982.

In 1891, when Ulverston's most famous son, Stan Laurel, was one year old, Mrs Pattinson wrote down her orders in a little accounts book. The amounts are small. There was, one assumes, no waste.

> Ribbon
> Lace
> 3 Feathers (at 3/6d each)
> Caps
> Cords
> Embroidery
> Fall net
> Beaver skin at 4/6d
> Hats (ranging in price from 1/2d to 14/9d)
> Flowers & Feathers
> Chiffon
> Feathers & Wings
> Velvetta

Elizabeth, daughter of a woodturner, was apprenticed to a milliner–dressmaker aged 15. 'I was surprised to learn that you had begun to learn to be a milliner,' went a letter from her cousin Jane. 'I hope you like it. It will be a nice pastime for you.' Judging by the accounts, it turned out to be rather more than a nice pastime. Since setting up on her own in 1884, aged 37, Mrs Pattinson had run a steadily lucrative business, assisted by her young niece, Maggie.

She soon diversified into general drapery – stockings, purses, mittens, flannel nightdresses, knickers, astrakhan, cashmere and calico. Orders for plumage continued, listed simply as 'Feathers' at 2/9d each; 'Wings' from five pence three farthing each; 'Quills' at 6 ½d each, and 'Birds' at 4/9d per dozen. Disappointingly, no species are given. Perhaps 'birds' were just that, to a milliner: a generic commodity, something requiring false eyes and wire supports. But there were also regular orders for 'Osprey' at 3/3d per dozen.

So here was the evidence. The osprey was worn in rural Lancashire, just as it was on Old Bond Street. Who was supplying these egret feathers? Mrs Pattinson formed the end of a long commodity chain: a chain that started in the remote heronries of Florida and the swamps of Venezuela, and ended 4,000 miles away on a small English peninsula, overlooking Morecambe Bay. The osprey plumes and other feathers were ordered from various wholesalers in the north, and from Annie Buckingham, a milliner and feather dresser from the larger Lake District town of Barrow. As I leafed through dozens of old bills, handwritten on fantastically elaborate headed paper, a network of interconnection and dependence emerged: the hat industry stretched like a web across Britain.

Who was buying and wearing Mrs Pattinson's hats? There were regular letters from Mary Anne Fenton of Low House, Windermere. Mrs Fenton was a 'faddy' lady, keen on feathered crimson bonnets and fancy astrakhan capes that concealed her girth. She rarely visited Ulverston, but conducted her fastidious shopping via post and railway.

A typically querulous letter begins:

Dear Mrs Pattinson,

My hat fits very comfortably but after the soft silk that would bend any way it feels rather stiff – I like it very much but am returning it to have some more trimming on – some loops from the crimson round to the other side to fill it up and I think if they were made of the plain velvet they would look well – just – little fancy bows on loops and I would like a bow at the back where the gauze is tied on to fill it up a bit – Mr F thinks it a beautiful hat but I think it a little juvenile – but the amendments will make it all right – the velvet both plain and ribbed is very pretty. Some thought – a bit of feather trimming would look nice – but leave it to you – I don't like great spreading bows – the crimson one is very nice . . . what a trouble I give you.

By 1897, Mrs Pattinson was managing to make a comfortable profit of two pounds a week, at a time when one pound was thought to be the bottom line for running a household. To a hard-grafting woman like this, the anti-plumage plea of Mrs Lemon and the SPB made absolutely no business sense. It was a frankly unreasonable demand. As long as there were ladies like Mrs Fenton who loved feathered hats, and as long as there were milliners to relieve them of their money, the SPB was fighting a losing battle.

There were five other milliners in Ulverston, a town of some 10,000 people. Most of Mrs Pattinson's customers would have been regulars, but their numbers were boosted by tourists. In the summer months, Ulverston's turreted railway station disgorged many hundreds en route to the Windermere steamboats at Lakeside. The Blackburn local branch secretary for the SPB might well have entered such a shop while visiting the Lakes, some 60 miles from her Lancashire home town. Perhaps Mrs Pattinson's was even the scene of a 'frontal attack'.

Hilda Howard was 21, unmarried and new to the post of Blackburn honorary secretary – a role she took extremely seriously. In 1904, she wrote a despairing letter to Mrs Lemon about the vicar of Blackburn's wife, Emily Thornton, who appeared in church week after week wearing a large, quivering osprey despite being sent SPB literature (and despite a 25 year ministry stint among the exquisite birdlife of Victoria, Australia). 'How can we expect mill-hands, shop-girls & domestic servants to discontinue the use of birds' plumes,' lamented Hilda, 'when such an example is set them by one occupying the position Mrs Thornton does?'

The previous year, Miss Howard had grasped the nettle and written to the portly Samuel Thornton, not only vicar of Blackburn but assistant Bishop of Manchester; great orator and man of influence. 'May I hope that Mrs Thornton will become a member of the society,' she asked, 'and use her influence to check the fashion which outrages the best instincts of womanly nature?' The 68-year-old bishop wrote back, and his letter gives a nice flavour of what the bird activists were up against.

> Thanks for the pamphlets you sent me on the Bird question . . . I confess that I have become – after considerable experience – <u>very</u> shy of joining societies of the kind you mention. They are liable to get into the hands of 'faddists' and extreme persons, who come to dominate their policy, and identify them with foolish and narrow and even calumnious utterances.

The SPB did, undeniably, attract women who were passionate about animal rights – and society in general was wary of ladies with passions. The bishop thought the feather issue 'far more suited to the considerations of the *leaders of Fashion* than of any other class of person'. 'If the Queen or Princess of Wales came to show the way, feather wearing would soon be discarded. To make it vulgar would be the best way to stop it.' As the bishop saw it, this was entirely a metropolitan matter.

26

The Countess Fabbricotti

In the spring of 1905, a woman with a past opened a hat shop at 5 South Molton Street, Mayfair. She claimed French parentage, had a New York accent and went by the Italian name writ large over the shop front: 'The Countess Fabbricotti'. Nobody quite knew what to believe about who she was or where she had come from, but her connections seemed impeccable. Fabbricotti was the other milliner I found in the National Archives database; the south to Mrs Pattinson's north. Her story was a tremendous web of self-fabrication.

'Never before in the British capital was there such a millinery opening,' gushed the *Chicago Tribune*, a foreign paper that knew a thing or two about the Countess's past. The shop's launch party resembled 'a drawing room reception in the height of the season'. Aristocrats, their wives, social leaders and hangers-on all crushed into a small space done up like a bower and hung about with extravagant hats. Three liveried footmen handed out tea and cake, directed by two debutantes. Carriages queued outside, disgorging London's biggest names in fashion. At the centre of the braying throng was the 'artistically jewelled' Countess Fabbricotti, a 'handsome' woman of 35, gowned in white muslin with a design of green leaves and white flowers.

The reporter noted that the price tags were 'even higher than her position in the peerage' (an arch reference, perhaps, to Fabbricotti's shady past). She was charging 'fabulous prices' for plain little toques. For a simple dress hat with plumes 'the Countess asks $50 – and gets it'. One hundred dollars (around £2,000 today) was considered 'a reasonable price for anything'. With brazen American chutzpah, the Countess had set her prices so exclusively high that everybody present felt they simply *had* to buy.

Everything was riding on this grand opening, for the splendidly named Fabbricotti had not a penny to her name. The woman seemed to have stepped straight out of an Edith Wharton novel. Like the Countess Olenska in *The Age of Innocence*, she was scandalously divorced from a European aristocrat (an Italian nobleman, ten a penny). And like Lily Bart in *The House of Mirth*, she was beautiful but penniless at a precarious age. Who was she?

After much digging around in census returns and shipping records, I discovered that the Countess Fabbricotti was born plain Anna Kingsley in 1866, to an Irish immigrant father and an Irish mother (not French, as she liked to tell people). She was educated in Chicago (not Germany, as her story went), and while her brothers became carpenters like her father, Anna had greater ambitions.

Since her divorce, she'd been romantically linked with a trail of admirers in New York and Long Island, but keeping up appearances did not come cheap. Anna Kingsley-Fabbricotti persuaded an heiress friend to give her a new start and bankroll her idea of a London hat shop. Princess Clara Hatzfeldt was a good business match for Anna: here was another self-invented woman. Born to a Sacramento grocer, Clara had been adopted, unofficially, by her childless uncle – the obscenely wealthy railroad baron Collis Potter Huntingdon. Because Clara 'longed to wear a coronet' (so said the *Illustrated American*), he arranged her marriage with a debt-ridden German nobleman, Prince Franz von Hatzfeldt.

When Huntingdon died in 1900, Clara was left a trust fund of $1 million. It wasn't enough. She promptly began an acrimonious suit for a 'daughter's share' of his vast estate, settling out of court the following year for $6 million. A Lafayette Studio photograph of 1903 shows the 'Princess' dressed as the Queen of Sheba for a fancy dress ball. Her nose is beaky, her gaze level and her small mouth spoilt.

Hatzfeldt and Fabbricotti: what better names to run an exclusive hat shop? 'We have been dreadfully hard up,' Anna Fabbricotti drolly told a reporter, 'and are doing this just to make money.' If the venture didn't work, she said, she would starve. 'She talks freely to her friends of the depleted state of her exchequer,' a journalist for the *San Francisco Call* noted with some awe. But clearly this tactic was paying off. 'As she is young and beautiful, she has everybody's sympathy.' She was also American, and happily free of British upper-class inhibitions. 'The old notion that there is anything discreditable in engaging in trade, even for a woman, is dying out,' Fabbricotti claimed. 'The fact is, it is becoming quite fashionable to make money.'

The Countess Fabbricotti ran her boutique very successfully between 1905 and 1909, when a wealthy Italian suitor swooped in to rescue her, as had been her fervent hope. Her heavy, leather-bound order books and accounts ledgers were given to Westminster Archives by a solicitor's firm in 1970, all buckled with damp. Here, in the columns of pounds, shillings and pence (plus one for 'bad debts') was primary evidence of hard work.

Not work with a needle: Anna Fabbricotti did not make the headgear herself. She had engaged a staff of Frenchwomen – 'there is no doubt they turn out the best hats and bonnets in the world.' Hats were bought wholesale on shopping expeditions to London, Paris and Berlin, then, with a flourish here and there, converted in-house into Fabbricotti specials with an astronomical price mark-up. Despite paying £88 interest a year on Clara Hatzfeldt's loan, her profits averaged £500; that is, around £50,000 per annum in today's money.

What she did was network assiduously among the upper classes. 'I have received more invitations to social affairs than I can begin to avail myself of,' she told a gossip columnist, ensuring a constant stream of many more. Her reward was their curiosity and their patronage. It appears that society could not stay away from 5 South Molton Street and its atmosphere of exclusivity; it was a little like a private club. Fabbricotti's alphabetical order books read like a Who's Who for racy Edwardian A-listers.

Emily Williamson started her Society for the Protection of Birds in Manchester, in 1889, because she was angry at being barred from the all-male British Ornithologists' Union. Its lady members vowed to wear no feathers, 'the ostrich and game birds excepted'.

When Emily's society merged with the Fur, Fin and Feather Folk of Croydon, in 1891, Etta Lemon *(right)* became the driving force behind the new SPB. The Victorian founders have gone down in history as genteel, elderly and out of touch – yet at its start they were in their prime.

Mother and children 'willowing' (lengthening) ostrich plumes by hand in their New York tenement, late at night. Work on a single plume might take a day and a half, requiring around 9,000 knots just to lengthen it throughout by one inch. In 1911, when this photograph was taken, this would earn the family three cents.

Young milliners at work. 'There we sit, all through the morning, afternoon and evening, stitching and trimming away, with the sun pouring in on us, and the room getting closer and closer until you can hardly bear it any longer,' one wrote anonymously to *The Times* in 1884.

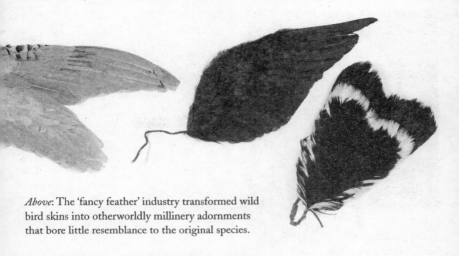

Above: The 'fancy feather' industry transformed wild bird skins into otherworldly millinery adornments that bore little resemblance to the original species.

Left: The 'bird hat' reached its apogee in the 1890s. Wild bird species around the world were brought to the brink of extinction by the highly lucrative plumage trade.

Right: The ostrich plume sorting room at London's Cutler Street warehouse, where raw bundles were inspected before fortnightly auctions. Cheap female labour was then used to wash, dye, thicken, lengthen and hand-curl the plumes.

In 1909, women's hats typically measured three feet high and two feet wide. Their preposterous growth was linked, in part, to female politics.

'A Bird of Prey' by Edward Linley Sambourne, satirising the Victorian woman's lust for avian adornment, was published in *Punch* in 1892, in support of Etta Lemon's campaign.

Right: 'Murderous millinery': for one ounce of the exquisite, airy plumage known to milliners as the 'osprey', four snowy egrets had to die. By 1903 an ounce could fetch $32 – twice as much as an ounce of gold.

Above: Queen Alexandra, fashion icon and wife of the adulterous King Edward VII, put her name to the birds' cause in 1906. Where she led, thousands of women would follow.

Above: Winifred, Duchess of Portland – president of the RSPB from 1891 until her death in 1954 – was vital for her influence in courtly circles. 'Winnie' was vegetarian and anti blood sports, yet married to a fanatical deer stalker.

Frank and Etta Lemon at home in Redhill, Surrey. When barrister
Frank helped draw up the SPB charter in 1891, he little guessed
his future would be so bound up with the birds. He and Etta
married a year later, formidable partners in work and life.

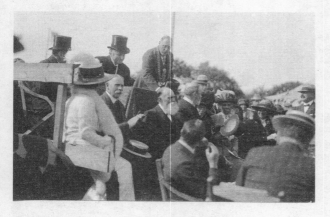

Colley Hill was saved from Surrey's developers by Mayor Frank
Lemon *(top, centre)* in 1913, the deeds presented to the parish by
Lord Curzon *(to his right)*. Curzon was staunchly supported in his
anti-suffrage campaign by Mrs Lemon.

Mrs Frank Lemon, Mayoress of Reigate, 1911-13 – and head of the East
Surrey Women's National Anti-Suffrage League. 'We believe that men and
women are different – not similar – beings, with talents that are complementary,
not identical, and that they therefore ought to have different shares in the
management of the State,' argued fellow Anti, Violet Markham.

East End factory girls dressed in Sunday best on a rare trip to the Sussex countryside, hosted by upper middle-class 'slummer' Milicent Ludlow (*front, far left*), in 1897. Emmeline Pankhurst came to see the vote as a 'desperate necessity' for exploited young workers such as these.

Millicent Fawcett *(bottom, centre)* and her law-abiding suffra*gists* were derided by Mrs Pankhurst and her militant suffra*gettes* as the 'spinster suffrage party'. 'Among these brave and devoted women there were a few who were not only plain but positively uncouth to the outward eye,' wrote Ray Strachey in her chronicle of the movement.

The hat stall at The Women's Exhibition, 1909 – an attempt to woo the public with a grand display of 'the feminine arts'. Bird-loving suffragettes wrote to Mrs Pankhurst *(centre, seated)*, begging that no 'murderous millinery' be included.

Suffragettes selling propaganda on street corners were enjoined by the Pankhursts to look their most elegant and feminine: the feathered hat was an indispensible part of their brand. These represent the Women's Freedom League, a splinter group of the WSPU formed in 1907.

Right: Anti-suffragette propaganda played on the mixed message of elegant women in feathered hats. Trust them at your peril, went the message. Just look at their millinery.

An Advocate for Woman's Rights.

A SUFFRAGETTE'S HOME

VOTES FOR WOMEN

AFTER A HARD DAY'S WORK!

Published by the Campaign Committee, National League for Opposing Woman Suffrage, Caxton House, Westminster. JOIN!

Left: The National League for Opposing Woman Suffrage stirred up national sentiment against suffragists. But most of the population already believed that votes for women would be 'a monstrous inversion of the natural order of things'.

Emmeline Pankhurst (*right*) in feathers and fur. A slave to fashion, she was unable to resist the shop windows of Regent Street. 'With your perpetual *come* on! *come* on!,' she once snapped to her friend, Ethel Smyth, 'you are as bad as a husband.'

The Pankhursts: Emmeline with her eldest, favourite daughter Christabel *(centre)* and second-born Sylvia *(right)*. In 1912 – a year of intense militancy – Christabel fled to Paris to avoid arrest, while Sylvia willingly endured prison and the hunger strike.

Suffragettes were required to parade the streets for publicity. 'We threw away all our conventional notions of what was "ladylike" and "good form",' wrote Mrs Pankhurst, 'and we applied to our methods the one test question: Will it help?'

In a desperate attempt to save the snowy egret from extinction, the RSPB women mimicked their rivals' methods in 1911 – but being ultra conservative, they refused to wear the boards themselves. These are hired men.

Starving egret chicks wait vainly for their parents, killed by plumage hunters. The RSPB's emotive campaign against the cruel 'osprey' used a series of shocking photographs by the Australian ornithologist Arthur Mattingley.

Women, not plume hunters, were to blame for the near extinction of snowy egrets in the Florida Everglades, according to the American magazine *Puck*. If women didn't wear the plumes, the birds would not be shot.

THE ANTI-SUFFRAGE OSTRICH
"The sun is *not* rising"

Left: By 1910 the League for Opposing Woman Suffrage had made great gains throughout Britain – so the suffragists hit back with a series of satirical cartoons. Here, the 'Anti' is willfully blind to the inevitability of future change.

Right: Virginia Woolf, suffragist and RSPB supporter, was incensed by the argument that women propped up the plumage trade. 'The birds are killed by men, starved by men, and tortured by men – not vicariously, but with their own hands.'

Left: Margot Asquith, wife of the new Liberal prime minister of 1909, was both anti-suffrage and indifferent to animal rights. 'Clothes are the first thing that catch the eye,' she was fond of saying.

MODERN INQUISITION

TREATMENT OF POLITICAL PRISONERS UNDER A

LIBERAL

GOVERNMENT

ELECTORS !

Put a stop to this torture by voting against

THE PRIME MINISTER

Left: The first forcible feeding took place in Birmingham Prison in 1909, ending the hunger strike of suffragette Mary Leigh. By 1913 there was increasing public outcry at the practice – thanks, in part, to WSPU propaganda such as this.

Right: At 5.30pm on Friday 1 March, 1912, hundreds of West End shop windows were smashed by suffragettes. 'Any unaccompanied lady in sight, especially if she carried a handbag, became an object of menacing suspicion.'

Left: Sylvia Pankhurst, committed socialist, addresses a bemused crowd from her new headquarters in Bow, London's East End, in 1912. She believed that her mother's movement no longer represented working-class women.

Left: Etta Lemon, painted in 1913. 'There was no point in fighting Mrs Lemon,' remembered one ornithologist. 'She would defeat you sooner or later.' After half a century at the RSPB's helm, she was purged in a bloody coup in 1939, at the age of 79.

Right: Emmeline Pankhurst, painted in 1927: newly appointed Conservative candidate for Whitechapel, in London's East End. Weakened by years of hunger strikes, she died in 1928, aged 69 – the year the Equal Franchise Act became law.

Some were famed for their looks. Millicent, Duchess of Sutherland, society hostess and committed social reformer, spends £6. 16s 6d on two hats at the shop's opening – as does the blue-eyed Lady Beatrice Pole-Carew, she of the celebrated Grecian profile. The Pre-Raphaelite beauty Lilian, Marchioness of Anglesey, visits every four days during the season, spending £70 on hats over 18 months (some £7,000 today). Lilian had sensationally bolted from her bejewelled and pomaded husband on their honeymoon, the divorce suit ending up in court (and in every newspaper). These are young women on whom all eyes are fixed; women whose faces sell popular postcards; women who are expected to appear in ravishing new outfits at every social occasion.

Other customers are sexual facilitators – throwers of notoriously louche and lavish house parties. Maud Cunard, social gadfly and ardent patron of the arts, is one. In 1905, Maud buys 24 new hats and nightcaps at up to £6 a time (around £600 a piece today). A surviving Countess Fabbricotti creation is held today by the Metropolitan Museum of Art – a beribboned 'boudoir cap' in peach silk and antique lace; an overtly come-hither siren call. Fabbricotti sells a lot of lace boudoir caps, at around one pound to six shillings apiece. They are her bread and butter. You could say that she is, herself, a sexual facilitator.

Her clients may be rich, yet they are also surprisingly mean. The *Chicago Tribune* reporter's claim that she asks $50 or $100 per hat turns out to be wildly exaggerated. The account books show that customers rarely spend more than two or three pounds on a single visit; sums in shillings are common, as are discounts. All purchases are made on account to be settled up later – or perhaps not. 'Bad debts' eat into her profit. Much of Fabbricotti's trade is in hat makeovers: refreshing one's look with a single feather or new ribbon. 'Blue straw toque retrimmed, 7s 6d'; 'Feathers on own black hat curled, 4s 6d.'

But women are also forced to keep apace with fashion, and hats are getting larger. The 'Merry Widow' picture hat – an absurdly voluptuous cartwheel laden with paradise plumes – becomes the compulsory new look when the operetta opens in London in 1907, starring dressmaker's daughter Lily Elsie, with costumes by Society couturier Lucile. When it opens on Broadway later that year, women stampede over the promise of a free hat for every coupon.

'A more ridiculous picture could scarcely be transmitted to future generations than a portrait of some of the huge structures, bristling with wings and tails, and flopping plumes of preposterous length, beneath which some women have been seen this year,' Mrs Lemon harrumphed in her 1907 annual report. They might as well be 'caricatures designed by bird protectors to bring the whole bird-wearing fashion into the contempt it so richly deserves'. But they didn't. The craze for the Merry Widow hat just turned up the heat on an inexorably ripening fashion, soon to reach its apogee.

How could a woman like Mrs Lemon infiltrate, let alone convert, a consumer circle as intimidating as Fabbricotti's? I admit to falling under the Countess's spell as I flicked through those order books with their roll call of titles. I was seduced by her customers – their wealth, beauty, scandals, lovers and connections. I was seduced by her hats; could feel the textures beneath my fingers – the slippery peach silk, the spring and flex of best Tuscan straw, those lolling, foamy ostrich feathers and the quivering gossamer of paradise tail. I, too, wanted to push open the white-painted door on 5 South Molton Street and find myself ushered to a decorative gilt chair opposite an ornate mirror. I was helplessly fascinated by this rarified world of inherited beauty and money. I did not want to think of Alice Battershall curling plumes at a kitchen table in Lever Street, choked up with dust at the end of the day; or of Mrs Lemon's earnest SPB pamphlets describing heaped egret corpses rotting in the Everglades of Florida.

Fabbricotti was offering something overwhelmingly irresistible. Intriguingly, there were not just professional beauties on her books but thinking women, too – females in the process of carving out a serious name for themselves. Plantswoman Lady Moyra Cavendish of Holker Hall in Lancashire, wife to a Liberal MP; the philanthropist and humanitarian worker Muriel Paget, founder of the Southwark Invalid Kitchen and SPB member;

and – most interestingly – the Duchess of Hamilton, co-founder in 1903 of the Animal Defence and Anti-Vivisection Society with feminist Lizzy Lind af Hageby.

Nina Douglas, Lady Hamilton, was also a member of the Society for the Protection of Birds. And yet despite the Duchess of Portland's best efforts, here she was, shopping regularly at the Countess Fabbricotti's little boutique, where ospreys bristled in the window and parrots' wings made elegant toques take flight.

The order books of the Countess Fabbricotti reveal the guilty parties. One pink osprey for SPB member Daisy Cornwallis West, Princess of Pless (extravagant spender and social reformer, England's 'most beautiful woman'), purchased on Friday 30 June 1905, for 12s 6d (around £60 today).

One week later, as the sun rose in the far distant Florida Everglades, a warden on duty for the Audubon Society motored his little boat over still waters to confront a notorious egret hunter and his two sons. By the time he got near, the men were climbing back into their schooner, limp snowy egrets swinging from their hands. Guy Bradley shouted across the water that he was going to arrest them – and was shot at point-blank range while standing in his boat on duty for the Audubon Society. Bradley's murder made international headlines: America's first martyr for the cause of bird protection.

The same week that Florida's bird protection warden was murdered, the playwright George Bernard Shaw took his seat at the Royal Opera House in Drury Lane for Puccini's new opera, *Madama Butterfly*. He found himself behind a woman who was obscuring his view: 'For this lady, who had very black hair, had stuck over her right ear the pitiable corpse of a large white bird, which looked exactly as if some one had killed it by stamping on its breast, and then nailed it to the lady's temple, which was presumably of sufficient solidity to bear the operation. I am not, I hope, a morbidly squeamish person,' he wrote to *The Times*, 'but the spectacle sickened me. I presume that if I had presented myself at the doors with a dead snake round my neck, a collection of black beetles pinned to my shirtfront, and a grouse in my hair, I should have been refused admission.'

To many eyes, such preposterous headgear undermined the thinking woman. It made her look unconsidered, even stupid. What price emancipation if she remained enslaved by fashion? What was the use of a higher education, if she still could not grasp 'this simple question of ethics and aesthetics', as Mrs Lemon so acidly put it? I was curious about the future lives of these Edwardian women, helplessly in thrall to the surface of things, and was surprised to discover that many of Fabbricotti's customers went on to do extraordinary, brave and adventurous things, spurred on by the First World War. Of course, they were facilitated by large private incomes. But these were not mere featherheads.

On Thursday 3 May 1906, Mrs Asquith – brilliant wit and socialite, second wife of the Chancellor of the Exchequer – was drawn irresistibly into the boutique on South Molton Street and spent £2 17s (around £280 in today's money). Two months later she was back again, buying millinery worth £4 4s (around £415). Tall, big boned, with a long, determined face, Margot Asquith understood the power of a good hat. 'Clothes are the first thing that catch the eye,' she was fond of saying. Having absolutely no compunction about wearing feathers, Margot was painted by society portraitist Philip de Laszlo with a large dead bird on her head. The painting was commissioned in 1909 to mark her powerful new role as the Prime Minister's wife.

It is intriguing to imagine an encounter at Fabbricotti's between Margot Asquith (who took a dim view of what she called the 'women's suffrage lot') and Emmeline Pankhurst. Given Mrs Pankhurst's predilection for West End shops, it is entirely possible that their paths crossed at 5 South Molton Street. 'No more irresistible magnet to Mrs Pankhurst than a sale,' remembered her friend, the composer Ethel Smyth; 'no severer trial to people who loathe gazing into shop windows than to walk down Regent Street with her any day. "With your perpetual *come* on! *come* on!" she once said to me angrily, "you are as bad as a husband"'.

Margot's husband, Herbert Asquith, was to become the arch enemy of the WSPU for frustrating again and again the cause of women's suffrage. The Liberal Prime Minister was 'the Official Wretch of the Woman Movement . . . the Public Hen-Peckee', as the novelist H. G. Wells put it. His fashionista wife, on the other hand, was a highly public symbol of the type of woman that both Mrs Lemon *and* Mrs Pankhurst were attempting to convert. With a prime minister and his wife who could not give a damn for *either* campaign, the WSPU and the SPB were going to face great obstacles in the battle ahead.

27

Royal Approval

1903–6

When the portly Bishop Thornton wrote back to Hilda Howard, suggesting that the Queen should be enlisted on behalf of the birds, he was right. 'To make it vulgar' – both to provincial ladies and to women like Margot Asquith – 'would be the best way to stop it.' And the surest way of making feather wearing vulgar was for Queen Alexandra, arbiter of taste, to 'show the way'.

The year 1903 was one of supremely murderous millinery. Hats were growing in diameter, the better to display the feathered pile-ups happening on top of women's heads. Now that magazines had started to use photographs, it was possible to actually *see* these birds, with their sharp little beaks, in detail that is shocking to modern eyes. The *Millinery Record* reveals how extravagantly complicated hats were becoming in September of that year:

A new feature in the mounting of birds and feathers may be called the double mount. Two plumes or two birds are mounted *almost as if both were trying to occupy the same space*. Two plumes are also mounted back to back, and toward the tips are drawn apart and fastened down. The curl of the long plumes, in which the fibres are turned toward the outside of the rib, is called the 'lobster curl'.

The lobster curl. These hats gave out a strange message indeed. There was a kind of anger contained in their spikes and furbelows; a sort of seething expression of frustrated power, potential and ambition. Paired with a neat 'tailor-made' suit, they were a cry for eye-to-eye attention. 'The trimming is the hat nowadays and the hat the trimming,' quipped a fashion commentator; 'thus reversing the order of things.'

Bishop Thornton was right. Without a signal from royalty, nothing would happen.

All through 1903, and the following year, there was talk at the SPB about branch secretaries gathering signatures for a petition to be presented to the Queen. The female suffragists had flung down the gauntlet in 1901 with their 'monster petition', and this should and could be outdone. The Duchess of Portland, under increasing pressure, made it clear she had no influence in this direction. 'I am afraid it is no use asking the Queen about a petition,' she wrote to Etta Lemon. 'But if it is drafted I will certainly send it to her.'

Mrs Lemon began, uncharacteristically, to falter. Might a petition the size of a garden roller look hysterical, the action of 'frothy fanatics'? It would not do at all to be confused with those 'wild women', as the suffrage campaigners were known. Might there be a more sober way of proceeding? She was persuaded by the men (and there were so many men on board these days) that an 'influentially signed', smaller petition would mean so much more. When Mrs Lemon looked back on the society's history, many years later, this was one moment she might have paused over. 'Influentially signed' meant endorsed by the men of science (Dr Bowdler Sharpe, Professor Cunningham, W. H. Hudson, J. A. Harvie-Brown, etc). It hinted at the beginning of a schism within the society: on the one side rational, scientific men; on the other, emotional, inexpert women.

Yet at the time, it must have seemed like a step forward – anything to push their cause in the corridors of influence. The petition was finally presented not to the Queen, but instead to the seat of real power: the

Privy Council, for incorporation by Royal Charter. While the ladies had been agitating about Queen Alexandra, it turned out that the men had, all along, been driving this charity in a slightly different direction. The prime mover was no less than Etta's husband, barrister Frank Lemon. He and chairman Montagu Sharpe, another barrister, had worked hard at drafting a textbook charter for the Privy Council – so correct in its detail and persuasive in its rationale that it was passed with record swiftness.

That all-important 'R' of the RSPB was won, to the society's immense satisfaction, in October 1904. They were now the *Royal* Society for the Protection of Birds. This was immensely prestigious for a charity barely 15 years old with an annual income of a few hundred pounds. 'It was very gratifying,' as Etta put it, looking back, 'that so young an Association should have conferred upon it this recognition of its character and aims.' It was a feather in their cap.

But under a Royal Charter, a woman could not legally hold the position of honorary secretary, and Mrs Lemon was forced to relinquish her 10-year reign to her husband, Frank. It was a small, essentially nominal thing, the committee reassured her; the inner core would now go by the self-important name of 'Council'. She would continue to run things just as before. But (and again, looking back) it was another small sign: a concession to the gradual takeover of the society by the men.

As for the Queen – it was decided that a 'memorial' would be less intrusive, more incisive than a great list of signatures. A memorial was a formal appeal for Her Majesty to take a public stance on murderous millinery. Much thought went into its oily wording – 'Your gracious influence', etc, etc – as there was strict protocol in writing to the Queen. Another year slipped by. Osprey sales soared in Mincing Lane, and Etta Lemon began to make a nuisance of herself once again. She flapped around the Duchess, barraging her with questions at insensitive moments.

'Dear Mrs Lemon, I have no idea as to the size & shape of petition – nor has the Duke – but we do not think it much matters!' wrote the Duchess irritably. 'Surely the Law Stationers would know what is customary. As long as it is easily read the Queen will not notice. I think the best time to send it would be after the Queen returns from Copenhagen & when all the funeral functions are over.' Etta Lemon seemed unaware that Queen Alexandra's father, King Christian IX of Denmark, had died in January 1906.

The 'Memorial To the Queen's Most Excellent Majesty' focused on the plumes of the egret and the bird-of-paradise – the two species most in danger of extinction. In the end it was signed by three names only: Winifred Portland, President, Montagu Sharpe, Chairman of the Council, and Frank F. Lemon, Honorary Secretary.

4 March 1906: 'Dear Mrs Lemon, I have sent the petition to the Queen & when I receive her answer I will let you know! Yours truly W Portland.'

Ten days passed. Etta waited, fidgety and apprehensive.

14 March: 'Dear Mrs Lemon – I have got an answer from the Queen but should like to talk it over with you will you come round & see me tomorrow – am wiring you.' The RSPB offices at Hanover Square had just that year been connected by telephone, but it didn't occur to the Duchess of Portland to call rather than write, nor to simply walk the length of Brook Street and visit them herself.

On Sunday 18 March, a letter was delivered, by hand, to the Portland London residence at 3 Grosvenor Square. The envelope was ripped open in haste, rather than slit with a silver letter opener, as one might have expected from Winifred Portland. Inside was a stiff, watermarked sheet from Charlotte Knollys, Lady of the Bedchamber and Private Secretary to Queen Alexandra. At last, here it was:

> The Queen desires me to say in answer to your letter that she gives you, as President, full permission to use her name in any way you think best to conduce to the protection of the Birds – You know well how kind and humane the Queen is to all living creatures, and I am desired to add that HM never wears Osprey feathers herself, and will certainly do all in her power to discourage the cruelty practised on these beautiful birds.

The Duchess, elated, forwarded the letter to the RSPB office. 'Dear Mrs Lemon, the Queen has given her sanction for this enclosed letter to be read out at the meeting tomorrow – I *am* so glad! It will do much good. Yours truly, WP.'

Finally! Queen Alexandra was on board – fashion leader, pin-up, inspiration to every class of British woman. It was an immense victory for the RSPB. The royal seal of approval carried, in those times, an extraordinary value. This letter was not just a decree that would sway the fashion houses; it was a passport to real influence in parliament. It would open the path to powerful legislation. Mrs Lemon filed it away meticulously, ripped envelope and all. Yet what first grabbed my eye as I unfolded the small sheet of typed paper was a correction in ink. The word 'little' had been scored out with a single, black line: '. . . cruelty practised on these beautiful little birds.'

It appeared that the Queen and her private secretary were embarrassingly vague on what the long-legged, hunch-backed, snowy egrets might actually look like. And if they didn't know, what hope was there of the average British woman knowing where her osprey came from – or caring?

There were, at this time, persistent rumours that the Duchess of Portland had been seen wearing osprey feathers – even rare owls' feathers. As soon as a rumour reached Mrs Lemon's ears it would be promptly reported to the Duchess, who would emphatically contradict it. 'Her Grace had never worn such feathers; and those who knew anything of her would never believe these idle stories, because the Duchess of Portland was a most true, conscientious, and consistent member of the society.'

It is true that the Duchess loved a good hat, often dressed with game feathers from the Portland estate. Like horsey-faced Margot Asquith, she had the bone structure to wear millinery with great flair. But the Countess Fabbricotti's clientele was not her circle. It was too liberal; too racy. In February 1906, Winnie had made the mistake of leaving the King's lover, Alice Keppel, off the guest list for a house party at Welbeck Abbey out of loyalty to Queen Alix, and as a result incurred the royal wrath. The King took it as a slight to himself, and the Portlands were not forgiven.

Perhaps Winnie was becoming staid, out of touch with the morally shifting times. There was a growing sense, in this modern era, that the female trailblazers of the 1880s and 1890s were relics of the past century. They had had their moment in the spotlight.

In 1906, the year of the landslide Liberal victory, the Duchess of Portland was 43; Etta Lemon was 46; Emily Williamson 51 and Eliza Phillips 82. They were a well-mannered lobbying group, still soldiering on. But their voices sounded, increasingly, as if from another epoch. Their anti-glamour campaign was becoming monotonous. And their worthy movement was about to be comprehensively eclipsed by a younger, more attention-grabbing, more exciting campaign.

28

The 'Suffragette'

1906

Foreign Secretary Sir Edward Grey, a vice president of the RSPB and fanatical bird lover, gripped the ornate lectern at Manchester's Free Trade Hall and stared levelly into the crowd. Two women had unfurled a calico banner between them, on which was daubed the slogan 'Votes for Women'. He could hardly believe what he was seeing -- or hearing. 'Will the Liberal government give women the vote?' called out one repeatedly in a fluting voice. Each was as young and as striking as the other. The meeting erupted, men shouting over the top of the women's question in angry cries. Suave and beaky, Sir Edward tightened his lips and waited for order. He was, as it happened, a supporter of women's suffrage. But to have a pre-election speech interrupted by ladies calling out and waving a home-made banner! It was unprecedented, and it was unacceptable. At a brisk nod, the Chief Constable of Manchester pushed through the audience towards the two women and 'invited' them to put their question in writing, so that it could be handed to the speaker.

Christabel Pankhurst, 25, and Annie Kenney, 26, rolled up their banner and waited patiently. When no reply came at the end of the meeting, Annie – a cotton factory worker – clambered up onto her chair and repeated the question in a cry: 'Will the Liberal government give women the vote?' They were instantly dragged out of the Free Trade Hall by burly stewards, the audience howling and jeering in their wake. As she passed a policeman, Christabel pursed her rosebud lips and spat.

Rather than pay fines for the outrage, the two chose a week in prison – and consequent martyrdom. They were released to a heroes' welcome (bouquets, songs of liberty, stirring speeches). Emmeline stood proudly by the daughter who had put women's suffrage on the front page of every newspaper. From now on, heckling of politicians, and a willingness to go to prison, became key tactics in the WSPU campaign to get the vote.

As the WSPU suffrage movement geared up, Mrs Pankhurst's shop, Emerson & Co, was finally wound down in 1906. Emmeline and Christabel moved south to join art student Sylvia in London, the better to influence parliament – just as the SPB had done in 1889, choosing London over Manchester as the centre of operations. The move to the capital marked a determined change of gear for the Women's Social and Political Union.

At 48 years old, Mrs Pankhurst was of Etta Lemon's generation. Yet she had her daughters as well as her ardent young followers propelling her forward. She had the thoroughly modern Christabel, all painted eyebrows and persuasive tongue, courting martyrdom to win the propaganda war. Mrs Pankhurst's eldest daughter in particular gave her softly spoken, genteel mother the momentum to step into the limelight at last.

The WSPU organised widespread heckling during the 1906 General Election. 'Pay no attention to those cats mewing,' male speakers cried in irritation as yet another woman popped up and started shouting questions in meeting halls and tents throughout the country ('Will the Liberal Government, if returned, give votes to women?'). These women would then be pounced upon by male stewards and dragged outside, their heavy hats tipped well over the face as a protection against missiles from the crowd (eggs, cayenne pepper, stones).

The Liberal candidate for Manchester North West, a young man named Winston Churchill, was particularly outraged by the idea of women's suffrage. 'They come here asking us to treat them like men,' he expostulated. 'That is what I particularly want to avoid. We must observe courtesy and chivalry to the weaker sex dependent on us.' Churchill could not open his mouth without being heckled for an answer to the women's suffrage question. 'Nothing would induce me to vote for giving women the franchise,' he replied with contempt. 'I am not going to be henpecked on a question of such grave importance.'

'These silly women', as they were known, were not the bluestocking matrons of last century's suffrage movement, caricatured as elderly spinsters in horn-rimmed spectacles and trilby hats. They were young, articulate, fearless – and attractive. 'If I might illustrate my meaning from football,' said one male suffrage supporter at a meeting in Redhill, home town of Mr and Mrs Lemon; 'both have the same goal, but the suffragettes are, perhaps, the forwards in the game, while the older suffrage societies are the backs and halves.' Many of them belonged to the same social circle as Churchill (son of a Conservative lord and an American heiress). When Alice Milne, secretary of the WSPU Manchester branch, visited the London office in October 1906, she was surprised to find it 'full of fashionable ladies in silks and satins . . . Ours was a movement for the middle and upper classes' – women who shopped at boutiques like Fabbricotti's.

The public could not get over its astonishment that these agitators were *ladies*. Ultra-feminine, exquisitely attired ladies. Their bonnets and hatpins usually made it into the first paragraph of every report on their latest exploits. Fashion had become political. At the opening of parliament in October 1906, 20 such ladies invaded the Strangers' Lobby and started making speeches in high, patrician voices, waving red flags about their heads, standing on the settees. 'Six stalwart policemen arrived at the double, and threw themselves into the mêlée,' reported the *Daily Chronicle*. 'The bodyguard was quickly dispersed -- leaving a trail of hatpins and hairpins behind them, and even bonnets.'

The belittling new term 'suffragette', coined by the *Daily Mail* in 1906, was immediately taken up by Mrs Pankhurst's WSPU as a badge of honour. Soon it became the word in every buzzing conversation, whether in solidarity or – far more commonly – appalled dismay. The RSPB's ageing personalities and small victories slipped off the front page and down the news agenda. The Queen had just decried in public the osprey, but nobody seemed to care. And like a Trojan horse, the 'suffragette' made her first entrance into the RSPB's annual general meeting that year in Hanover Square.

Through twirling moustaches, the Marquess of Granby warmed up his sedate, bird-loving audience with a little joke about suffrage. 'Where ladies are in a majority it is somewhat difficult to deal with them!' Granby was referring to the recent WSPU deputation that had gone to call on the new Liberal Prime Minister, Sir Campbell Bannerman. For an hour the women had waited on the doorstep while the PM hid inside, refusing to open the door of 10 Downing Street. 'If many of the ladies who were now making strenuous attempts to wear the breeches were at the same time to *give up wearing egrets*,' continued Granby, pausing for laughter, 'they would do more to extend their influence in the world than they would do by many of the methods adopted in the agitation for women's rights.'

The conservative core of the RSPB, male and female, was horrified by the spectacle of well-dressed women making a strident exhibition of themselves. It went against every natural, God-ordained principle. As a murmur of complacent 'Hear hears' ran around the AGM meeting room, a renegade got to her feet. Miss Clara Mordan, 62, was a wealthy heiress whose father had invented the propelling pencil. This perhaps gave her the confidence to speak out more boldly than most – and especially on this contentious subject. 'From a wide acquaintance with women suffragists,' said Miss Mordan (freshly recruited to Mrs Pankhurst's WSPU), 'I can confidently assert that they are of the class of women who are the *most* in sympathy with the objects of the Bird Society.'

Frank and Etta Lemon's eyes might, for a brief moment, have met. From within their own ranks! The 'suffragettes' were precisely the sort of women – and this was clear to all who had witnessed the rallies around Westminster – most likely to *wear* murderous millinery. Few of them seemed to go out without a flock of long-tailed parakeets or half an

Acadian owl upon their heads. Miss Mordan sat, avoiding hostile stares. But the cat was out of the bag. There were close and growing links between animal rights issues and the suffrage cause; it was inevitable that humanitarian and feminist movements would share sympathisers. The RSPB attracted educated, fervent, brave women who were not afraid to swim against the tide of popular taste. This was the society's strength. But if their members were also clandestine cardholders for the suffrage movement, militant or otherwise – well, this might also damage the society's reputation.

The glaring crossover in membership, once pointed out, seemed suddenly to threaten all that Mrs Lemon believed in. She *was* the RSPB. She and Frank. It was theirs, moulded in their image, a mouthpiece for their conservative values. It could not admit this insubordinate, unnatural, deeply troubling element.

'When the suffragettes began the campaign, they were mistaken for notoriety hunters, featherheads, flibbertigibbets,' reported the *Daily Mirror* that October. 'Now that they have proved they are in earnest, they have frightened the government, they have broken through the law, they have made votes for women practical politics.'

Like most of her circle, Etta Lemon did not believe in votes for women. But rather than keep quiet, she was willing to risk her good name in fighting against this pernicious cause. There was no time to lose.

PART 4

Votes

29

Onto the Street

1907

They woke to the sound of drumming rain.

By two o'clock on the afternoon of Saturday 9 February 1907, as thousands of women were gathering as instructed at Hyde Park Corner, a fine, soaking drizzle had settled in. The streets squelched underfoot – horse dung, ostlers' refuse, sawdust and road sweepings mingling and clinging to long hems of tweed and astrakhan, cotton twill and mink. Sodden white banners proclaimed their political goals in vivid scarlet lettering: 'Willing and Able', 'Representation our Goal', 'Not Indirect but Direct Influence'.

Why had bitterly cold February been chosen for this day of all days? Kate Frye's entire family told her she would be mad to go in the procession in this rain, and so all morning she procrastinated nervously. Twenty-nine years old, with striking, dark features, Kate was a middle-class grocer's daughter, living with her parents in North Kensington, waiting for life to get going. She had joined the New Constitutional Suffrage Party (NCS) with their cautious blessing – her father was a former radical Liberal MP for North Kensington and a believer in women's suffrage. Kate had planned to dine first at the house of some fellow members, but couldn't bring herself to leave home. It was such an unknown, momentous and rather alarming adventure.

'We all had lunch. I knew I was going all the time – but couldn't go,' she wrote in her diary. The clock ticked; cutlery scraped. Beyond the house, through the wet streets of the capital, knots of women streamed from all directions towards the Achilles statue at the edge of Hyde Park. Still Kate sat at the dining table. 'Off to wash my hands. 2 o'clock,' she wrote. This was the time for the march's start. 'Then as I washed I made up my mind I would go rain or no rain.' Out she dashed, hat pinned firmly onto heaped coils of dark hair, running through the puddles to Notting Hill Gate station, her apprehensive older sister, Agnes, hurrying after her. They would try to join the procession.

At Piccadilly Circus they heard the faint strains of a band – so, the march had started. It must be processing towards them – and then it was upon them, pouring round the corner into Lower Regent Street, a 'swarm of roughs' dancing around the male brass band that lead the procession. The crowd surged closer to get a good look. 'Dignified and really impressive,' Kate thought; 'it was a sight I wouldn't have missed for anything.' She was craning her neck for her group, the NCS. Celebrated suffragist Eva Gore-Booth – today heading the factory girls' contingent from Manchester – actually *spoke* to them; told them it was coming. The excitement mounted.

'I shrieked out when I saw Miss Doake's red head in the distance and we dashed up to them and asked if we could join in,' Kate wrote in her diary later that night. 'It felt like boarding an express train. We walked three abreast – Miss Doake, Agnes and I.'

Down Lower Regent Street the column of women walked, three or four abreast, stopping all the traffic at the height of a shopping Saturday. Past the great department store of Swan & Edgar; past jewellers Frazer and Haws, and the exclusive court hairdressers Unwin and Albert.

A reporter for the *London Daily News* struggled to describe this orderly, purposeful mass of women surging past department store windows full of the spring fashions. It was, he wrote banally, 'as if they were out on a gigantic shopping expedition, and determined not to miss the cheapest bargain.' But none paused to look at the goods on display.

Ralph Cleaver, an illustrator for the popular *Graphic* newspaper, was in the crowd, sketching rapidly. Never had an outdoor public demonstration afforded such scope for so many improbable silhouettes. Women were self-consciously eating sandwiches. Women were vaulting Regent's Park railings, with a flash of ankle, or struggling with heavy pennants that flapped wetly in the weather. The artist's eye was drawn endlessly to the tops of these women's heads. Each female face – whether spectacled, jowly, sweetly feminine or determined New Woman, was framed by its headgear. The marching column of 3,000 suffragists was topped, uniformly, by feathered hats.

The extraordinary sight of women of all ages, classes and professions marching side by side, in appalling weather through muddied streets, had attracted hundreds of spectators. The women looked ahead stoically, tried not to catch the eyes of heckling men in the crowd ('Where's yer sweetheart?'; 'Wot abart the ole man's tea this orternoon?') and felt the unfamiliar, excruciating sensation of parading their beliefs and their bodies, unchaperoned, before the male gaze. Just to take part, to be one face buried in all those others, was an act of great courage. 'I felt like a martyr of old,' wrote Kate, 'and walked proudly along. I would not jest with the crowd – though we had some jokes with ourselves.'

Reporters ran alongside, staring at the mingling of the classes. Heading the long procession were, inevitably, those at the top of the social hierarchy – 'ladies of spirit and culture', as the London Daily News man put it – figureheads for the many different suffragist societies on the march. 'Here comes the class!' the hecklers cried, as the women splashed through the mud in satin slippers. The auburn-haired Lady Frances Balfour, president of the National Society for Women's Suffrage (NSWS), quite the poshest suffragist in Britain; Lady Jane Strachey, leaning on a stick, her five adult daughters accompanying her for the National Union of Women's Suffrage Societies (NUWSS); Lady Emily Lutyens, theosophist wife of the famous architect; Lady Cecilia Roberts, friend of the young Mahatma Gandhi and president of the Women's Liberal Federation (WLF). The radical temperance campaigner Lady Carlisle plodded along, her notoriously beautiful daughters carrying heavy standards in their fearsome mother's wake. Then came university women from Oxford and Cambridge, artists, members of women's clubs and yet more anti-alcohol temperance advocates.

Women had travelled through the night from all over Britain, representing invisible trades in cities that Westminster's politicians rarely gave a passing thought to. Bradford, Leicester, Warwick, Nottingham, Bournemouth; cigar makers, power loom weavers, clay pipe finishers, shirt makers, textile workers, hank and bobbin winders. From Manchester, doing the thing in style, came a hired electric cab packed full of young men 'like sardines in a box' who were there to support their 'suffragette sweethearts'. Every few minutes, a broad Lancashire shout would go out from the cab windows to the bedraggled women – 'Are we downhearted?' And a cry would come back – 'No!'

There were just two mounted policemen accompanying the march of 3,000. No one, at this early stage, had much to fear from the ladies. And if they could have looked into the future – just four days into the future – they might have been astonished at the violence soon to be meted out, women against police and police against women.

'The policemen were splendid,' wrote Kate Frye, and why would they not be, escorting such upright gentlewomen? Another marcher wrote warmly about the constable walking alongside her – 'an evident sympathiser'. He bought their suffrage literature, he collected procession badges 'and stowed them away in his helmet "for the missus", who would have been with us, he explained, but for the "kiddies"'.

A cavalcade of motorcars and carriages brought up the rear, including one belonging to celebrity actress and new recruit, the sloe-eyed Mrs Patrick Campbell and her daughter, Stella. 'Mrs Pat', who was about to take the lead role of Ibsen's 'unwomanly' Hedda Gabler at the Royal Court theatre, cradled on her lap a tiny dog with bulging eyes known as Pinkie Panky Poo.

They moved as one body like a military battalion – along Piccadilly, down Lower Regent Street, east along Pall Mall to Trafalgar Square, then finally along the Strand to the classically imposing Exeter Hall where rousing speeches were made. The stark, vertical flourishes on their heads bristled (so it might have appeared) with intent. Touches of red and white splashed the procession – rosettes, scarves, posies bound with white handkerchiefs – the colours of Millicent Fawcett's NUWSS. 'The Military Type,' noted Ralph Cleaver, drawing two quick portraits of glossy haired, purse-lipped young women with a riot of plumage quivering on their heads: 'General and her Aide'.

As Kate Frye's contingent passed the luxurious Carlton Hotel at the bottom of Haymarket, their banners now battered like broken wings, she saw two 'quite smart men standing by the kerb' staring at her and her friends. 'I say look at those nice girls,' said one to the other, within earshot, '– positively disgraceful I call it.' Lady Frances Balfour, self-conscious at the head of the procession, had her own moment of mortification when she passed by the Savile Club and saw her disapproving husband, the architect Eustace Balfour, and his friends all watching. She 'hated this appeal to the Mob' with bands and martial airs – but she marched anyway. To Kate Frye it felt momentous: 'we were making history – but after all I don't know, I am sure, what will come of it.'

Many of the women taking part on Saturday 9 February were conservative of temperament and modest of character. They were pillars of philanthropy; they worked selflessly in their communities. Walking the streets of central London for hours in driving rain, bearing banners, eating on the hoof with no husband's arm to cling to – this was behaviour so astonishing that most spectators watched them pass in shocked silence. It was so unfeminine! And yet the women taking part were the epitome of femininity. 'Crowds watched and wondered,' wrote suffragist Rachel 'Ray' Strachey, whose brilliant sister, Pippa, had choreographed the day – 'and it was not so dreadful after all.'

'Nobody can suppose that most of the women who took part can have done so for sport or for the pleasure of the thing,' wrote the *Manchester Guardian*'s correspondent that evening. 'It requires some courage for a woman to step out of her drawing room into the street, to take her place in a mixed throng for a cause probably distasteful to many or most of her acquaintances, and to see herself pilloried in the newspaper the next morning by name as one of the "Suffragists".'

The Jewish writer Israel Zangwill, champion of the oppressed, thought they needed to be more courageous still. Suffragists were going to have to 'lower themselves to the manners of men', he told them in his Exeter Hall speech that afternoon. The women sitting before him needed, he said, to become 'unwomanly in order to promote the cause of womanhood'. They themselves must 'do the dirty work'. It sounded almost as if he was trying to provoke them into militarism. 'Ladylike means are all very well if you are dealing with gentlemen,' declaimed Zangwill, 'but you are dealing with politicians.'

Sitting in the crush of women, Kate Frye thought the chief speaker 'splendid and most witty'. But he was in deadly earnest.

What would become known as the 'Mud March' was the brainwave of the constitutional suffragist Millicent Fawcett, leader of the NUWSS, now 60 years old and still doggedly lobbying parliament. It was a first. Never before had British women paraded the streets in such numbers – and in such an eye-catching manner. Mrs Fawcett had come to realise that her generation, the 'old stagers' as she put it, had to adopt new methods to remain in the public eye – just as Mrs Lemon and Mrs Phillips had come to realise with the RSPB. There was now strong competition from the more glamorous and racy WSPU; hundreds of young women were defecting weekly to this militant society with its battle cry of 'Votes for Women!'.

And so, in refusing to invite Mrs Pankhurst to take part in the procession *at all*, Millicent Fawcett had stolen a march on the so-called 'suffragettes'. Millicent knew that she and her circle were ridiculed as the 'spinster suffrage party'. How nice it was to show the Pankhursts, *mère et filles*, that they were by no means all 'stick-in-the-mud dodos'. (As it was, Christabel couldn't resist joining the throng, nor giving interviews to reporters throughout the march.)

In the eyes of the press, the suffrag*ettes* and the suffrag*ists* were one and the same. They were interchangeable; there was no distinction. But in this the press was wrong. The militancy enshrined at the heart of the Pankhursts' WSPU – tactics that were already landing women in

Holloway Gaol – was deeply disturbing to the well-mannered majority of suffragists, and wholly distasteful to Mrs Fawcett.

'If you went to a dinner party,' recalled former militant suffragette Lady Ricardo, 'you were terrified of who you'd sit next to, and you could feel it coming round gradually to them saying "Oh . . . these *awful* women, did you see that somebody did so-and-so", and you *had* to say that you quite agreed with what they were doing . . . It was rather a nightmare.'

Mrs Fawcett's march through the mud, just days before the opening of parliament, was an attempt to show that they were not all 'awful women'. Swiftly, Mrs Pankhurst set about eclipsing it. The following Wednesday 13 February, just four days later, she held the first 'Woman's Parliament' at Caxton Hall, Westminster, which turned all too quickly from a consideration of yesterday's King's Speech (no provision for women's suffrage, yet again) to a fracas outside the House of Commons, lead by a deputation 'ready for Parliament or prison'. After the bonhomie and goodwill of the Mud March, these were ugly, violent scenes – both for women and for the police.

Westminster had been expecting Mrs Pankhurst's 'deputation' – a marching procession of some 400 women – and a solidly helmeted police cordon was waiting in the dusk on the green outside the abbey. The constables could hear them getting closer, singing as they marched to the tune of 'John Brown's Body':

> *Rise – up – women! For the fight is hard and long,*
> *Rise in thousands, singing loud a battle song,*
> *Right is might and in its strength we shall be strong,*
> *And the cause goes marching on . . .*

At a shouted order, the police strode towards them, pushing through the ranks of the procession to turn the women back. The suffragettes rallied quickly and pressed forward again. This time they were met with a body of mounted police – the London Cossacks – coming towards them 'at a smart trot'. All hell broke loose. Shouting women were pushed to the ground and under hooves; clothes were torn, hats rolled along gutters, bruised female bodies clambered to their knees and up again to keep pushing towards the Houses of Parliament. Again and again they were driven back by the heavy policemen, pursued onto pavements and down side roads, crushed up against railings and dragged out of doorways. The cold night air rang with high screams and gruff curses.

To Emmeline Pankhurst, fragile but determined in the dreadful mêlée, there seemed to be 'hundreds on hundreds' of police, on foot and mounted. The struggle, 'quite indescribable for brutality and ruthlessness', went on for an incredible six hours. At its core was a group of female militants recruited in advance from the north of England, women who had been briefed closely on their roles in quasi-military style. They proved to be astonishingly resilient. Fifteen suffragettes managed to fight their way through to the Strangers' Lobby of the House, where they began to hold a meeting. In all, 57 women and two men were arrested, including a dishevelled but triumphant trio: Emmeline, Christabel and Sylvia Pankhurst.

Locked in a claustrophobic cell in the back of a horse-drawn 'Black Maria' was a 44-year-old married woman from Leicester. Alice Hawkins sat clutching her best hat on her knees as the police carriage jolted over the cobbles to Westminster police station, her heart still thudding with adrenalin. The filthy seat was so narrow she had to perch sideways in the darkness, and she strained to glimpse the streets outside through a narrow grille. She fought down panic and claustrophobia.

Alice had travelled down to London from the East Midlands by steam train that morning for the WSPU meeting in Hyde Park – her first. There she had been persuaded to join that afternoon's 'deputation' to Westminster, and now here she was, six exhausting hours later, about to be sentenced to prison. In 'boots and shoes' all her life from the age of 13, Alice Hawkins was a fervent union campaigner for better working conditions for women. At home were six children aged from 11 to 22, plus an in-and-out-of-work husband. The family could not afford to lose their main breadwinner. Unlike the many smart, young, metropolitan suffragettes she had met that day, Alice had first-hand experience of why women needed the vote. She knew about their derisory wages, long working hours and lack of promotion.

Here is another Alice; one who must represent Alice Battershall and the sweatshop workers of Britain at this point in our story, because the WSPU no longer did. The dictatorial Christabel Pankhurst had decided that politicians 'were more impressed by the demonstrations of the feminine bourgeoisie than of the female proletariat'. She and her mother had decided to court wealth and influence to this end. But since it was hard to get their more bourgeois members to resort to 'unwomanly' tactics, it was accepted that fearless working women from the industrial heartlands had their uses – women such as Alice Hawkins.

Alice was surprised to discover that 14 days in Holloway Gaol elevated her to the status of a heroine. In the early hours on the day of the prisoners' release, some 200 supporters gathered outside the turreted gateway. The London Excelsior Band had been hired to play rousing tunes to reach the women in the cells. This London prison, recently transformed to take women only, would play a growing part in the suffragette propagandist drama.

At 9am they appeared, one by one, walking out beneath the portcullis. Twenty-eight women – martyrs all – released to shrill cheers (the remaining prisoners, including the Pankhursts, would be released a week later). They were marched with a swagger down Camden Road and into central London for a breakfast – already a suffragette tradition, where supporters of the cause (including, on this day, George Bernard Shaw) bought tickets to attend and congratulated them on their bravery.

Alice, in the church-going clothes she had worn to make her journey to the capital over a fortnight earlier (silk shawl, two ropes of jet beads, hat crowned with a modest ostrich feather), stood to read out a letter she had received in prison from her local MP, the Labour Party co-founder Ramsay MacDonald. He said he was sorry that Alice had been 'run in', but he also criticised the women's actions, saying that it would do serious damage to the cause of women's suffrage.

Did she pause to reflect? The first thing Alice did, once safely home with her socialist husband Alfred, two daughters and four sons, was to invite Sylvia Pankhurst to speak in Leicester to the women in the shoe industry. One year later, Alice Hawkins had graduated to keynote speaker at a mass WSPU rally in Hyde Park.

Like an inexorable tide, 'Votes for Women!' began to grip the female population. With the militants creating headlines on one side, and the constitutionalists winning sympathies on the other (the Mud March had been a brilliant publicity coup), women that had 'never before given a thought to public questions' began to be roused. 'The Cause' promised to release them from economic dependence; from conventional limitations; from 'all the multitude of trifles which made them hate being women and long to have been men'. But most of all, it promised a thrilling excitement. For a pent-up young woman like Kate Frye – unmarried, living at home – it made her feel a part of something glamorous and urgent. For a hard-pressed working mother like Alice Hawkins, it made her feel heroic, important – as if she *counted*. It gave women a voice – and it gave them a social life.

Edwardian men, whatever their class, had their clubs. Now women might have theirs, too, without the worthy straightjacket of philanthropy, or social work, or animal rights that had been the lot of their Victorian mothers. There were suffragist plays, suffragist badges and sashes, suffragist magazines and endless suffragist meetings. For the militants, the excitement was all the more intense: marches, megaphones and 'ever recurring crises', wrote Ray Strachey, which 'seemed to have a glamour greater than the light of common day'.

There was something of the Evangelical movement in the way these women whipped up their sisters' enthusiasm. The meetings that multiplied in halls and drawing rooms, in schools and chapels, at street corners and on village greens 'did not seem like the dull and solemn stuff of politics'. Rather, they were 'missionary meetings', wrote a nostalgic

Strachey (looking back two decades after those 'great years'), 'filled with the fervour of a gospel, and each one brought new enthusiasts to the ranks'.

Such language and sentiment – such *sacrilege* – was noted tersely at the Surrey breakfast table of Frank and Etta Lemon as they scanned the daily newspapers with appalled fascination. The antics of the militant 'suffragettes' – particularly the egocentric, posturing tactics of that Pankhurst woman and her daughter Christabel – were insufferable. But what could be done to neutralise them? One morning that February, Mrs Lemon's eye fell upon a letter in the anti-suffrage *Times* from the prominent do-gooder Sophia Lonsdale, who said, 'I think we should be *doing* something.'

'I have lived in this small town for forty years,' she wrote – Lichfield, near Birmingham – 'and I believe I know every woman of education in the place, and I hardly know one who is in favour of women's suffrage.' Etta Lemon felt much the same way about the tight-knit town of Redhill, where she and Frank had lived now for 15 years at Hillcrest, a gabled house bordering the common and its heathland.

In her letter, Miss Lonsdale backed suggestions in recent *Times* columns for an anti-suffrage petition; she would, she said, gladly pay for the expense. By 20 February, she was able to announce via *The Times* that a committee had been formed to promote the petition. There was an honorary secretary, but they did not intend to hold unladylike public meetings, only to collect signatures 'in the quietest and speediest manner possible', using newspaper publicity and women's existing social networks.

Sophia Lonsdale, 53, was a woman in the Etta Lemon mould: daughter of the Canon of Lichfield, a devout and selfless unmarried woman who had given her life to philanthropy. In all this, she was thoroughly High Victorian in spirit, and enjoyed a womanly sphere of influence that needed no 'Votes for Women' leg-up. To ladies like Sophia, the vote 'would destroy, rather than add to' this special influence.

'She was at her best when she had some big battle to fight,' noted her obituary some 30 years later, 'and it is not too much to say that she invariably came out victorious.' Miss Lonsdale had flung down the gauntlet. Within a fortnight, a record 37,000 signatures had been obtained in opposition to women's suffrage, and a petition presented to parliament.

30

The Antis

1908

'What woman of genius will be our leader?' asked the journalist Miss Frances Low.

A woman was wanted who would lead the fight against women's suffrage. A strong and articulate, organised and efficient woman – but not so strong or articulate, organised or efficient that she thought she should have the vote. 'There are thousands of good, quiet women who feel as I do,' continued Frances Low in February's *Spectator*, 1908, 'but who are inarticulate.' If the momentum of last year's petition was to be sustained, an anti-suffrage organisation needed to be formed. But who would grasp the nettle?

You might think that this would be a toxic invitation, something so counter-zeitgeist that no woman would be willing to touch it. And if you read the suffragists' literature – both the contemporary magazines such as *Votes for Women* and the rose-tinted histories produced after the First World War – you'd be forgiven for thinking that their movement was inexorable, irrepressible and irresistible. But in truth, it had minority appeal. The vast majority of British women had no interest in politics, the franchise or Westminster. Their interest lay firmly at home. And those women who resisted the vote (the anti-suffragists or 'Antis', as they became known) were, on the whole, intelligent, resourceful – and feminist. Strange as that sounds to us today, it was not an incompatible position.

When I started researching Margaretta Lemon, I'd assumed that she would be in favour of women's suffrage. Of course she would. This 'redoubtable' personality, a woman not afraid to swim against the current, renowned for her public speaking and 'masculine' dominance of the field – how could she not get behind the ultimate battle for equality? But then I discovered an urgent clarion call in the *Surrey Mirror*.

27 June 1908

Sir – May I be allowed to make known through the columns of your newspaper that I am prepared to furnish information concerning the National Anti-Women's Suffrage Association to any one desirous of combatting the Women's Suffrage movement. I have joined the Central Organising Committee of this Association, and shall be glad if 'anti-suffrages' women in the neighbourhood who wish to add the weight of their opinion to the protest against the demand for the extension of the Parliamentary franchise to women will communicate with me.

Reluctant as one is to turn aside from the legitimate and useful work of all kinds that is needing the energy, time, and thought of women, it is now becoming absolutely necessary for all women who are of opinion that to extend the franchise to their sex will work irrevocable mischief to human progress, to the British Empire, and to women themselves, to voice that opinion, and to clearly and definitely state the reasons upon which the opinion is based. – Yours, etc., MARGARETTA L. LEMON (Mrs F. E. Lemon). Hillcrest, Redhill Common.

The language is pure Lemon – the same withering and indignant tone that she uses against the plumage trade, or when attacking 'feather-bedecked' women and those slippery shop girls. I admit that Mrs Lemon's vehement anti-suffrage stance, and her leading role in trying to crush both suffragists and suffragettes, shocked me. Etta was not the pro-women heroine I'd imagined she was, despite her leading role in founding an all-female conservation society. Yet the more I researched the anti-suffrage movement – hugely significant at the time, but now a forgotten women's campaign – the more I came to understand that, for a large majority of Edwardian women, being anti-suffrage did *not* necessarily mean anti-feminist.

Discovering this letter in the *Surrey Mirror* gave me both a key to Etta Lemon's character and a key to understanding the fundamental conservatism behind the RSPB. There was also something else. Remarkably, the rise of the women's anti-suffrage movement, and its eventual takeover by the men, closely mirrored the birth, growth and final bloody coup within the RSPB.

What woman of genius *would* lead the charge? The Countess of Jersey, impeccably connected political hostess, discreet wife of a Conservative politician and banker, answered the call. She was persuaded to chair the inaugural meeting of the Women's National Anti-Suffrage League at the Westminster Palace Hotel on 21 July 1908. The setting is significant: the very same venue as the RSPB's annual meetings. Perhaps it was Mrs Lemon who suggested it – because she was there, sitting on a gilt and plush chair, along with a few dozen other women of influence, education, breeding and energy.

One month earlier, the new Liberal Prime Minister, Herbert Asquith, had challenged the suffragists to prove that votes for women had popular support. Both factions had responded magnificently to the challenge. First came Mrs Fawcett's NUWSS, with an immense procession along London's Embankment on the Saturday afternoon of 13 June. Young Kate Frye was there again, carrying a rather more beautiful and robust banner for her North Kensington society, so heavy it made her feel 'completely done' by the time she reached the Royal Albert Hall.

Ten thousand women had marched through the capital with eight hundred Arts and Crafts-style embroidered banners. 'They have recreated the beauty of blown silk and tossing embroidery,' wrote an impressed male reporter for the *Morning Leader*. 'The procession was like a medieval festival, vivid with simple grandeur, alive with an ancient dignity.'

Not to be outdone, Emmeline Pankhurst's WSPU retaliated with their own stunningly well-organised 'Women's Sunday' in Hyde Park one week later, on 21 June. This time *30,000* women in decorous white dresses gathered and paraded. An even bigger crowd of public bystanders attended, as if it were a great day out, snapping up WSPU souvenirs in purple, white and green and buying fairground-style refreshments. Among the brass bands, suffrage singers and banner parades were 20 outdoor platforms, erected in a great circle around the park. And there was ex-Holloway inmate Alice Hawkins, now a keynote speaker, ostrich feather quivering as she earnestly told the crowd about women's working conditions in Leicester's boot and shoe industry. Neither event had any effect on the new Asquith government, but the evident surge in suffragist numbers rattled the Antis.

Four weeks later to the day, in that ornate meeting room at the Westminster Palace Hotel, the novelist Mrs Humphry Ward rose to her feet to speak. In view, she declared, of 'the spectacle of marchings and counter-marchings . . . on behalf of the suffrage cause up and down England', it was time for anti-suffragists to bestir themselves.

Eighteen ladies were nominated to serve on the executive committee, including Lady Jersey as chairman, Mrs Ward as chairman of the literature committee and Miss Gertrude Bell as honorary secretary. Mary Ward we have met before: the novelist and champion of women's education, who wrote under her married name of Mrs Humphry Ward, was responsible for the plea against women's suffrage in *Nineteenth Century* magazine back in 1889. The adventurer and archaeologist Gertrude Bell was an extraordinary woman by any standards. She had just published a book on her journeys through Syria, and was briefly in London between expeditions to the Ottoman Empire and Mesopotamia. Another influential executive was Violet Markham, a wealthy social reformer passionate about women's training and education (held by a pro-suffrage friend to be 'a real feminist'). And there was Etta Lemon: a woman with a proven track record in growing a society, lobbying parliament and effective public speaking at home and abroad. In this she was almost unique. By definition, Antis were disinclined to step onto public platforms and raise their voices. Mrs Lemon had spoken at international women's conferences; had been praised by one 'grateful' male journalist for her 'discriminating advocacy' (as opposed to the 'passionate and headlong declamations' of other female speakers).

The executive committee made a formidable team. An upper-middle-class leadership with strong links to political aristocracy – the exact model, as it happened, of the RSPB. Perhaps it was no coincidence that Lady Jersey was also an RSPB member and her husband a vice president (he was, too, a prominent Freemason, just like Frank Lemon). They all shared the potent Lemon cocktail of Christianity, conservatism and charity. Anti-suffragism was the obvious destination for well-to-do late Victorian women active in the charitable world. It was also the natural refuge for women of exalted social status, who did not want the vote because they had never needed it. Lady Waldegrave, Lady Jeune, Lady Ashburton, Lady Londonderry, Lady Wantage, the Countess of Ilchester, Lady Glenconner, Lady Sheffield . . . the list went on.

As for working-class women – there was only token interest in enlisting them. The Antis felt confident that they could speak *on behalf of* poorer women. And they were confident that the vast majority of working women's horizons did not extend beyond their own four walls.

At a later Anti rally in the packed Royal Albert Hall (in direct imitation of the suffragettes), Violet Markham succinctly summed up their position: 'We believe that men and women are different – not similar – beings, with talents that are complementary, not identical, and that they therefore ought to have different shares in the management of the State.' Women were eminently capable of holding high office, she maintained, but a 'fruitful diversity of political function' was sought, not a 'stultifying uniformity'.

And so this powerful female arsenal prepared, perversely, to range its guns against its sisters. They were, most of them, of an age. Etta was now 48; her Victorian reflexes were entrenched, and she shared them with those sitting in the Westminster Palace Hotel on that late summer's day.

They were instinctive conservatives all, hard-wired to respect male authority, mistrust reforms and fear social anarchy.

Mrs Lemon had a nagging anxiety she was no longer 'in the van', as they called it in those days: in the vanguard. She was already in the process of being marginalised within her own bird protection society. The men were taking over at the RSPB on all fronts. An important bill had been drawn up to halt the importation of wild birds' plumage, and it was only right that their leading man of influence, the 74-year-old Liberal Lord Avebury, should steer it through the House of Lords (where it was passed that very day of the inaugural Antis meeting, 21 July), and then the Commons (where it would be read the next day, 22 July, then shelved for lack of time). Etta Lemon's work for the birds was far from done, but here was a different, equally compelling cause requiring her energy. A cause that might propel her to centre stage once again.

The Times leader on 22 July 1908 celebrated the founding of the Antis, and exhorted the ladies on: 'They must fight the suffragists, male and female, with their own weapons. They must meet organisation by organisation, agitation by counter-agitation, and argument by argument.'

'If you have an influential position, socially or professionally, we want you' announced Emmeline Pethick-Lawrence to a packed Exeter Hall. Here was one of the Anti's arch enemies at work: a woman seeking perplexingly similar supporters, ironically from the very same social circles. Rows of elegantly attired ladies tilted extravagant hats towards each other in whispered confabulation. 'Well-connected' members were urged to make a list of 'every woman of good position', including her name and address, making it 'easy to write a letter from headquarters'.

This was a recruitment meeting for the WSPU. The Wis*poo*. The woman holding forth on the platform we have met before, in the late 1880s, taking cockney girls in the rag trade out of the London slum and into the countryside for a holiday. Emmeline Pethick-Lawrence was the *other* Emmeline of the suffragette movement, responsible for raising the game of Mrs Pankhurst's WSPU and turning it into a finely tuned, brilliant publicity machine. Without 'Pethers', we might not today remember the name of Pankhurst, or 'Pank' as she was affectionately known.

Emmeline Pethick-Lawrence had heard about Mrs Pankhurst's militant movement while living in South Africa. Intrigued, she and her husband had returned to London in 1906 to meet this woman who shared both her Christian name and convictions – and she was smitten.

'All the Pankhursts behaved as if the Cause was a religion which demanded total commitment,' she remembered. Mrs Pankhurst had, she thought, 'a temperament akin to genius. She could have been a queen on the Stage or in the Salon'. But Mrs Pankhurst was trying to run a movement from a kitchen table. Immediately, 'Pethers' and her husband, Frederick Lawrence, offered to rent offices for the society within 3–4 Clement's Inn, Holborn (where they had a flat), so that the WSPU could operate from central London. As the RSPB had discovered 15 years before, a central London office was vital if they were to be taken seriously. Women could not expect to influence the establishment if they tried to run a movement from home.

Like the Lemons, Emmeline and Fred Pethick-Lawrence were a couple closely united by vehement values and shared work. They were, like the Lemons, childless, workaholic thrusters in life. Like Frank Lemon, Fred was a Cambridge man and trained in the law, but unlike Frank, Fred's fortune meant he did not need to practise. Like Etta, 'Pethers' was principled, methodical and a natural leader. Unlike Etta, she was stylish, always elegantly attired in the Aesthetic style – and she had bags of flair. It was 'Pethers', not 'Pank', who introduced the pageantry, colour and music that did so much to popularise votes for women. It's interesting to speculate how the RSPB might have triumphed with the aesthetic oomph of a Pethers, rather than the finger-wagging conservatism of an Etta.

Fred Lawrence brought his love for detail, mapping out and planning the demonstrations and big schemes. A former editor, he created the WSPU newspaper, *Votes for Women* (a tool swiftly copied by the Antis). In 1911, the paper ran a series of photographs of the centre of operations at 3–4 Clement's Inn, in which they managed to make a series of small rooms look like a government wing in Whitehall. In the 'National Strategy' room, a large map of the British Isles was pinned to the wall, marked with local divisions. There was a financial secretary's office, where Pethers helped raise the modern equivalent of £3 million in just five years. Every photograph shows a calm and orderly hive of activity: young women in crisp white shirts and wide Edwardian hairstyles are bent intently over their business – typewriter, ledger, telephone exchange, hand-cranked duplicating machine.

By the end of its first fiscal year, in February 1907, the WSPU had 47 branches, mostly in London and the Home Counties (a social pattern shared by the Antis, and one that remained constant). It had raised an annual income of nearly £3,000. It also had a dictatorship. Mrs Pankhurst had dramatically torn up the WSPU draft constitution at the AGM that October and announced (to stunned surprise) that they were now in the ranks of an army, of which she was the permanent 'Commander-in-Chief'.

Christabel Pankhurst wrote the editorial in the first edition of *Votes for Women* that month: 'The founders and leaders of the movement must lead, the non-commissioned officers must carry out their instructions, the rank and file must loyally share the burdens of the fight.' There was no room, she said, for 'pettiness or personal ambition'. There was no compulsion for any woman to join. But those who did 'must come as soldiers ready to march onwards in battle array'.

Not all women who had been roused by militancy wanted to be militants themselves. The membership of Millicent Fawcett's NUWSS had begun to increase almost as fast as that of the WSPU. Since the Pankhursts had turned up the heat on their subversive activities, the secretaries of the older suffrage societies found themselves 'worked off their feet'. Every post brought applications for information and membership. 'Where we were formerly receiving half-crowns and shillings,' wrote Mrs Fawcett in her memoir, 'we were now getting £5 and £10 notes.'

The constant sideshow of suffragette spectacle knocked everything else off the front page. These women were so audacious! Such as the day two beautifully dressed ladies, Miss Muriel Matters and Miss Helen Fox, chained themselves to the grille of the Ladies' Gallery at the House of Commons, before addressing appalled MPs sitting below. They had to be carried away, the grille still chained to their bodies, 'jabbing the sergeant-at-arms with a hatpin' until a blacksmith could be found to unfetter them.

On another occasion, a suffragette steam launch had sped up the Thames to the Commons' riverside terrace at teatime. As 'seven hundred MPs, clerics, constituents and a host of delightfully dressed women friends sat in the cool shade, sipping tea, eating strawberries and cream, cress sandwiches, and other dainties', reported *The Times*, they were interrupted by a woman drawing alongside with a megaphone, through which she began to 'harangue' the MPs with good humour. This was Flora Drummond, a woman known as 'the General' for her love of military uniform.

Or there was the day that six large, horse-drawn vans had arrived at the House of Lords and flung open their doors. Out stepped from each a 'dozen daintily clad suffragettes who immediately began to hold a meeting' (public meetings being forbidden within one mile of the Houses of Parliament). All of London – apart from the Home Office – laughed.

As the constitutional suffrage leader, Millicent Fawcett wrote to *The Times* in October 1906 (before the WSPU had ratcheted up the violence), that 'far from having injured the movement', the Pankhurst's suffragettes had 'done more during the last twelve months to bring it within the realms of practical politics than we have been able to accomplish in the same number of years'.

About the Antis, she felt great frustration. So many of their leaders were impressive women who might otherwise be pro-suffrage – but here they were, offering a 'splendid field for chaff' with their ill-conceived arguments about separate spheres and God-ordained roles. Mrs Humphry Ward was an admirable thinking woman who had, Mrs Fawcett felt, 'somehow wandered into the wrong camp'.

She went on to predict, correctly, that 'future generations will probably mete out no very kindly judgment to the women who petitioned against women'.

*

Against this backdrop of suffragette stunt and spectacle, the Women's National Anti-Suffrage League sprang briskly into action. These were women who had past form in getting things done. The Countess of Jersey was already chair of the Victoria League, founded in 1901 with the aim of building links across the empire with like-minded women. If she could do it globally, she could surely do it nationally. Women needed to be roused from their complacent inertia and thoroughly (if ironically) politicised.

First, another petition: 337,018 signatures were gathered by the end of 1908; a cause for jubilation, as this was larger than any suffragist effort in the past 30 years. Next, their own newspaper. The *Anti-Suffrage Review* was launched in December 1908, and there was no shortage of Anti writers to fill its pages. Then it was a matter of building up the branches through old-fashioned social networking – something Mrs Lemon was able to advise on. From the first Anti cell in Hawkhurst, Kent, to the second in South Kensington, London, the movement spread rapidly: 26 branches by the end of 1908, 82 by April 1909, 104 in July 1910.

But it wasn't quite like the RSPB. The local secretaries were far wealthier, more grandly titled and less inclined towards agitating and public speaking. Here lay the great difficulty for the Antis. Its female supporters refused to mount platforms, attend meetings or pen leaflets. This was partly a logical extension of their ladylike refusal to tangle with parliamentary politics, but it meant that the league found itself handicapped. Its supporters believed in 'true' rather than 'new' womanhood: devotion to family duties and inconspicuous public service. They were not going to make a spectacle of themselves by noisily resisting the franchise.

This left the propaganda battle to the likes of Mary Ward, Violet Markham and Etta Lemon. Women of mettle. Women of conviction. Of course, the glaring irony in all this was that the Antis were women *made* for the world of politics. They were self-evidently capable of politicking – but they lacked the youth, glamour and *passion* of the suffragette movement. There was no comely Christabel Pankhurst capturing the imagination of the young; no 'Pank' or 'Pethers' capable of stirring an audience's emotions to fever pitch. No woman ever said of an anti-suffrage meeting that it 'sucked up my soul like a tide' – as did suffragette Lady Constance Bulwer-Lytton about her all-consuming 'hobby', the WSPU.

The Antis were, in a sense, their own worst enemies. For while the Pankhursts were writing fresh and modern-sounding editorials in *Votes for Women*, the Antis were huffing and puffing in convoluted paragraphs for the conservative press. Mrs Ethel Harrison, head of the Hawkhurst (Kent) Antis, wrote 'The Opponent's View' in *The Queen*, 1908. Women had, she said, 'waited long for some word or sign from the constitutional suffragists to curb and restrain this flood of frothy effervescence' from militant 'irresponsibles'. 'But no word or sign has come. So it is that the women of our League find a duty thrust upon them to speak plainly their mind, and to say openly what they think of a movement which seems to them morbid and retrograde.'

The trouble with suffragists, wrote popular novelist Marie Corelli, was that they were *unfeminine*.

> If a bevy of dainty, beautiful, exquisitely dressed women were to quietly enter the Lobby of the House of Commons, and there plead with tuneful eloquence and reasonable dignity for their 'suffrage', they might not so bedazzle and bewilder the members as to cause these gentlemen to lose their heads entirely – even to the extent of granting them anything and everything on the spot!

Jeering at suffragists for being unfeminine monsters dressed in tweeds and trilbies, with facial hair and hobnailed boots, was a very old joke indeed – one long enjoyed by misogynists. It was beneath Marie Corelli, and her outpourings did no service to the Antis. But did she have a point? Many suffragists (and suffragettes) *were* young and beautiful but, as Ray Strachey wrote, 'it cannot be denied that among these brave and devoted women there were a few who were not only plain but positively uncouth to the outward eye'. It was the old-style, dogged supporters, in the campaign now for forty years, who all too often let the side down. The sort who looked 'awfully strong-minded in walking dress', with 'short petticoats and a close round hat and several dreadfully ugly arrangements' (as one suffragist wrote uneasily to another of a fellow supporter). These sort of women were 'abominable, and most damaging to the cause'.

Very well, then. If the Antis thought them all to be unwomanly and unfeminine, then the suffragettes would hit back. It was just a small question of rebranding. And so the great WSPU propaganda wheels at Clement's Inn began to turn. Floor plans were drawn up, costumes and banners designed, strict editorials written on dress code. Un*womanly*? Unable to dazzle, daintily? It was too delicious a challenge for Pethers and Pank. The public had seen nothing yet.

31

The Feminine Arts

1909

You could not mistake the colours. The outside of the Prince's Club, an elite ice skating rink in Knightsbridge, was festooned with flags in purple, white and green. Inside was a fair, so they promised, with 'feminine arts' and refreshments. And you might well be curious, after so much unusual publicity, to see what lay within – whatever your stance on women and the vote.

For weeks now, suffragettes had been parading the streets of West End London, advertising this twelve-day event: young girls with fluttering maypole ribbons, women side-saddle on white horses or dressed as historical heroines. An all-female marching drum and fife band had caused a sensation from Harrods to Hyde Park: 22 youthful musicians in gleaming black shoes and uniforms with white frogging. 'The first Amazon drum and fife band which has ever existed,' reported the News of the World. Gawping crowds in bowler hats and flat caps choked the roads around Montpelier Square.

Cunningly, political slogans were absent from the banners, which read simply, 'Exhibition – Prince's Skating Rink, Knightsbridge – May 13 to 24.' But you would have been a fool not to recognise those colours. Every marching woman was dressed in the livery that was now de rigueur for WSPU members: purple for dignity, white for purity, green for hope.

Promoting the colours *above all* was Emmeline Pethick-Lawrence's master stroke. It created an instant political message that no longer needed words; a message that could be understood 'by the most uninstructed and most idle of passers-by', as the exhibition programme explained. The pinched West End milliners on their lunch break understood those colours; the jaded shop girls staring out of plate glass windows, too. 'Again and again we have seen how the colours arrest attention and evoke enthusiasm; how they . . . call forth a response from the work-weary faces of men and women in the crowded ways of great cities.'

At 2.30pm on Thursday 14 May, 1909, the double doors of the skating rink swung, heavily, open – and into a space the size of three tennis courts surged a curious crowd of men and women. The men were important, for the event was calculated to show that suffragettes were not the dangerous 'shrieking sisterhood' as portrayed by the popular press, but wives, mothers and sisters like any others: women safely occupied in familiar female pursuits (embroidery, jam making, baby clothes, art); women dedicated to creating beautiful things, not destroying them.

This, on the surface, was how it appeared and the crowds stared, astonished, about them. A warm, ultra-feminine spectacle had somehow been conjured from this most masculine of sports halls. Pennants in purple, white and green shimmered from the skylit roof, heraldic flags jutted from the walls, and a series of garlanded murals on wooden panels encircled the whole. It was like entering a cathedral – or a stage set.

The murals were the work of Sylvia Pankhurst, Emmeline's artistic second daughter, who had interpreted the words of a psalm – 'They that sow in tears shall reap in joy' – with a series of winged female figures. In one, a winged woman sowed grain with a flight of doves above her. Simple, graceful and biblical, it would have made a fitting symbol for the RSPB. Instead it was pressed into use on behalf of the vote.

For Mrs Lemon, the exhibition's much promoted branding was bitterly ironic. For what use was it allying yourself with nature, or indeed with angels, if you wore the plumage of endangered birds on your head? Etta Lemon had reason to take a beady interest in the Women's Exhibition of May 1909, as she knew that there were plans for a large millinery stall where 100 hats would be sold to raise money. She had many informers in the suffragette ranks – and regrettable as this membership crossover might be, it was also useful.

Since early that year, *Votes for Women* had been soliciting goods for this big fundraising event. 'Will members please remember that their contributions . . . must be sent in before 6 May. Hats, veils, or scarves suitable for the millinery stall must be sent to Mrs Reginald Potts, 8 Victoria Road, Kensington.' Mrs Potts was the honorary secretary for the WSPU's well-heeled Kensington branch, and she began to use her leverage at the millinery counter of various big department stores. Liberty, Derry & Toms and Peter Robinson all succumbed, donating valuable summer stock. By 1909, the typical suffragette was their kind of shopper – smart, independent, a woman about town. But since many WSPU members were also RSPB members, the vexed question of feathered hats reared its head.

The hat stall at the Women's Exhibition is important, for it was here that Emmeline Pankhurst crossed swords with Etta Lemon. Up until now, the two had (as far as I could tell) kept a wary distance. But here, at this highly visible junction of ethics and aesthetics, the two dealt each other a metaphorical parrying blow.

Well-to-do members of the WSPU had been urged, via *Votes for Women*, to 'obtain contributions to the millinery stall from their milliners', with the observation that 'many of our members must have accounts with the big hat shops'. They did. The hat was an important part of the suffragette's battledress, and a highly symbolic part. If you study the monochrome photographs of these women *en masse* in the suffragette archive, it is the hat that dominates – whether laden with roses or topped with aggressive-looking albatross feathers. In 1909, women's hats typically measured three feet high (trimmings included) and two feet wide, and their preposterous growth was linked, in part, to female politics.

The ever-elegant Emmeline Pankhurst insisted that if they were to win the nation over, suffragettes must ensure that they were the best dressed, most alluring women at every social gathering. Last century's New Woman in her assertive straw boater (slightly masculine, undecorated, hard-edged) had produced the caricature of unmarriageable spinsters in trilbies, an image that now had to be purged. And so, by personal example, Emmeline and Christabel Pankhurst assiduously promoted large, fashionable hats. If you were both powerful *and* feminine, went the message, then you had the best of both worlds. So central was the hat to her brand that Mrs Pankhurst took a keen, controlling interest in the millinery stall at the Women's Exhibition.

'I feel myself impelled to put in a plea for the birds,' wrote Miss Clara Mordan to *Votes for Women* in February 1909, 'and to suggest that women should take the opportunity of dissociating themselves from "Murderous Millinery".' Clara was that Trojan horse who had entered the RSPB annual meeting in 1906 – a 66-year-old lesbian heiress, unmasked by Mrs Lemon as a bird-loving suffragette. Now, though, this RSPB Fellow was proving her use. 'A hat and bonnet stall in which ospreys and the stuffed bodies of birds were conspicuous by their absence would be a wonderful demonstration of the merciful ingenuity of women,' wrote Clara, parroting the crisp language of Lemon.

Her letter prompted a flurry of concerned correspondence. 'I should like to range myself on her side, and also plead for the birds,' wrote a Miss B. Hake the following week. 'Would it be too drastic a suggestion to make that those who are in charge of the millinery stall at the exhibition would refuse to accept any hats or bonnets with the bodies of stuffed birds or ospreys in them? The sickening sights one sees so much of in the present-day millinery makes me feel impelled to second your correspondent's admirable letter, and I trust her humane suggestion will not pass un-noted.'

Votes for Women was usually conscientious about replying to letters; the paper was professional in tone, intelligently edited and respectful of readers. What is more, Clara Mordan was an important donor to the cause. Since joining the WSPU in 1906 she'd handed over a total of £759 of her fortune (around £723,000 in today's money) in various donations to the 'treasure chest'. But neither Pethers nor Pank would engage with these pleas in print and thus alienate their millinery trade advertisers.

'Dear Sir,' wrote Joan Baillie Guthrie, a fortnight later. 'I was for some years a Fellow of the Bird Protection Society, and only recently resigned in order to give my annual subscription where it was even more needed, to the WSPU. I am one of the links of four generations who have refused to wear the plumage of any poor feathered beauty, killed solely to adorn a featherless biped's hat.'

Joan Baillie Guthrie – 'Lavender' to family and friends – was 19. Her father had died in the Boer War and money mattered. She, her mother and her sister had signed up to the suffragettes the previous year, and they were all utterly seduced by the camaraderie and excitement it offered. Lavender – in charge of the soda fountain bar at the Women's Exhibition – would go on to embrace extreme militancy. We shall meet her again.

The news that Miss Baillie Guthrie had *resigned* from the RSPB, severing the family connection and transferring her one guinea a year to the Pankhursts, was chilling news to Mrs Lemon. Her society was haemorrhaging members – to death, mostly, but here was a new and most pernicious claim on the young. 'Perhaps it is because we are fighting so hard for liberty,' continued Lavender in *Votes for Women*, 'that so few of our members transgress in this way against the birds, which are surely Nature's best type of joyous freedom.'

Lavender was deluding herself. A full-page advertisement in the same issue, from ladies' outfitters Charles Lee & Son of Wigmore Street, advertised a series of hats simply heaped with avian body parts. 'Charming Hat in Burnt Straw, lined with most becoming shades of Brown; the Wings, which form the only trimming, are of a beautiful shade of Blue, finished in front with handsome Jet Ornament. Price 59/6 [£290 in today's money].' 'Chic Little Toque, in a lovely shade of Old Blue, with handsome Wing at side in the most beautiful colourings. Price 35/6 [£175].'

When Lord Avebury put the Plumage Bill before the House of Lords the previous year, he had read out, to surprised members, some trade figures for the twelve months of 1907. These included over 28,000 bird-of-paradise skins, together with snowy egret feathers from an estimated 190,000 birds. At the June sale alone, 1,386 crowned pigeon heads were sold at the Commercial Sale Rooms, while one firm shifted over 20,000 kingfishers among a sales lot of 'miscellaneous bird-skins'. That year's fashion for one dramatic feature on a hat meant that long, curling lyre bird's tails and the immense quills of albatrosses sold in vast numbers.

While the House of Lords was listening to Avebury's second reading of this bill ('of a somewhat peculiar nature,' as he put it, 'but the circumstances are exceptional'), the curtain rose on a one-act comedy at the Royal Court Theatre. *Tilda's New Hat* by George Paston opened with a jam factory worker lolling on a sofa in a shabby Clerkenwell tenement house, pinning long black ostrich feathers onto her hat to the stern disapproval of her puritanical mother, Mrs Fishwick. 'I wouldn't have been seen with a thing like that on me head. A nice chip bonnet, trimmed with ribbon and tied under me chin, me hair neatly parted and gathered in a chenille net behind.'

Tilda belongs to a 'feather club', and it is her turn for the plumes. She lives on Chapel Street, a mile north of Alice Battershall's home at Lever Street, and she occupies the same world. But instead of dreaming of rescue by a rich admirer, as a working-class girl might have done back in 1885, Tilda's plucky self-sufficiency is celebrated. 'Give me me independence!' Her hat is a symbol of self-indulgence, self-worth and sexuality. It was a sly feminist play, very modern, and it transferred to three consecutive West End theatres, each audience stacked to the upper circle.

The RSPB was handicapped because it was founded on a negative. The whole campaign involved *not* wearing feathers. There was an absence at its core. This was hard to promote, hard to celebrate and hard to make visual. There was not much humour in it. Etta Lemon and her redoubtable ladies were losing the propaganda battle to the suffragettes, who had a positive at the core of their argument. They wanted to *get the vote*, and they were going to show that they deserved it. Theirs was an all-consuming positive, and the suffragettes were expected to promote it at the expense of all other causes.

In her autobiography of 1914, Emmeline Pankhurst explained the 'instant appeal' of the WSPU compared to the other suffrage associations. 'In the first place,' she wrote, 'our members are absolutely single minded; they concentrate all their forces on one object: political equality with men. No member of the WSPU divides her attention between suffrage and other social reforms.' No dabbling in philanthropy, no agitating for green spaces or lecture halls for the working classes, no emotional schemes to protect cats, dogs or birds.

'There is not the slightest doubt that the women of Great Britain would have been enfranchised years ago had all the suffragists adopted this simple principle,' Mrs Pankhurst continued. 'They never did, and even today many English women refuse to adopt it. They are party members first and suffragists afterward; or they are suffragists part of the time and social theorists the rest of the time.'

Narrowness of focus was Mrs Pankhurst's ideal, and foot soldiers had to be seen to obey the 'Commander-in-Chief'. Thus, Margaret, Lady Brooke, the Ranee of Sarawak – keynote WSPU speaker at the Women's Exhibition and long-standing member of the RSPB – had to look down on an audience of quivering aigrettes, paradise plumes and exotic wings jostling for air rights at the Prince's Club skating rink, and keep firmly to her script. Her brief was to convert 'unconventional friends and wobblers' to the cause. Margaret's dear friend and personal parrot-sitter, W. H. Hudson, would not have been able to contain his contempt had he been there.

Standing on the speaker's platform alongside the Ranee of Sarawak was a diminutive woman with a camera, tripod and glass plate negatives, photographing the sea of upturned, earnest faces. Christina Broom had official permission to record the Women's Exhibition, and before the double doors had swung open and the crowds poured in, she asked each stall to pose for her. She knew by now what postcards sold well with the ladies. Suffragette memorabilia was a fast-growing market at her stall in the Royal Mews of Buckingham Palace. Broom was 47, self-taught, self-employed and the family breadwinner. She wasn't remotely a part of the

WSPU's world, but her location had caught her up in it. Her roving lens was unobtrusive, and sympathetic to its subjects. Christina Broom's suffragette photographs seem as fresh and vivid today as when her shutter snapped in May 1909.

At the sweets stall, she homed in on all that was saccharine and dainty. Coconut ice, butterscotch, chocolate and candied mice; nine heavily corseted women lined up behind a puckered white cloth; eight seriously feather-laden hats, two whole birds included. These were women dressing for *women*. 'Perseverance Keeps Honour Bright' reads a placard behind them. American sister suffragists had sent fudge and candies across the Atlantic for the stall, which raised a grand £109 (around £10,400 today).

Broom's lens captured quietly subversive touches: little dolls on the toy stall dressed in purple, white and green, clutch *Votes for Women* newspapers. Poisonous spiders scurry over snow-white broderie anglais. A thicket of jewelled hatpins bristle in the foreground, four or five inches long. Then there is the reconstructed prison cell (entrance 6d) where the public could push open a studded door and glimpse a suffragette prisoner, in arrow-flecked uniform, sewing coarse cloth.

The Women's Exhibition was deemed 'a brilliant success' in *Votes for Women*. It raised a whopping £5,664 (roughly £542,000 today) for the 'War Chest' campaign fund – and as a public relations stunt it worked. The shrieking sisterhood was transformed into industrious purveyors of 'charming art and needlework, flowers and farm produce', wrote the *Morning Post* reporter; 'evidence, if any were needed, of the ingenuity and determination which characterise members' of the WSPU'. Pethers and Pank had cleverly taken up the concept of women's work – and subverted it.

One ex-suffragette was scathing about the effect of stunts like this on the women's cause. Teresa Billington-Greig had left the WSPU in disgust when Emmeline Pankhurst appointed herself its autocratic commander. She and many others had gone on to co-found the non-violent Women's Freedom League (colours white, green and gold), and she wrote a harsh critique of the Pankhursts' society. 'It has gradually edged the working class element out of the ranks. It has become socially exclusive, punctiliously correct, gracefully fashionable, ultra-respectable and narrowly religious.'

She might as well have been describing the hat stall at the Women's Exhibition. This, too, was captured with Christina Broom's unerring eye. Some two dozen hats perch like heavily decorated wedding cakes on pedestals. All shriek of femininity, of gracious garden parties and high society summer outings – and all are exquisitely heaped with artificial flowers. There is no murderous millinery, not a swallow's wing nor an osprey in sight – at least, not in the official photograph. Perhaps the arguments of Clara Mordan were heeded, or perhaps a little financial leverage was applied. That April, a month before the exhibition's opening, Miss Mordan donated £100 to the WSPU.

And there was a more personal victory for Mrs Lemon. At the centre of the photograph, gazing dispassionately at the camera lens, is Mrs Pankhurst. She holds in her hand a pretty hat of Tuscan straw and rosebuds. On her head she wears not paradise, not osprey, but ostrich. A humanely harvested, curling plume is wrapped around her velvet crown.

32

The Advice of Men

1910

On Friday 6 May, King Edward VII shuffled to his bedroom window in Buckingham Palace to play with his canaries – and fainted. These tiny caged birds, forever bursting into frantic song, were a source of solace and delight to the harassed, corpulent and asthmatic Bertie, now aged 68. More beloved still was his white-haired terrier, Caesar. A chauffeur remembered how the King would shake his stick at Caesar in mock severity. 'You naughty dog,' he would say, very slowly. 'You naughty, naughty dog.' 'And Caesar would wag his tale and "smile" cheerfully up into his master's eyes, until His Majesty smiled back in spite of himself.'

By midnight on Friday 6 May, Caesar's master was dead. His queen felt as if she had been turned into stone. 'That horrid Biarritz', Alix believed, had killed her husband of 47 years. Court mourning was declared until 18 June, followed by a further period of half mourning, in which tones of black, grey, dull mauve and white could be worn. Whole cities turned black overnight – men, women and shops. The smart department stores of London were 'literally besieged from morning to night', reported the *Illustrated London News*. From the mid-Atlantic, women sailing home on the luxury liners *Mauretania* and *Lusitania* placed hurried orders via the on-board showrooms of Messrs Russell & Allen, their measurements flashed by the new wireless telegraphy straight to Bond Street. Disembarking passengers could pick up the whole mourning ensemble at the Welsh port of Fishguard.

In the City of London, Abraham Botibol's feather workers toiled around the clock, dying white ostrich plumes jet black. In the West End, dressmakers and milliners worked their way through a glut of orders. A 'critical Frenchwoman' remarked with amazement to a reporter that 'no woman in London lacked a mourning hat before midday on Saturday. The little English milliner has risen splendidly to the occasion,' observed Madame. 'But,' noted the *Linlithgow Gazette* wryly, 'how that poor "little milliner" worked.'

It went down in the fashion annals as the 'Black Season' – though many men felt that this obsession with dress at such a time wasn't quite seemly. What is more, it would literally get in the way: a hat the size of a 'cart-wheel' would not only destroy the view of everyone behind, thought the *Sheffield Telegraph*, but would 'mar the reverent feeling proper at such a time in the nation's history'. The women ignored them. The 'Mourning Hat' was – according to the *Evening Standard* – 'the Crux of the whole toilette'.

Mrs Pankhurst, no royalist, was not among the public mourners on Tuesday 17 May, the day of the funeral. She had great sorrow of her own, as her 21-year-old son Harry had died of a spinal inflammation that January. She had now lost a husband and both sons; only the Pankhurst women remained. But as a mark of respect, she delayed a scheduled 'monster demonstration' of 10,000 marchers, and the WSPU magazine appeared with a black-bordered portrait of Queen Alexandra on the cover. The WSPU headquarters' cache of Edward VII one pennies, his jowly face hand-stamped with 'VOTES FOR WOMEN' on each coin, would now become collector's items.

Society descended upon the Royal Ascot races that June dressed flamboyantly in black. Ladies looked 'like giant crows or morbid birds of paradise strutting at some Gothic entertainment', wrote the future fashion photographer Cecil Beaton, then a young boy. 'Fashions tend to extremes before being dropped,' mused Beaton, 'and the elaborate headgear had now become like the last spurt of a Catherine wheel. These vast picture hats, perhaps set on one side of the head and piled high with black ostrich feathers mixed with osprey, or black paradise feathers combined with black tulle, were worn not only in mourning for a king but for a glory that had gone forever.'

King George V – institutionalised by the Navy, self-effacing, uxorious – could not have been more different to his father. 'Not only has his name never been mixed up with any scandal,' wrote a commentator, but George shunned all 'rich upstarts and merely rowdily amusing vulgarians and sycophants' (in other words, his father's circle). What father and son *had* shared was a lust for shooting, and a disgust for the idea of women's suffrage.

At a Windsor reception, the new king shared his views with the Prime Minister's wife. 'In a loud cheery voice he explained how he would chop all their hair off, give them hard labour and then, with a slight lowering of the voice, repeated what his father had thought so witty.' The suffragettes, he told Margot Asquith, were known as 'the un-enjoyed'. Margot was also anti-suffrage, but she was not amused: 'I have no great taste for stale jocularities and no available social laughter but I did my best.'

'The King is a very jolly chap but thank God there's not much in his head,' wrote Lloyd George to his wife. 'They're simple, very very ordinary people and perhaps on the whole that's how it should be.' Queen Mary – real name May – was equally repressed and retiring, but rather better educated, with a taste for the fine arts. Her hallmark was a large, swathed bosom and a neat, unfashionable 1890s toque on a tightly curled coiffure. She was a known supporter of the anti-suffrage movement, and immediately forbade any of her ladies-in-waiting from being involved with those awful women.

May was not sentimental like her mother-in-law, but fortunately for the RSPB she shared Alix's compassionate streak, having spent much of her youth working for her mother's charities. She had a particular horror of caged birds. The Duchess of Portland took discreet steps to ensure that May's wardrobe would be purged of all feathers before next year's durbar and the royal tour of India (on which George V would shoot 39 tigers, 18 rhinoceroses and four bears).

What, at this time, was Mrs Lemon doing? I searched in vain for her voice in 1910. At the crowded annual RSPB meeting in the Westminster Palace Hotel, this tumultuous year of industrial strikes and political upheavals was reviewed through the prism of bird protection. Mrs Lemon sat entirely mute as one man after another rose to his feet to talk. Lord Avebury held forth on the frustrations of getting another hearing for the Plumage Bill; the colonial expert James Buckland harrumphed about the illicit export of bird skins from the colonies (from India, cases labelled 'sheet music', 'examination papers' and 'cow hair' had been found to be bulging with thousands of dead birds). The MacLeod of MacLeod, owner of the Island of St Kilda, despaired of the bird cruelty done out of ignorance by his islanders, who slaughtered puffins and fulmars routinely on their nests for food.

The Duchess of Portland was absent from the AGM, yet again, and without her Mrs Lemon seemed to lack boldness. Winnie's presence gave her tacit permission to operate as in the good old days, when women ran the show. The once so forceful Eliza Phillips was an old lady of 87, writing letters from her house in Croydon. Emily Williamson was absorbed with her social work in Manchester. It was time to face up to the fact that this was no longer a women's society – and perhaps, more importantly, no longer Mrs Lemon's society.

'Quite prevented from going to London,' her Grace had telegraphed from Welbeck Abbey; 'so grieved to cause such inconvenience, but hope you can find someone to present the prizes.' Etta wasn't even chosen for this – the dishing out of nature essay prizes. The honour went to Julia, 64-year-old Marchioness of Tweeddale (after whom the exquisite purple-throated sunbird had been named – *Leptocoma sperata juliae* – by her first husband, the ornithologist Arthur Hay, on his final expedition to the Philippines). No one had named a bird after Mrs Lemon, nor would they.

That year she had *not* been chosen to attend the Fifth International Congress of Ornithologists in Berlin; instead, Henry Dresser took her usual place (an aged ornithologist and owner of a colossal collection of bird skins and eggs). Now that the old impulse to collect birds with a shotgun had turned, imperceptibly, into a desire to record them using binoculars and a notebook, the field was becoming rather crowded. Bird books and societies were proliferating; *Punch* had declared bird feeding 'a national pastime'. And now there was bird ringing.

Mrs Lemon objected forcibly to this new and invasive practice, started in 1909 by a young ornithologist obsessed with migratory patterns. Harry Forbes Witherby, a former Blackheath neighbour and now editor of the new *British Birds* magazine, wanted to track how far swallows flew. Where did they end up? And did they return to the same spot? Similar schemes were started that year by the University of Aberdeen and *Country Life* magazine. 'Systematic' was the buzzword of the new male bird enthusiasts. Systematic, and scientific – not sentimental.

Which left Mrs Lemon, bird and nature lover, feeling excluded and unwanted when she went about bird protection the old-fashioned way – by putting the birds, not the scientists, first. Lighthouse resting ledges were her idea; the network of 22 keen-eyed 'watchers', too, who policed breeding reserves. The campaign against feathered hats was still hers to drive; the threat to exotic birdlife more urgent now than ever before. But how did one hold public interest in a campaign that had been rumbling on now for 20 years? How did one keep to the forefront of national debate? The Humanitarian League had recently bemoaned the fact that 'great social and political interests' (women's suffrage, the Irish Home Rule question) were taking all the attention from the 'so-called minor subjects'. Mrs Lemon, who had just turned 50, was not content to become a minor subject.

Sitting stiff-backed in the throng of top hats at the Westminster Palace Hotel was Lord Curzon of Kedleston, former Viceroy of India and amateur expert on exotic birdlife. *He* was not content to become a minor subject either. Since his humiliating return from Delhi in 1905, when he was refused an earldom and excluded from the cabinet, he had virtually retired from Westminster. Curzon was in search of a cause, something more exciting and political than his vice presidency with the RSPB. Now he thought he knew what it might be.

George Curzon was a man who liked women. He preferred to socialise with women. Behind the cool, inflexible, imperious facade was a robust libido, and he was given to pursuing full-blown affairs. As his lover Elinor Glyn (sister to couturier Lucile) observed, he liked women 'rather in the spirit in which other men like good horses or fine wine . . . not as equal souls worthy of being seriously considered'.

In 1906, his devoted, submissive wife Mary had died aged 36, leaving three small daughters. 'Give me a girl that knows a woman's place and does not yearn for trousers,' Curzon had written to Mary, an American heiress, before they were married. 'Give me, in fact, Mary.' Two years after her death, despite constant back pain from an early riding injury (and the tight metal corset he wore for relief), the 50-year-old widower embarked on a passionate, clandestine affair with the married Elinor Glyn.

He also threw himself back into politics. As an instinctive Anti, Curzon had put his name to the Men's Committee for Opposing Female Suffrage back in December 1908 – but compared to the go-ahead women's league, the men had failed to distinguish themselves. Unlike the women, who had hatched a 'Forward Policy' to promote women's roles in local government, the men's approach was fundamentally negative. In a box at the Women's Library today, deep within London's School of Economics, is a slim wallet of Men's Committee handbills and pamphlets: shameful evidence of a misogynistic campaign.

'What would Queen Victoria say if she were alive now?' goes the headline to one of the men's handbills, quoting the deceased monarch's antediluvian arguments made in 1852. ('We women are not made for governing,' she had said; 'and, if we are good women, we must dislike those masculine occupations.') As a queen, Victoria 'acted upon the advice of men', the Men's Committee argued. 'Save suffragist women from themselves, and other women from suffragists!' reads another leaflet. While all this was being produced, Curzon had been keeping a weather eye on what the ladies were up to.

When it was clear that the women's organisation was the healthier of the two, their membership having doubled to 10,000 by July 1910, he staged a takeover. The Men's Committee was briskly wound down and Lord Curzon transferred his attentions to the women's league. He brought with him the 70-year-old statesman Evelyn Baring, First Earl of Cromer and former British consul general to Egypt (infamous for trying to free Egyptian women from the subjugation of Islam and the veil). These two imperial old hands flung themselves into the fight, with all the virile authority of former British rulers in India and Egypt. But they underestimated the women.

The first hint of trouble arose when the novelist Mrs Humphry (Mary) Ward telephoned Lord Cromer to register her alarm at the provisional title for the new organisation: the National *Anti-Woman* Suffrage League. Then came Lady Jersey, erstwhile women's president, writing to Curzon in great pique from Lake Como that 'Lord Cromer's name already appears on the stationary of the new League as "President"'. She wanted a commitment to a guaranteed quota of women on the executive committee *and* in the office, on equal standing to the men. Curzon and Cromer were surprised, then increasingly annoyed by Lady Jersey's attitude. 'Inclined to ask much too high a price,' wrote Cromer to Curzon; 'unfriendly, not to say aggressive.' But since the Men's Committee had already been dissolved, 'the Women's League rather have the whip hand of us'.

All this had a worryingly familiar feel to Etta Lemon, zealous honorary secretary for the East Surrey women's Antis. As with the RSPB, once the women had done all the hard work, the men stepped in to run the show. Curzon wanted their networks, but complained that the women had no campaigning experience. It was true that outdoor speaking was beyond the pale for most, while indoor speaking was limited to the drawing room. 'It was our fate, as antis, to attract all the ultra-feminine and the lady-like incompetents,' remembered one woman.

Curzon's main thrust behind the takeover was that the Antis needed money if they were to make an impact – no less than £100,000 (£9.5m today). An absurdly excessive sum, surely (the RSPB operated quite respectably on a whisker of this amount: £1,330 in 1910). But Curzon was an ambitious man, and this was his new pet project.

His initial appeal was successful, but his top-notch fundraising backfired. When *The Times* published the league's list of 103 names on 21 July 1910, over a third were peers and peeresses (and seven of these peers were vice presidents or fellows of the RSPB). The suffragists gleefully rounded on the league as an aristocratic and plutocratic male conspiracy. This charge was being borne out, quietly, in the Antis' office. While Curzon and Cromer took elaborate care to ensure that at least a façade of equal participation was retained (seven men and seven women on the board), covertly they plotted for male domination. On 26 September, Cromer told Curzon he thought it 'politic' to give Lady Jersey some special post like vice chairman. 'I do not think much harm would be done, for certainly, so long as I am President, I will take very good care that I am always present at the meetings of the Committee, so as to take the Chair.'

Cromer also thought it important to 'keep the Women's Association in a good temper' because 'they are far more efficient than the men'. Yet the two men connived to slowly strip them of their power. They felt it important to have a man in charge of the headquarters at Caxton House, plum in the heart of Westminster's clubland. 'MPs and others who call for information will, as you rightly say, expect to find a man,' the white moustachioed Cromer told Curzon in August. Again, Lady Jersey was incensed. Women were much better at office work, she pointed out, and more easily obtainable. 'A first class man may be better than a first class woman,' she wrote, 'but a first class woman is better than a second class man!' Cromer compromised with an 'economical' woman to 'deal with details'.

So Miss Lucy Terry Lewis became the league's office secretary, with the inexperienced Mr Scott as 'Organising Agent' on a handsome £300 a year. Within a month they were at loggerheads: Miss Lewis had left Mr Scott with nothing to do. 'I really think that the whole of this business is likely to drive me into a premature grave,' Cromer wrote wearily to Curzon on 4 November. Three days later, Scott resigned.

The Anti archives of Cromer and Curzon have been preserved simply because of who these two men were. Far less has survived from the women's side of the story, but the men's letters give silent voice to female frustrations during this power struggle between the sexes. The two men continued to commiserate knowingly on the difficulty of working with women, and particularly with Miss Lewis. 'I am physically incapable of doing eternal battle to all these rampaging women,' wrote Cromer to Curzon on 15 December 1910. 'With her ideas of the way to treat the male sex, Miss Lewis ought really to be a Suffragist; it is a mere accident that she has drifted into our camp.'

And therein lay the central, delicious irony in all of this. Working for the Antis, whether in the office or out on the road, had the effect of honing women's political skills. Of giving them more, not less of a voice. When Miss Lewis was dismissed in January 1911, a woman in the mould of Etta Lemon stepped forward to take her place. Even her name had a formidable ring: Miss Gladys Pott.

A 44-year-old, 'not particularly feminine' spinster, Gladys was the daughter of an archdeacon and only sister to many brothers. She had started out as organising secretary to the Berkshire Antis and initially refused to speak in public, claiming she didn't know how – but other women in the league trained her up and soon she was holding the floor in debates all over London and the Home Counties. In December 1911, young suffragist Kate Frye went to watch Miss Pott in action at a pro- and anti-suffrage debate in Notting Hill. 'A most harsh, repellent and unpleasing woman,' wrote Kate in her diary. 'She began by saying we should not get sentiment from her and we did not.' Curzon and Cromer warmed instantly to Miss Pott. She was conscientious and self-effacing, industrious and modest. Just as the name of Mrs Lemon was synonymous with the RSPB, 'Miss Pott' was to become a byword for the Antis. She devoted herself wholeheartedly to the cause.

*

On a bitterly cold night in Manchester in November 1910, Violet Markham shared the public stage with Lord Cromer. The elderly statesman held forth in a voice of absolute authority on 'the qualities mainly required to govern the people of India', while he fixed the audience with penetrating, hooded eyes, his trademark monocle flashing. Markham, 38, kept an admirably impassive face while Cromer listed women's failings, but inside she was simmering. 'Extreme sentimentality,' he began, 'vague and undisciplined sympathies, hasty generalisations, based on inexperience and inaccurate information . . . qualities which are, broadly speaking, characteristic of the majority of the female sex.'

Violet Markham was beginning to suspect that Cromer and Curzon didn't want women to have the vote because they were fundamentally *anti-women*. She was not alone. Mrs Humphry Ward, speaking in conservative Croydon the same month about her 'Forward Policy', warned that she 'did not always agree with the arguments commonly used against women's suffrage'. She was *not* one of those who thought that 'the suffrage question was settled when the women who asked for the vote were bidden to go home and mind their domestic duties'.

There was one negative argument that did unite both male and female Antis, an argument they returned to again and again: women were the weaker sex. 'The addition of the women to the Parliamentary Franchise with no *physical force* would inevitably affect their prestige,' said Mrs Ward, speaking in Reigate at the invitation of Mrs Lemon. Parliament was not just a debating chamber, it was the male force behind it: the heft that controlled the natives in British India and Egypt and East Africa, the strength that subdued civil uprisings on home turf. Women, for all their skill in local government, were deemed 'weak citizens'.

In a private doctor's room in London, Mary Frances Earl, of 39 Raglan Road in the county of Dublin, laid her hand on the Bible and began to describe what had happened to her on the afternoon of Friday 18 November 1910. Some 400 WSPU members, invited by Mrs Pankhurst, had met at Caxton Hall, coming from all over Britain and Ireland to mark the opening of parliament. The hope was that the Conciliation Bill, a bill to enfranchise a million property-owning women, would finally get a fair hearing this session. When word came that Asquith had killed the bill, Emmeline Pankhurst urged her audience to follow her to the House of Commons, where she would deliver yet another petition to the Prime Minister. The women went – and the police were waiting for them. 'The scene down there was terrible,' said Mary Earl, a 40-year-old doctor's wife and mother of two children,

> but the most terrible part to me was the disgusting language used to us by the police, who were, I understand, brought specially from Whitechapel. In the struggle here the police were most brutal and indecent. They deliberately tore my undergarments, using the most foul language – such language as I could not repeat. They seized me by the hair and forced me up the steps on my knees, refusing to allow me to regain my footing. I was then flung into the crowd outside.

The testimonies gathered by Dr Jessie Murray and journalist Henry Brailsford on behalf of the WSPU, to be forwarded to Winston Churchill at the Home Office, were unanimous on the physical might of the police. 'For hours one was beaten about the body, thrown backwards and forward from one to another, until one felt dazed with the horror of it,' another woman testified. 'One policeman picked me up in his arms and threw me into the crowd saying, "You come again, you B–B–, and I will show you what I will do to you."'

Breasts were clutched and twisted, groins were kneed and skirts were lifted. Onlookers were incited by the police to join in. 'Do what you want with her!' the police called, throwing woman after woman jeeringly into the crowd. It was all done in the most public way, one victim testified, 'so as to inflict the utmost humiliation'. The ugly, animal scene was spun out for five hours; a scene of what today we would call sexual assault. In 1910, these middle-class suffragettes – 'well-dressed, in furs', according to a journalist witness – barely had the words to describe it as they gave their testimonies.

A photograph in the *Daily Mirror* the next day showed a slender woman on the ground, large hat pushed backwards, gloved hands covering her face, her WSPU band rucked up under her arm. Towering over her is a top-hatted gentleman and a police officer. Ada Cecile Wright was one of Emmeline's well-heeled intimates; an upper-class woman with a useful house in Westminster. Too late, Churchill ordered the *Mirror* to be seized and the photograph's negative destroyed.

The Home Secretary refused to authorise a public enquiry into the alleged police brutality. His grave mistake – which he did not repeat – had been in asking for policemen from Whitechapel and other East End districts to back up parliament's more gentlemanly 'A Division'. These were officers more used to dealing with public house brawls, brothels and striking factory workers; officers, in other words, from the world of Alice Battershall. Privately, Churchill put the WSPU's gathered testimonies before Sir Edward Henry, Commissioner of the Metropolitan Police.

Sir Edward strenuously denied it all. 'The police are even accused of using their heavy helmets to batter the women,' he wrote in irritation.

> I have had a helmet with all its trappings weighed and find that it is only three and a half ounces heavier than an ordinary silk hat. What may have happened is that when a Constable's helmet was knocked off by a woman he, in his convulsive effort to secure it, may have struck someone with it, but not necessarily intentionally, and certainly a helmet that weighs only 11 ounces cannot be considered heavy.

Parliament had shown the women its physical supremacy. The afternoon of 18 November 1910 went down in the suffragette annals as 'Black Friday'. It was a dark end to a dark year.

33

Maternal Weakness

1911

Mrs Lemon moved magnificently back into the limelight this coronation year. She rode into high office on her husband's coat tails, as wives were then expected to do. 'Married women have all the plums of life!' the veteran suffragist Lydia Becker once complained to Mrs Pankhurst – and this *was* a plum. The year 1911 turned out to be not just George V's, but Etta's coronation year, too. On 9 November, the affable councillor for the borough of Reigate, Frank Edward Lemon, was unanimously voted mayor.

Frank was known to fellow councillors for his courtesy and hospitality, his ability and application, and his able and impartial manner. An official portrait shows a man rather more thickset than in his youth, still with a gentle face, pale blue eyes staring out from pale lashes, small mouth kindly composed beneath a neat, blonde moustache. The heavy chain of office lies in elaborate loops over his shoulders and chest – a piece of regalia effortlessly worn by a Freemason accustomed to dressing up.

A mayor in England, in 1911, held a powerful and hugely respected position. The new mayor was lucky in his wife, noted the *Surrey Mirror* – and perhaps he would not have been elected without such a woman at his side. 'The Mayor-elect will have the advantage of the hearty cooperation and loyal support of Mrs Lemon, a lady of singular charm and culture, and one who is well known and held in high esteem for her many activities on behalf of societies and institutions that are national in their aim and character.' In other words, the mayor's wife was no mere provincial do-gooder.

The official photographic portrait of Mrs Lemon at this time has her toying with a wreath of artificial flowers, but the strong face and unflinching dark eyes suggest she would as soon sweep the whole lot to the floor and take to the podium. She is appropriately (if slightly uncomfortably) attired in satin and lace: very dignified, very Victorian. After her name are the letters MBOU (Member of the British Ornithologists' Union; she was one of the first women members admitted in 1910) and FZS (Fellow of the Zoological Society, which admitted women in 1826). Status mattered to Etta Lemon. She was a woman in her own right, not just the mayor's wife.

But as such, she had her duties. The Lemons had lived all their married life in Redhill and were intimately involved with their community. The small, neighbouring towns of Redhill and Reigate were flanked by the Surrey North Downs in a spot of exceptional beauty, 20 miles south of the capital. It was – and still is – prime commuter belt. Staid and gracious Reigate was where the gentry lived. Redhill, with its mainline train station, seethed with self-confident shopkeepers and tradesmen. The Lemons' house stood aloof from the bustle down below, high on a hill capped by a glorious heathland of gorse, heather and bracken.

Hillcrest was an exhilarating home for a bird lover. Its upper gables looked north towards the distant ridge of the Downs, and south onto the wide expanse of Redhill Common. But nieces and nephews remember it as oddly claustrophobic, too – a series of small, gloomy, downstairs rooms crammed with uncomfortable, dark furniture. The home is still inhabited today, and so one summer's afternoon I walked up the steep hill and rang the doorbell, hoping to be allowed a look around. A pair of outrageous golden sandals lay next to children's wellington boots in the entrance porch, and a bird bath stood by the front door.

Catherine Hutchison had never heard of Mrs Lemon – but she had, of course, heard of the RSPB, so she let me in. The family hadn't lived here long, and had just finished purging the house of its Victorian past. The series of gloomy rooms had been knocked through to bring in the light, as is the modern way. The basement was now damp-proofed and carpeted, but a tiny, Victorian time capsule scullery remained intact, with worn brick floors and a coal-hole. In the attic bedroom, the floorboards still bore grooves from two narrow beds.

Basement and attic were once the domain of Ada and Ellen, Etta's housemaid and cook. These two unmarried women granted Etta Lemon her freedom. It was Ada and Ellen who looked after those reception rooms with heavy fireplaces and prickly horsehair sofas; Ada and Ellen who fed the local worthies around Hillcrest's mahogany dining table – the doctors and vicars, committee heads and sanitary inspectors, teachers and newspaper editors. Some came more eagerly than others, for there was always a lengthy grace before meals – and no alcohol. Mrs Lemon believed in temperance.

Standing in the modern, open-plan kitchen, looking at the distant North Downs through a wall of glass, I tried hard to channel the Lemons. Catherine suddenly remembered an envelope of old papers they had inherited on buying the house, kept in a drawer upstairs. She'd never bothered to look at it properly before, and I tried to contain my excitement as she emptied the contents onto the kitchen counter. Inside was a truly extraordinary cache of Lemon family photographs and legal documents. Why had they been left at Hillcrest? Probably because nobody else had wanted them – not even the RSPB. It was as if, in the absence of children, the house was their rightful inheritor. Hillcrest *was* the Lemons. For 60 years, between 1893 and 1953, it was the backdrop to an unusually closeknit marriage.

One photograph in the envelope intrigued me. Taken outside the front porch, Frank stands with his foot on the bench, eyes on the camera, in a commanding pose. Etta sits in an entirely subservient position, dwarfed by her flower-topped hat, her long skirts spread wide. She looks stoically into the distance. She is the quintessential Victorian wife.

As lady mayoress, Mrs Lemon exemplified perfectly the 'Forward Policy' of the female Antis. Local government, with its 'splendid opportunities for civic betterment and uplifting of the race' (as Violet Markham had put it) was the perfect forum for her formidable talents. She was known locally not just for her role with the RSPB, but as local secretary for the RSPCA, head of Reigate's British Women's Temperance Society, head of the local Red Cross and co-secretary of the Anti-Suffrage League.

Now that Frank held high office, however, Etta was obliged to step back from her Anti activities. While Mrs Pankhurst pushed forward with 'the glorious battle', as she called it, Mrs Lemon could not be seen to be political. By simply embodying womanly capability, with all possible dignity, she tried to send out a strong message to the local faction of the 'shrieking sisterhood'.

Surrey was 'rather a nest of suffragettes', according to a local accountant. Within a 20-mile radius of the Lemon's home resided some of the more notorious names of the campaign for the vote. Militants fresh out of prison recuperated at the Woking home of the composer Ethel Smyth, who that year wrote 'The March of the Women' for the WSPU. They were also hosted at Emmeline and Frederick Pethick-Lawrence's Dutch-style country idyll, The Mascot, in South Holmwood. Strange things happened at The Mascot, went the rumours – unnatural goings-on between women.

The village of Peaslake fairly swarmed with WSPU members, including Marion Wallace Dunlop (no-nonsense in tweeds; the first imprisoned militant to go on hunger strike in 1908) and Hilda Brackenbury (a formidable general's widow, whose two daughters had each served six weeks in Holloway).

Reigate and Redhill's leading suffragist, Helena 'Nellie' Auerbach, was a highly prominent source of irritation to Mrs Lemon, since she moved in the same philanthropic circles and was a firm believer in words, not deeds. Auerbach had no children and rattled around in an immense house bought with her mercantile husband's South African profits, while devoting herself to the cause. She was treasurer for Mrs Fawcett's powerful NUWSS, president of the Jewish Women's Suffrage Society and persistent champion of local women's rights during Frank Lemon's mayoralty.

The well-heeled suffragists of Surrey were matched, like for like, by its Antis. The county seethed with them; with the most prominent Anti of all – Lord Curzon – stirring up support from his sporadically rented country pile, Reigate Priory. The first suffragette novel was that year written just 10 miles north of the Lemons, in Sanderstead, Croydon. Constance Maud, a rector's daughter, was amused by the Antis on her doorstep and had some wicked fun in recreating one for *No Surrender*. The fictional character of Lady Gertrude Thistlethwaite is 'a vision of pale blue chiffon and lace, crowned by an enormous hat of nodding white plumes' (a jibe at the typically 'unconsidered' dress of the upper-class Anti). Lady Thistlethwaite trots out all the stale Curzon and Cromer arguments in a high treble – 'it will be the death of chivalry', and 'as there are certainly a million more women in England than men, before we can look round we shall be under petticoat government'.

Surrey's nest of suffragettes can be tracked down today through the 1911 census – a census that women were encouraged to boycott by the Women's Freedom League. 'No vote, no census' is scrawled across many forms. 'No persons here, only women.' This was the first census that householders themselves were required to fill out; the first to ask more penetrating questions about people's lives. The government was anxious about the imminent decline of Britain's 'imperial race', and wanted to find out whether the lower classes were having more children. The 'Inquiry into Marital Fertility' required the head of the household to state the total number of children born alive to the present marriage, those children still alive and those who had died. 'None,' wrote Frank Lemon on the evening of Sunday 2 April 1911. 'None', and 'None'. In the space for Margaretta Lemon's profession, he struck a dash with his pen.

The message of the National League for Opposing Woman Suffrage was that being a mother was the only importance a woman required. The earlier Women's League emblem showed a mother reading to her young son and daughter. Such women were well balanced, educated and intelligent, it implied. They did not need the vote to make them happy, too. (The WSPU emblem, by contrast, was a winged woman blowing a horn.)

Childless women were largely regarded as unfortunate and neurotic. 'The happy wife and mother is never passionately concerned about the suffrage,' wrote the bushy eyebrowed bacteriologist Sir Almroth Wright, in an extraordinary letter to *The Times* in March 1912. Under the heading 'Militant Hysteria', he argued that not only childless women, but menopausal women, too, were unhinged and a menace to society. Think, he asked his readers, of 'the serious and long-continued mental disorders that develop in connection with the approaching extinction of a woman's reproductive function'. Wright concluded that peace would come again only when the present surplus of women (around one and a half million) had gone to outposts of the empire and found husbands.

Furious letters poured in to the editor. Clementine Churchill, prosuffrage wife of Winston and mother of young Diana and Randolph, wrote: 'After reading Sir Almroth Wright's able and weighty exposition of women as he knows them the question seems no longer to be "Should women have votes?" but "Ought woman not to be abolished altogether?"'. Mrs Humphry Ward was appalled to discover that Curzon and Cromer had turned the 'odious letter' into a pamphlet for Anti propaganda without so much as consulting the women. She and Violet Markham wrote instantly to *The Times* dissociating themselves from Wright's repugnant views.

No doubt Mrs Lemon, breakfasting at Hillcrest's mahogany dining table, also read Sir Almroth Wright's letter in *The Times*. Perhaps, at some level, it hurt. Etta was 51 and childless. The birds had fulfilled many of her maternal urges; they had kept her busy. But they were not enough.

Her sentimental, nurturing streak came to the fore that Christmas, when she hatched a 'gigantic' children's party at the imposing municipal buildings in Reigate. Nobody had done such a thing before. Greeting the children as they swarmed through the imposing redbrick entrance, Mrs Lemon 'captivated the hearts of her numerous guests' with her 'gracious words of welcome and kindly smile', wrote the reporter for the *Dorking and Leatherhead Advertiser*.

With small party hats perched 'grotesquely' on their heads, Frank and

Etta lead the noisy horde into a room with a Christmas tree. Mrs Lemon held up a finger. Silence fell. 'We are all in fairy land,' she said. 'In fairy land strange things happen. Just watch and see.' The lights were switched off and 100 children held their breath. Then the Christmas tree burst into brilliant, electric life.

Frank Lemon became known as 'the children's mayor' for instigating these parties, but they were the work of his wife. This is the woman remembered by RSPB office colleagues as 'The Dragon'; the woman so terrifying that a director of the Natural History Museum hid down a stairwell, rather than face her with a bee in her bonnet. The Christmas party was commemorated by a photograph in which Mrs Lemon stares fondly at a boy in a papier-mâché wolf mask (star of *Little Red Riding Hood*). This boy was their nephew.

Hugh Lemon was born in British Malaya in 1900 to Grace and Arthur, Frank's younger brother, a governor in the colonial service. Aged five, he was shipped back to the mother country to boarding school. Hillcrest was where Hugh spent his school holidays, smothered by the loving attentions of Aunt Etta and Uncle Frank. When Hugh's mother, Grace, swept in with patronising airs on sporadic visits, invariably wearing a hat laden with exotic plumes, Etta was said to have bristled with rage and jealousy. She disapproved of Grace's warped values: a woman who would travel only by first-class rail, but who begrudged money for Hugh's school uniform. The plumed hats were the final straw. Perhaps Grace wore them as a mute challenge to this woman who had stolen her small son's affections.

Five weeks before the May coronation of King George V, the Lemons boarded the steam train at Redhill for the RSPB annual general meeting in town. They were furious. Frank was clasping a copy of the *Daily Mirror*, open at a review of the latest Gaiety Theatre production. It carried a photograph of Gabrielle Ray, 'one of the most beautiful actresses on the London stage' – and one of the most photographed women of the era. On her head was a hat fairly bristling with an alleged '£50-worth of "ospreys"'. This was the type of news story that drew the Lemons ever closer together; the glue, as it were, in their marriage.

The picture of the 'monstrous' hat caused a gratifying sensation at the Westminster Palace Hotel. 'I think those present at this meeting would do well to send some sort of protest,' said Frank, holding up the article, 'to the manager of a theatre who will allow such a thing to appear upon the stage.' This would, of course, be the job of his wife, unpaid society administrator and writer of fulminating letters.

Gabrielle Ray was starring in *Peggy*, a show about a hotel manicurist who sets her sights on snaring a rich husband. It was just the sort of twittering, vacuous role model the suffragists wanted to thrust aside, and it played to packed audiences at the Gaiety for nearly a year. Mrs Lemon's protest was probably thrown, with a grunt, in the wastepaper basket – *Peggy* was simply mirroring what women were wearing on the street that year. 'One of the most important articles of spring and summer will be osprey or aigrette,' reported *Millinery* trade magazine that February, 'which is returning to favour, partly on account of the lower price which has obtained since the last sales, and partly because this decoration is the *enfant chérie* of all French milliners.'

The year 1911 was remembered for many things – a severe heatwave and drought; the National Insurance Act finally pushed through the House of Lords; King George V crowned Emperor of India at the lavish Delhi durbar. It was remembered as a year of unprecedented industrial unrest. A total of 872 strikes broke out 'like foot-and-mouth disease' all over Britain: Singer sewing machine factory workers; National Railway men; the entire transport network of Liverpool; dockers, carters and miners; jam makers, biscuit makers and picklers; men, women – even schoolboys.

Yet 1911 also marked the zenith of the giant 'picture hat'. It did not get any bigger. From now on, hats would begin to shrink. It also marked a peak in the rampant consumerism of the Edwardian (or New Georgian) woman. 'The demand for heron feathers and aigrettes, both in black and white, is exhaustless,' came the Paris report for July's *Millinery* magazine, ' – so much so that one wonders how it can be supplied.'

Appalled, the bird women put their heads together. The audacious idea for the sandwich-board protest came from Mrs Lemon's friend, the 56-year-old novelist Florence Henniker – aristocrat, passionate anti-vivisectionist and muse of author Thomas Hardy (whose wife, Emma Hardy, was a keen suffragist). Florence had seen the suffragettes parading in the street with boards advertising events slung over their shoulders, attracting both jeers and grudging admiration. She had noted how Lady Gertrude Stock's National Canine Defence League had bravely stopped a dog-muzzling bill by employing 'sandwich-men' to parade outside the Houses of Parliament. Could not they attempt something similar for the birds? She, the Honourable Mrs Henniker, would foot the bill.

Of course, it was out of the question that they might carry the boards themselves. To ally yourself with a 'sandwich-man' would be a dreadful travesty, for this was a desperate rank of person. Anyone who had fallen to wearing placards to advertise another's goods was deemed the 'bearer of the most pathetic insignia of poverty and failure'. Such men were readily for hire – but what would the placards say?

Etta Lemon felt that everything that *could* be said had *already* been said. But there was one thing they might yet do.

That August, as the West End's macadam turned sticky under the sun's burning rays, a procession of ten gaunt men marched slowly towards the summer sales. They wore a strange, otherworldly garb of sage green 'gaberdines' and priest-like birettas, and they carried their billboards not slung upon their bodies, but high above their heads, supported on iron shoulder clamps. Their expressions were sombre – whether because of what they were publicising, or because of their station in life, was unclear.

'The Story of the Egret' read the leading man's shoulder board. The next showed a beautiful white 'osprey' adornment of the sort advertised by the *plumassiers*, captioned 'The Badge of Cruelty'. Then came six crisp photographs showing the life cycle of the snowy egret, from nest building, to nuptial display, to brutal extermination (a corpse on the ground, the chicks starving to death). The gruesome story was rounded off with another fashionable 'Badge of Cruelty' headpiece, and a final placard of bold text. It was an unmissable stunt, and as they walked slowly past the seductive windows of Regent Street and Bond Street, shopping women in white lace and pastel chiffon wheeled round, intrigued. Others ducked haughtily into department store doorways, screening out the offending images with their parasols.

The photographs *were* shocking. They brought to the egret's nest the same forensic lens that had pried into working women's homes for the 1906 Sweated Industries' Exhibition in Bayswater, London, or exposed the conditions of New York's feather workers to illustrate Mary Van Kleeck's report. You could ignore the many column inches written on murderous millinery, but you could not ignore the photographs. The Australian ornithologist and photographer Arthur Mattingley had presented them to the RSPB, and these black-and-white images were to prove the society's most valuable piece of propaganda. While the sandwich-men marched, the pictures were also being pasted up at 100 London and suburban railway stations. Other towns would follow suit.

By imitating Mrs Pankhurst's WSPU, the RSPB had finally embraced modern shock tactics. If only they had done so sooner. Languishing in the hold of several ships in the Victoria and Albert Docks that sweltering August – where mountains of food rotted and stock slumped in value by the day – were 618 *tons* of bird-skins and feathers. The striking dockers had brought London, and its commodity auctions, to a standstill.

Of all the efforts employed by the RSPB over the previous two decades, that single image of a nest of starving egret chicks, beaks agape, was thought to be the most effective. It would strike (so Mrs Lemon imagined) like a thunderbolt into a woman's heart. The dominant instinct in a woman was held to be maternal – but there were exceptions.

For just as Arthur Mattingley was scaling a red gum tree in swampy New South Wales with his half-plate camera to capture those deeply affecting scenes of egret family life and death, Emmeline Pankhurst was boarding a trans-Atlantic liner for a lucrative American lecture tour while her 20-year-old son, Harry, lay ill with a spinal inflammation. Delicate and sensitive Harry, a farm worker, was known as 'the only girl in the family'. Christabel saw her mother's decision to leave her sick son as a 'necessity', since she had to earn money to pay for his nursing. A more embittered Sylvia saw it as a question of priorities. 'So ruthless was the inner call to action that . . . there was never a moment of doubt as to where she should be substituted – on the platform or by the bedside of her son,' she wrote of her mother, 20 years later. 'The movement was paramount.'

Harry died in January 1910. Four years later, Emmeline despatched her wayward youngest daughter, Adela, to Australia, rather than have her join forces with a resentful Sylvia and her new East London Federation of working women. Adela was given £20, some warm clothes and a letter of introduction. 'Of course, now all is settled,' Mrs Pankhurst wrote to her; 'I have pangs of maternal weakness, but I harden my heart.' Mother and daughter never saw each other again.

'Mummy's a Suffragette' went the caption on a popular Anti postcard of a baby crying piteously for its mother. Here, too, it was assumed that mothers were the women most susceptible to Anti propaganda. A favourite trope was to show a domestic household upset by an unnatural suffragist mother: the husband holding baby gingerly on his knee while the wife strides out to a political meeting, or else returning from a hard day's work to find no food on the table and his wife nowhere to be seen.

Britain's birth rate was slowing – while Germany was building itself up, inexorably, for war. There was a dawning recognition that Britain, too, must strengthen herself for possible conflict, something that the Antis used to their advantage.

'The German man is manly, and the German woman is womanly,' thundered Lord Cromer at one of his Anti rallies. 'How can we hope to compete against such a nation as this, if we war against nature, and endeavour to invert the natural roles of the sexes? We cannot do so.' Women were 'race regenerators'. They had a duty to breed; to fill the nest with eggs.

The suave cabinet minister and baronet Sir Charles Hobhouse –

ETTA LEMON

prominent Anti and future champion of the Plumage Bill – announced in the Commons that 'The absorption of women in politics would prejudice the number, character and vigour of our future race, would lead to the limitation of their capacity and inclination for maternity, and to their unwillingness and incapacity to manage their home – and home was the primary and eternal unit of social life in all countries.'

Hobhouse, a hay fever sufferer, received in his morning post the next day a letter filled with grass seed and pepper: a little gift from the suffragettes.

The lady mayoresses of England and Wales received in *their* morning post a photographic leaflet showing the life cycle of the snowy egret – corpses, starving chicks and all. Of these, 150 mayoresses wrote back to Mrs F. E. Lemon of the RSPB, promising to 'sympathetically' purge their wardrobes immediately.

At the close of this tumultuous year, on 15 December, suffragette renegade Emily Wilding Davison was arrested outside Parliament Street post office while trying to force a piece of flaming linen steeped in paraffin into a letter box. She had, so she claimed, done the same to two other London postboxes earlier that day and was acting entirely on her 'own responsibility'. No woman had yet used fire in the campaign for the vote. Within a year, arson would be commonplace. Her reckless act of militancy was, wrote Mrs Pankhurst looking back, 'prophetic'.

34

Peak Rage

1912

'I am what you call a hooligan,' Mrs Pankhurst announced to Carnegie Hall – and 3,000 New Yorkers laughed in delight. This petite, middle-aged lady, dressed in a mauve and green velvet coatdress, with flowing sleeves and a white lace blouse, looked to them 'as if she were ready to pour a cup of tea in an English vicarage'.

How she tickled them – and how she moved them. 'The little Englishwoman,' as the *New York Times* called her, had captured the heart of her largely female audience on her first lecture tour of America in October 1909. Reporters who'd been expecting England's most notorious militant to be a 'bold, coarse, aggressive, unfeminine woman', found themselves listening to a speaker of 'attractive voice, of refinement, and of rare ability'. A hooligan!

But she was. Her appearance was the perfect disguise.

In February 1912, Mrs Pankhurst felt that the suffrage movement had reached 'crisis point'. Asquith – in a typically craven move – had used the King's Speech to announce a surprise reform bill for men only. This was an extraordinary piece of treachery, thought the *Saturday Review*: 'With absolutely no demand, no ghost of a demand, for more votes for men, and with – beyond all cavil – a very strong demand for votes for women, the Government announce their Manhood Suffrage Bill and carefully evade the other question! For a naked, avowed plan of gerrymandering no Government surely ever did beat this one.'

Mrs Pankhurst, who was again raising cash by lecturing in America, was more explicit. *'Protest imperative,'* she cabled to WSPU head office. Back home, she came up with a plan of action. She wrote a veiled note to her friend Ethel Smyth: 'On Friday there will be an unannounced affair, a sort of skirmish, in which some of our bad, bold ones will take part.'

Women huddled in winter furs thronged the wide streets that branched off Piccadilly Circus. It was five o'clock on Friday 1 March: prime shopping time. The windows of the International Fur Store on Regent Street enticed consumers with astrakhan, chinchilla, sealskin and Arctic fox. At Liberty, the silhouette was long, loose and exotically coloured, a radically new look that was all the rage since Diaghilev brought his Ballets Russes to Covent Garden the previous June: harem pants, embroidered Russian dresses, Cossack coats and jewelled diadems for the liberated woman's head.

At Swan & Edgar, on Piccadilly Circus, Paul Poiret's 'hobble skirt' was still in vogue; a difficult fashion to wear, for the tiny, geisha-like steps it imposed on a woman. Just when the struggle for female emancipation had reached a new height of militancy, it was ironic that ladies should choose to wear skirts that were so restrictive.

Nobody noticed the women who lingered in front of shop windows, their hands concealed within soft fur muffs. They looked just like any other fashionable shopper huddled up against the cold, breath frosting the air as they gazed at the luxuries within.

As St James's Church struck the half hour, a loud crashing and splintering of plate glass sang out along the length of Haymarket and Piccadilly. Shoppers screamed and scattered; horses shied, dragging carriages across the road. Feathered hats fell from window displays and rolled into gutters, dusted with sparkling shards of glass. Shop girls stared, open-jawed in shock. *Women* were calmly, deliberately, breaking windows with little toffee hammers – a tool normally used for breaking up slabs of confectionary. Caped policemen ran this way and that, arresting and dragging the culprits away. But it was not the end.

Before the police had reached Marylebone police station with their arrests, the ominous noise resumed again, this time on Regent Street. A furious rush of policemen and bowler-hatted pedestrians charged towards the scene – but then exactly 15 minutes later, a *third* relay of women began breaking the windows in Oxford Circus and down the length of Bond Street. At half past six, it was the turn of the Strand.

The militant suffragette Charlotte 'Charlie' Marsh later remembered how she perfected the technique, by wielding her hammer 'broadside'. 'I walked down the Strand as though I was playing hockey, and I just boldly went on like that, and I did at least nine windows.' Charlie was among the 121 women arrested for breaking nearly 400 shop windows, causing an estimated £5,000 worth of damage (around £454,000 today). The shopping quarter of London 'plunged itself into a sudden twilight', reported the *Daily Mail*. 'Shutters were hurriedly fitted; the rattle of iron curtains being drawn came from every side. Guards of commissionaires and shopmen were quickly mounted, and any unaccompanied lady in sight, especially if she carried a handbag, became an object of menacing suspicion.'

Three days later, on the morning of Monday 4 March, the suffragettes surprised everybody by setting to work on Knightsbridge. They smashed nearly every shop window they passed.

This was beyond the pale. In the space of a weekend, between Friday and Monday, Mrs Pankhurst lost the support of the public – and made headlines from New York to New Zealand. 'Never since plate glass was invented has there been such a smashing and shattering of it as was witnessed this evening,' reported the *New York Times*. A harsher penalty was urged upon the leader of the WSPU for inciting this violence with her now infamous 'argument of the broken pane of glass' (she herself had smashed a window at 10 Downing Street). The suffragettes had 'brought the country to a state which was not allowed in any other civilised land', blustered a magistrate.

The Antis were in ecstasies. 'These wild women,' Curzon pronounced, 'are in a sense the most capable recruiting sergeants that we could have, and every one of them is an unconscious agent for our cause.'

Why did they do it? Many of the businesses they targeted were their advertisers and personal couturiers; the streets their favoured recruiting grounds. The West End was more justifiably a battleground for the anti-plumage RSPB ladies, handing out 'Badge of Cruelty' pamphlets and mobilising sandwich-men parades. But for the suffragettes, fashionistas par excellence, it seemed wilfully perverse. Mrs Pankhurst's argument, that voting store owners were responsible for the acts of MPs, did not wash with the public. To the vast majority of British citizens, this was pure vandalism.

Millicent Fawcett was furious. All that careful, constitutional work towards gaining a measure of suffrage for women – undone, as she saw it, in the space of one hour. She wrote swiftly to Chancellor Lloyd George, begging him to remember, in the light of the 'deplorable proceedings of the Militant Suffragists', that the guilty were 'a small and decreasing minority'. There were, she reckoned, just a few hundred hard-core women whose names came up before the magistrates again and again. She pleaded for him not to punish 'the great mass of law-abiding suffragists for the faults of the small section of law-breakers' by withholding his support for the Conciliation Bill that would extend the right of women to vote.

Who were the window breakers; those 'bad bold ones' at the WSPU's core? The Brackenbury daughters, Georgina and Marie were two, Surrey neighbours of the Lemons; Mrs Janie Terrero, a composer from Pinner in Essex, was also among them. 'Arrested March 1st 1912 for window-smashing; sentenced to four months, endured forcible feeding,' reads Terrero's entry in the *Suffrage Annual and Women's Who's Who*, along with 'Recreation: Croquet'.

Zoe Proctor, sister of the formidable headmistress of Surbiton High School, was also sent to Holloway for her relatively minor deed that day. Inspired by Christabel Pankhurst's impassioned speech urging women to take action, she had timidly tapped her toffee hammer against several small panes of an old-fashioned silversmith's shop on the Strand, breaking them all.

There were also angry aristocrats in their number. The Honourable Evelina Haverfield, an instinctive horsewoman who had perfected a technique of making police horses sit down during demonstrations, had attempted to lead mounts out of a police cordon. There were, too, bird-lovers with other axes to grind. Joan 'Lavender' Baillie Guthrie, former RSPB member, was sentenced to six months' imprisonment in Holloway for wilful damage. The window she had chosen belonged to Garrard & Co, the famous jewellers in Albemarle Street. It was a protest at the opulent Edwardian lifestyle she had come to abhor.

Remarkably, the damaged shops continued to advertise in *Votes for Women* and court the suffragette's custom, despite the WSPU's vexed relationship with the law. For Swan & Edgar, Liberty, Pontings *et al*, it was business as usual within the week.

If 1911 was the year of 'peak hat', 1912 was the year of peak rage. Window smashing were followed by outbreaks of arson, which was followed by physical assault. In vain, Mrs Lemon continued her dogged campaign to push a bill through parliament to halt the trade in exotic bird-skins. But how could the RSPB compete with a distraction of this magnitude? All eyes were on the suffragettes. All papers were obsessed with the disappearance of Christabel Pankhurst, who had (so it was said) swapped a close-fitting pink straw hat for the large floppy one she habitually wore and vanished into thin air. The florid-faced Chief Inspector Scantlebury had 100 detectives on her case: she was wanted for conspiracy. Where *was* Christabel?

The RSPB's central committee was united in its antipathy towards the Pankhursts and their wild women. But it was also increasingly infuriated by the House of Commons. For 20 years now, the British Royal Society for the Protection of Birds and the American Audubon Society had been campaigning, separately, for legislation to thwart the milliners. The plumage trade had fought back robustly on both sides of the Atlantic –

but in America the bird lovers had prevailed. First came the Lacey Act in 1900, making it a crime to poach and sell protected species. Now, in 1912, came the Plumage Act, 'to prohibit the sale, hire or exchange of the plumage and skins of certain wild birds' – which stopped them from leaving or entering the country.

Women graciously disembarking from liners at New York's docks were appalled to have all 'ornamental feather trim' removed from their hats by newly empowered customs officials. The conservationist Thomas Pearson, driving force of the Audubon Society, gleefully noted the 'hundreds and even thousands' of women being 'relieved of their decorations so proudly borne aloft as evidence of recent visits to London or Paris millinery-houses'. When the *Lusitania* docked, one passenger was followed to her downtown hotel and her feather hats seized as she checked in.

While this made for titillating headlines in the *New York Times* – 'Hold up of Five Hats' – the motivation behind the act was deadly serious. Here, finally, was a cast-iron law for Britain to emulate. But the British government seemed to want only to listen to the protestations of the plumage trade. Its most vigorous defender was Charles Downham, managing director of Sciana & Co, ostrich and fancy feather merchants. Downham spent long hours before Parliamentary committees demolishing arguments put up by the bird 'faddists and fanatics'. The exotic feathers were, he said, 'harvested' humanely. What's more, it was a highly valuable British trade.

That year, farmed ostrich plumes worth £2.2 million, weighing a total of 428 tonnes (the weight equivalent of a shipment of 250 cars), were exported from the Cape to Great Britain – the largest gross income for plumes ever seen. This was nearly three times the amount imported by France, and five times that of Germany. In the same year, £772,000 worth of ostrich plumes were processed and re-exported from Britain, the bulk destined for the United States. It was a massive industry. If the trade for exotic bird skins was stopped, Downham argued, it would have a knock-on effect on the fortunes of the ostrich feather.

The Board of Trade kept a protective eye on the feather industry. But its new president, Sydney Buxton, was in a difficult position – he was also honorary treasurer for the RSPB. Buxton wondered if a compromise could be brokered between the bird lovers and the feather dealers. He set up a 'Committee for the Economic Preservation of Birds' (a brilliantly twisted title), and he invited to his table representatives of the millinery trade, the London Chamber of Commerce, the Zoological Society and the Selborne Society – that old, antagonistic rival of the RSPB.

The Reverend Francis Orpen Morris – he who had once accused the women of stealing his Plumage League idea – was long dead. But the Selborne Society had continued to develop in its idiosyncratic way, and was now, astonishingly, making its bed with the plumage trade. Better to work with it than against it, went the thinking. Perhaps captive-bred birds could supply the needed feathers? It was an unprincipled move that disgusted Mrs Lemon, and she sought to distance her own society at once. When the Board of Trade invited the RSPB to join its new committee, Mrs Lemon refused to take part. This was highly embarrassing for Sydney Buxton, a man with a foot in each camp.

The truth was that the plumage trade's reputation had been damaged by the long campaign against murderous millinery, and particularly by the crusade against the osprey. It was beginning to seem a furtive and rather grubby business. To bolster its reputation, the trade began to strike back with its own propaganda. The most inventive of these leaflets gave the testimony of one Léon Laglaise, a French plumage hunter working from Venezuela. Monsieur Laglaise vowed he had seen with his own eyes hundreds of egrets bred in wire pens, their moulted nuptial plumage gathered from the ground. The RSPB responded with all the contempt that such a fanciful report deserved. Back and forth the arguments went; back and forth. *The Feather Trade: The Case for the Defence* (1911). *Feathers and Facts: A Reply to the Feather-Trade* (1911). It resembled a boxing bout, or a debate between suffragists and Antis.

Now the Liberal government appeared to be siding with the plumage men, with a view to obstructing the RSPB's cherished goal of legislation.

At the end of 1912, a crisis meeting was called at the Westminster Palace Hotel, and the RSPB council came to a grim resolution: 'that the Honorary Secretary be empowered to take any step which might appear desirable to *frustrate the efforts* being made by the Plumage merchants.' The Honorary Secretary was Frank Lemon – but this meant, of course, his wife.

Mrs Pankhurst had uttered a similar battle cry at the Royal Albert Hall before the window-smashing episode: 'I incite this meeting to rebellion! Let each of you be rebellious in your own way.' Did anybody hear the echoing battle cry of the RSPB? Given the background of unfolding anarchy in Britain that year – the 'great unrest', as it became known – feathers were not high on the nation's agenda. Mrs Lemon, who had so many other concerns as wife of the Mayor of Reigate and behind-the-scenes Anti, might have felt a momentary sense of weariness. But if she did, she pushed it aside. The success of the Audubon Society had filled her with a new determination.

America's Plumage Bill had been passed because of the impassioned pleas of conservationists to politicians. One ornithologist, Henry Oldys, had chastened the heart of Congress by standing up and making a passionate, eloquent speech. The spirit of the age was, he said, marked by ignorance, cupidity and supineness – a toxic combination that was steadily exterminating creation. 'History will not listen to the plea, "It was not my business",' he cried. 'It will answer: "You were there and could have prevented it; therefore, it was your business. You failed to do your duty. The only explanation is that you were corrupt, ignorant, or weak."'

This was the same spirit that drove the Pankhursts. It *was* their business. Nobody else was going to do it with such urgency, and with such passion. And so Sylvia Pankhurst, dismayed by the direction the WSPU was taking, decided to strike out on her own.

Her mother seemed to have gone mad. In October 1912, she had summoned the Pethick-Lawrences – the inspired driving force (and ready cash) behind the WSPU – and told them that their services were no longer needed. 'Mrs Pankhurst was the acknowledged autocrat of the Union,' Fred summed up, looking back. He was, he said, 'shattered'. But as a man among female leaders, it was felt he was surplus to the cause. His wife, 'Pethers', was more phlegmatic. 'There was something quite ruthless about Mrs Pankhurst and Christabel where human relationship was concerned. Men and women of destiny are like that,' she added. 'The Pankhursts did nothing by halves!'

The cartoonists got to work. 'Are you a Peth or a Pank?' hisses an elegant, osprey-wearing suffragette to another in a darkened private club (*Punch* magazine). The WSPU was riven by infighting and slander. Christabel was in exile in Paris, urging on her adoring followers back home to greater acts of violence: electric cable cutting, cricket pavilion burning, the slashing of train carriage seats. When Sylvia, recovering from the horrors of force-feeding at Holloway Gaol, visited her sister, she found her strolling around Parisian shops, her tiny Pomeranian dog 'Wispoo' tucked under one arm. She felt that she and Christabel had nothing in common any more.

Sylvia Pankhurst was an angry woman, and she alighted upon an equally angry corner of London to heal her wounds. Unlike her sister and her mother, Sylvia had not deserted her socialist principles. She wanted to reconnect with the working-class roots of the women's suffrage movement, and she chose to do so in Bow. Here, in London's impoverished East End, she could reinvent herself not as the slighted, less attractive middle Pankhurst sister – but as a heroine and saviour of working-class women.

She rented an empty baker's shop at 198 Bow Road, erected a platform outside and painted 'VOTES FOR WOMEN' across the front in gold. Then she turned straight away to face the bemused street and began to address it. Being a Pankhurst, she had ensured the presence of a photographer to capture these first moments of the 'East London Federation' of the WSPU. The images show a suspicious but not unfriendly small crowd – mostly sharp-faced boys in caps, with hesitant women hovering on the fringes. Sylvia leans forward from the scaffold: theatrical, confident.

This wasn't a Victorian slummer lecturing them about temperance and hygiene. It wasn't a missionary or a social worker. Sylvia Pankhurst was calling for equal pay for equal work and an end to the 'sweating trades' – the ostrich feather curlers, the hat box and artificial flower makers, the fur pickers and so on. She believed that, with the right encouragement, women like Alice Battershall could bring about change themselves; they didn't need a Christabel in a paradise hat to plead on their behalf. The women of Bow turned out to be surprisingly receptive – and highly protective of their new champion.

Christabel was infuriated by her sister's perverse insistence on fighting alongside working-class women. It was, she wrote to her, 'a mistake to use the weakest for the struggle! We want picked women, the very strongest and most intelligent.' But Sylvia, sensitive middle daughter of the suffrage movement's most powerful matriarch, felt strangely at home among the oppressed and downtrodden. Having weathered an arguably damaging upbringing, she found her solace among the women of Bow.

35

The Feeding Tube

1913

The prison authorities typically gave a hunger-striking suffragette three days. Three days to come to her foolish senses while plates of hot food were held under her nose. Three days of coaxing, castigation or punishment – perhaps in the solitary confinement cell, hands cuffed in front of the body, palms facing outwards. And when she would not budge (and none of them would, on point of honour), she would be lead to the prison doctor's room.

The first published testimony of forcible feeding came from Mary Leigh, a 24-year-old, dark-eyed teacher of 'sturdy constitution', imprisoned in Birmingham's Winson Green Gaol after hurling roof slates at Mr Asquith in September 1909. What Mrs Leigh saw in the doctor's room was enough, she said, to terrify the bravest. In the centre of the room was a stout chair resting on a cotton sheet. Against the wall, 'as if ready for action', stood the matron and eight wardresses. A nervous junior doctor was also on hand. The senior doctor addressed her with authority. He had, he said, been ordered not to release her, even on medical grounds. If Mrs Leigh still refused to eat, he would have to compel her to take food by 'other measures'.

She refused. 'I was then surrounded and forced back on to the chair,' she told her solicitor, 'which was tilted backwards. There were about ten persons around me. The doctor then forced my mouth so as to form a pouch, and held me while one of the wardresses poured some liquid from a spoon.' Physically worn out from the struggle, Mary Leigh recovered for two days in her cell – yet worse was to come.

The wardresses returned, forced her onto the narrow bed and held her down, two women at each limb. The doctors then produced a rubber tube, two yards in length, which they began to insert clumsily up her right nostril. The pain was so dreadful that she screamed repeatedly. Three of the wardresses burst into tears and the junior doctor begged his senior to stop, but these orders came from the government, and the tube had to be forced 20 inches into Mrs Leigh's body until it reached her stomach. Standing upon a chair, the chief doctor held the rubber tube high and fitted a funnel to its end. Into this he poured liquid food: a pint of milk mixed with beaten eggs.

Mary Leigh, die-hard militant, felt herself begin to suffocate. In mounting panic, she struggled and kicked, but they held her down. 'The drums of my ears seemed to be bursting,' she said. 'I could feel a horrible pain in the throat and the breast.' When at last the tube was withdrawn, it felt 'as if the back of my nose and throat were being torn out with it'. The ordeal was repeated daily, using alternate nostrils, for five weeks.

By 1913, around 1,000 suffragettes had been sent to prison, and hundreds began using the hunger strike as a political tool. It was excellent propaganda. Along with her daughter Sylvia, Mrs Pankhurst turned fasting into an art form, unnerving the politicians and securing a quick release. But she did not receive quite the same rough treatment as builder's wife Mary Leigh. Once out of the foul, urine-smelling remand cells of the police office, Emmeline would be transferred to a category A Holloway cell and allowed her own furniture, eiderdown, warm clothing and writing equipment. Plates of superior food would be placed, temptingly, before her.

And so the drawn-out game would begin, until the infuriated prison authorities considered keeping this wasting, bird-like, fervent woman alive with the rubber tube. But they never managed to get near her. In May 1912, she threatened her would-be force-feeders with an earthen toilet ewer and was promptly released. Incarceration had an inflaming effect on Mrs Pankhurst. She described herself as 'a human being in the process of being turned into a wild beast'.

There is something peculiarly avian about the ritual of force-feeding. The probing long tube, the deep delivery of slithery nourishment: it puts one in mind of a long-billed bird (the snowy egret or the cormorant) feeding its young with invasive force.

Popular cartoonists illustrated the drama of force-feeding with savage humour. One postcard shows the male prison warden, his recently scratched face bandaged, holding a prone woman by the ankles while the prison doctor pours 'SOUP' down a funnel forced into her mouth. The cheerful doctor's foot rests masterfully on the woman's chest, while her hips are held down by a '1CWT' block – a hundredweight, or eight stone. 'Feeding a Suffragette by Force' reads the caption.

The WSPU hit back with its own poster: 'The Modern Inquisition: Treatment of Political Prisoners Under a Liberal Government.' At the centre of six black-garbed persecutors is a slender, well-dressed woman writhing in terror. Over her head is the feeding tube, held high. 'Electors! Put a stop to this Torture by voting against the Prime Minister.' Since the new century dawned, there had been gruesome posters showing canine vivisection; there had been emotive photographs showing the slaughter of the snowy egret; and now, here were billboards showing the barbaric torture of women. How had society come to this?

'They prize open my mouth with a steel gag,' wrote Sylvia Pankhurst to her mother from Holloway Gaol in February 1913, 'pressing it in where there is a gap in my teeth. I resist all the time and my gums are always bleeding . . . My shoulders are bruised with struggling whilst they hold the tube into my throat and force it down.' Sylvia had feared for her emotional state, but was relieved to find it was just her digestion that was suffering.

This could not continue. There was public revulsion, and the government was increasingly uneasy. In April 1913, three and a half years after the first force-feeding, a new bill was rushed through parliament just in time for Mrs Pankhurst's next prison sentence. The 'Cat and Mouse' Act, as it quickly became known, ruled out feeding prisoners by force. Instead, it released hunger strikers until they had recovered, then recaptured them. The cat played with the mouse.

It made not a jot of difference to Mrs Pankhurst. April 1913 was her most triumphant hour yet, a highly public trial in which her nimble mind had the judiciary tied up in knots. She was accused of inciting to commit a felony, namely the February bombing of Chancellor Lloyd George's new house in Walton-on-the-Hill, Surrey (five miles distant from the Lemon household). Truthfully, she had nothing to do with the outrage, and the only trace of the culprits was two broken hat pins, a hairpin and a ladies' galosh – but Emmeline Pankhurst was quick to claim responsibility. 'We have blown up the Chancellor of the Exchequer's house . . . to wake him up,' she announced to the press. 'I have advised, I have incited, I have conspired.'

Then came the blow. She was sentenced to an unprecedented three years in prison. 'Shame!' cried her supporters, crammed into the Old Bailey courtroom. 'Shame!' They clambered onto their chairs in the confusion and began to sing the 'Women's Marseillaise' as their leader was led out of the dock, a wardress on either side. *March on! March on! Face to the dawn, The dawn of liberty . . .'*

Emmeline was plunged into a new rhythm of incarceration, hunger strike, release and rearrest. This was the year she served 42 days in 10 separate imprisonments. Ironically, the Cat and Mouse Act helped to keep this 54-year-old permanently in the public eye.

After a much-publicised nine-day hunger strike at Holloway, a swarm of detectives and journalists followed a 'half-alive' Mrs Pankhurst to her friend Ethel Smyth's house in Woking – not too far from the Lemons of Redhill. Here the government's 'cats' prowled, crouching in hedgerows, peering through windows, standing motionless under umbrellas, waiting for the mouse to recover her health.

'She was heartrending to look on,' reported Ethel Smyth, 'her skin yellow, and so tightly drawn over her face that you wondered the bone structure did not come through.' Her burning eyes were sunk deep; her cheeks were flushed dark. What horrified Ethel most was a 'strange, pervasive, sweetish odour of corruption'. She dearly hoped that Mrs Pankhurst – 'the most meticulously dainty of beings' – was unaware that her body gave off this smell. 'She would have minded that almost more than anything.' Really it was Ethel who minded: the hearty, tweedy composer had long nursed a private passion for her feminine idol.

Forty-four days later, a frail Emmeline was rearrested attempting to get to a WSPU meeting at the London Pavilion. Five more days of hunger strike ensued, followed by seven days' release on a special 'licence'. On Mrs Pankhurst's sixth day of licensed freedom, suffragette Emily Wilding Davison rushed in front of King George V's horse at Epsom Derby with the cry: 'Votes for Women!' This renegade member of the WSPU (arrested 9 times, force-fed on 49 occasions) was thought to be trying to attach a purple, green and white banner to the royal horse's bridle as it thundered round Tattenham Corner. Davison died from internal injuries four days later, on 8 June 1913.

All of smart society had been watching. Queen Alix's thoughts were for the horse, Anmer (who escaped with bruised shins), and for the jockey (concussed with broken ribs). She sent Herbert Jones a telegram, wishing him well after his 'sad accident caused through the abominable conduct of a brutal lunatic woman'.

Mrs Pankhurst was determined to attend Emily Wilding Davison's funeral on Saturday 14 June, but as soon as she left her Westminster sanctuary she was promptly rearrested. And so the WSPU's 'Commander-in-Chief' missed this minutely choreographed procession – a mass of 6,000 women following the hearse: those in black with bunches of purple irises, those in purple carrying red peonies, and a long column of women in white with Madonna lilies (all of these last in hats, many topped by a wind-ruffled osprey, as the old news reels show). She did not have the gratification of seeing the public mourning this unknown young woman; silent citizens craning their necks as the hearse went past. It was the suffragette movement's most effective propaganda moment yet.

While Emmeline Pankhurst began a gruelling 'thirst strike' at Holloway, she might have felt that she was no longer at the heart of this great movement. She was its figurehead, yet she was also somehow superfluous. Hands other than hers were now orchestrating arson attacks and marches; voices other than hers were shaping the WSPU's new paper, *The Suffragette*, and writing slogans for propaganda posters. Physically diminished, out of sight, Mrs Pankhurst was no longer at the helm.

36

Dumb Creation

1913

A country scene: 20 glossy horses are trampling the turf to clicks and calls of encouragement. These animals are walking, slowly – heavy carthorses, their fetlocks and forelocks groomed to a fluff, brass tack shining against the great wishbone curve of leather collars. Men and boys in Sunday best (waistcoats, white shirts, ties) lead their charges gently along the green to Reigate Town Hall. As they pass the mayor and mayoress, they doff tweed caps deferentially. Unhurriedly, the horses pass the admiring judges. Women in provincial summer hats – complicated arrangements of flowers and ostrich plumes – dance attendance on municipal clerks and aldermen in straw boaters.

It was Etta Lemon who started an annual parade for the horses of Reigate's Corporation in 1912, and the event was typical of her. The celebration of working horses and working men; the RSPCA judges honing in on animal welfare rather than gleaming tack; the orderly procession, prize-giving and tea. While Mrs Pankhurst was seeking martyrdom through hunger strikes ('O kind fate that cast me for this glorious role in the history of women!'), Mrs Lemon's feet were resolutely on the ground. And so her narrative does not – cannot – take flight in the same way. The restlessly theatrical Emmeline eclipses Etta's quiet moments of satisfaction.

These two women of the same age, so attuned to the idea of greater good, so passionate about their particular causes, no longer seem to occupy the same sphere. Emmeline is almost an abstract idea, a demi-deity. As Lloyd George exclaimed about the Pankhurst leadership: 'It's just like going to a lunatic asylum and talking to a man who thinks he's God Almighty.' Etta continues to embody what she knows best: the conservative, Christian values of the late nineteenth century. If Mrs Pankhurst is the jewel-green parakeet on the wing, calling out with piercing, insistent voice, Mrs Lemon is the brindled woodcock on the ground, hunkering down beneath the shadow of the raptor high above.

England was changing. It wasn't just the newly assertive spirit of protest among the working classes: the strikes, marches and industrial unrest bringing Britain to its knees. Nor was it just the arson attacks of 1913, particularly outrageous because they were committed by *women*. The targets – St Catherine's Church in Hatcham, London; a Liberal politician's mansion in St Leonards-on-Sea, Sussex; Rusholme Exhibition Hall in Manchester – were reduced to jagged, smoking silhouettes that unnerved the public, incensed the Home Office and sold newspapers. There was an unsettling feeling that the very countryside itself was changing: the soft, green counterpane of rural England.

On the afternoon of Saturday 31 May, 1,000 spectators gathered above Reigate on Colley Hill – an exhilaratingly high spot at the spur of the North Downs, with far-reaching views over the wooded Weald of Sussex and Surrey. An early summer breeze swayed the tall stems of lady's smock and buttercup, and the tread of human feet upon closely nibbled downland released the scent of chamomile and thyme. Pink-purple orchids would be pushing up any day now, observed Mrs Lemon from her vantage point in the mayoral carriage, for the larks were in full voice, high up above. The crowd knew her well as a vigorous campaigner, a formidable woman in her own right. But she was also a wife, and today her place was at her husband's side. She stole a proud glance: Mayor Frank Lemon, imposing in his gold chain of office and dark Victorian tailoring, looking down upon the crowd with his customary genial smile. And standing next to them on an improvised podium, urbane in brilliant black top hat and frock coat, was Lord Curzon of Kedleston

– RSPB vice president and leader of the National League for Opposing Woman Suffrage.

Mrs Lemon might have been forgiven for savouring her achievement on this early summer's day. To mark the crowning moment of her husband's reign as mayor, Lord Curzon had been persuaded to travel to Reigate to conduct the ceremony. Curzon's beliefs chimed absolutely with their own. The Antis were growing: by 1913 there were 270 league branches, with over 33,000 members. (Mrs Fawcett's non-militant NUWSS had by now 50,000 members; the Pankhursts' WSPU just 2,000.) The wave of suffragette militancy was playing directly into the Antis' hands. Thirteen paintings slashed at Manchester Art Gallery last month! The North Oxford Cricket and Bowling Club green disfigured by acid! Lloyd George's house at Walton-on-the-Hill had been bombed in February, scarcely a mile and a half from Colley Hill. League members were confident of victory. But Mrs Lemon was not a woman to rest on her laurels, and she knew that there were other, more important battles ahead.

With smooth authority, Lord Curzon addressed the sea of upturned faces. London, he said, was growing. Britain's capital was 'spreading out to clutch at them'. The crowd murmured, shifting on its feet. Never more at home than on a podium, Curzon warmed to his theme. He had, he said, been unpleasantly struck by the changes observed on his drive down this afternoon. The city was encroaching on the countryside. London was 'like a great octopus, stretching out its tentacles in order to lay hold on the rich pastures and leafy lanes'. The attending journalists wrote furiously. 'We must defeat it,' Curzon cried, pausing for cheers from the crowd. 'For on a glorious spot like the top of this hill, we find breezes blowing that are enough to give new life to an entire people!' (More cheers.)

Lord Curzon then spoke of the invisible casualties of Britain's success story. The country, he said, needed its green spaces. They were needed for the *people* (and it was, right now, political to say so): 'as an outlet for our urban population, stunned by the noise, jaded by the excitements, fatigued by the burdens of life in the towns of England.' But they were also needed to protect Britain's wildlife. This vice president of the RSPB knew about declining bird populations in the south-east; the rare cirl bunting, the plum-bellied Dartford warbler, the red-backed shrike with its chuckling, scolding song. He knew that their alarming disappearance from the hills of Sussex and Surrey had nothing to do with the fashion for feathers in hats.

To applause, Lord Curzon handed Frank Lemon the title deeds for the land on which they stood. The 60 acres of Colley Hill would henceforward be stewarded by the National Trust, now in its 18th year. It would not be built upon. The ridge would serve as a green buffer zone against the encroachment of London. Blackheath and Croydon had long ago been swallowed; the great octopus would *not* consume Redhill and Reigate.

This would be Mayor Lemon's most enduring legacy: an invaluable contribution to the preservation of the English countryside and its wildlife. He had overseen the raising of an immense £5,500 to thwart the speculators and developers – but could the tide of progress and expansion be turned back? Colley Hill was a tiny spot on a fast-changing island. Motorcars were everywhere, sending up plumes of dust; road surveyors were cutting down miles of hedgerow. Curzon was harking back, nostalgically, to a former age; an age before the countryside of England was 'cut up in plots for the building of houses'.

Fear of suburbia was replacing fear of the slum. The 'red rust' creep, as writer E. M. Forster put it, was the coming reality. 'Life's going to be melted down, all over the world,' predicted Margaret Schlegel in the novel *Howards End*, published in 1910. 'London is only part of something else, I'm afraid.'

Etta Lemon responded to the threat by retrenching. Like a hen, she sought to protect her chicks. Rather than making her disquiet known through militancy, she focused on things that would make a small but significant difference. The wider political picture was, in any case, beyond her control. In March 1913, the Plumage Bill had come before the House of Commons a second time. It received two readings but was shelved in June, derailed by trade interests. This was the month that the skins of some 77,000 egrets, 25,000 hummingbirds and 162,000 kingfishers came under the hammer in Mincing Lane.

On hearing that the bill had been dropped, yet again, Gertrude Ansell – a militant suffragette and passionate member of the RSPB – went straight out and smashed a window at the Home Office in frustration. The 52-year-old businesswoman promptly received a month's prison sentence, which she began with a hunger strike.

Mrs Lemon reacted differently.

Long dismayed by the large numbers of migrating birds dying at lighthouses, disorientated by the bright lights, she came up with the imaginative idea of lighthouse perches. 'Bird refuges' – great slats fitted around each tower – were erected in 1913 at Alderney, the Isle of Wight and at three points around the Welsh coast. To the east, guarding the sandy mouth of the Humber estuary, another lighthouse was fitted up. The perches were to be dismantled and cleaned twice a year after each migration. For this Lemon-like level of detail – a necklace of pristine perches at Britain's jagged extremities – the RSPB bore all expenses.

Etta Lemon was deeply rooted in Redhill and Reigate, but her responsibilities were spread wide across the British Isles. The system of 22 'watchers' at ten breeding spots around the country was her idea and special responsibility. She communicated with her 'boys' by letter and she visited them in person – from Dungeness to Cumberland, Anglesey to the Orkneys. Hen harrier, chough and buzzard; rock pipit, whimbrel and sandpiper – all were safer thanks to Mrs Lemon's personal perseverance.

After Lord Curzon's speech up on Colley Hill, a spectacular pageant unfolded against the backdrop of the North Downs. Along the old Pilgrim's Way came a Chaucerian procession of friars and nuns, knights on horseback, ladies riding donkeys, coarse-cloaked peasants and lords in doublet and hose. The 1000-strong crowd followed this theatrical parade (influenced, it must be said, by the suffragists' own pageants), down the slopes to a field at the foot of the hill. And here, among the ox-eye daisies and cow parsley, the citizens of Redhill and Reigate enjoyed some very old English games: tilting at the quintain, Morris and maypole dancing. The sun set slowly, and the surrounding woodland released its scent of bluebells. Later still, the nightingale could be heard, and as the mayor and mayoress's carriage finally left the scene, ethereal glow-worms drifted among the tall grasses.

This pre-war scene is suffused with an innocence that already felt fragile, elegiac. Its mood was captured again at Mrs Lemon's annual horse parade in August that year; the names of the men's horses – even the names of the men themselves – seem to belong to another, gentler, pre-industrial world. Tom Brewer and Nobby, John Apps and Taffy, Tom Withers leading Champion and William Jennings with Jolly – all walked their horses slowly up to Mrs Lemon, who presented each man with a card, and each horse with a carrot.

A photographer for the *Surrey Mirror* captured the scene, giving us the only blurred, off-guard picture we have of her. Mrs Lemon is smiling spontaneously, transformed by this moment of intimate contact between carter and horse. Gone is the severe, beaky glare. Etta Lemon, in the act of handing out a carrot, is almost beautiful. 'The love of dumb creation by the mayoress is well known,' reported the *Surrey Mirror*, in the language of the time, 'and this was amply demonstrated at Saturday's successful Parade.'

Prizes were announced and the usual good-humoured speeches made. 'If next year the men paid the same attention to the *hinder* part of their horses as they had this year to the *fore*-part,' summed up Mr Clarke for the RSPCA, 'my brother judge and myself would have even more difficulty in deciding as to where the prizes should go.'

But by the following August, all these horses would be gone, requisitioned for the Front. Most of Redhill and Reigate's young men would be gone, too.

PART 5
Power

37

At War

1914–18

A Channel passenger ferry – one of the last – chugs towards Southampton in the fading September light. Standing on the deck is a frail woman in a Tuscan straw hat, its silk veil tied tight under her bony chin. She grips the rail with gloved hands, her face to the wind. Next to her is her daughter, elegantly dressed in Parisian fashion, fur collar turned up high. A Pomeranian dog quivers under her arm as the ship engine booms. Grey herring gulls fill the sky like ash rising from a bonfire, wheeling and turning in a heavy cloud.

The upper deck is thick with bundled-up passengers: refugees, invalids, nurses, officers. There isn't a spare bench to be had. One hundred miles to the east of Paris, the Battle of Marne is about to begin. Thirteen thousand British men will be torn apart by shellfire in four days; nearly two thousand will die. One month into the war and the human cost is rising. But it should be over by Christmas. That is what everyone is saying.

Travelling in the other direction come thousands more men bound for France and the trenches. Volunteers, most of them, roughly trained and hungry for action. And horses – the war needs many more horses. Fifty thousand carthorses and hunters make this choppy crossing in the first six weeks of war, columns of them nervously walking onto the waiting vessels at Southampton.

Emmeline Pankhurst is ready to face her country again. She is frail, her skin a little yellow, but she is no longer a fugitive from the British police. Six days after declaring war on Germany, the Home Office freed all imprisoned suffragettes. In return, Mrs Pankhurst has brought the WSPU militants to heel and called a truce. 'The hatchet is buried,' she announced, 'but we know where to find it.' Suffragette violence is on hold. She and Christabel are now free to return home from Saint-Malo and from Paris.

'So ends, for the present, the war of women against men. As of old the women become the nurturing mothers of men, their sisters and uncomplaining helpmates.' She writes this in the foreword to her 1914 autobiography, a book dashed off during interludes of recovery from her many hunger strikes. But she doesn't *quite* mean it. For this war will present opportunities for women; Mrs Pankhurst is convinced of it. There will be power for the taking.

How near are they now? Emmeline strains her eyes at the horizon. St Catherine's Lighthouse on the Isle of Wight has been extinguished, along with any winking lights along the coast. The Edwardian watering holes have been snuffed out. Restlessly, she anticipates her first speaking engagement at the Brighton Dome two weeks hence. Christabel will take to the stage at the London Royal Opera House in three days' time: a heroine's welcome after two years of exile.

Mother and daughter stand side by side on deck, talking. They cannot sleep. There is work to be done. Pacifism, they both agree, is a luxury the country cannot afford. Britain's women must free up their menfolk for war – by taking on the men's jobs themselves. There will, no doubt, be strong resistance, but Mrs Pankhurst is renowned for her tenacity. This, then, is to be her new crusade.

Mrs Humphry Ward, Anti leader and famous novelist, sits at her Hertfordshire breakfast table with *The Times*. She is furious that the suffragists appear to have stolen the moral high ground since war was declared. Women are knitting and sewing for soldiers 'with such a perpetual running accompaniment of suffragist self-laudation that they might as well embroider the sacred name of Mrs Pankhurst or

Mrs Fawcett on every sock and every muffler,' she writes tartly in the *Anti-Suffrage Review*, 'so as to give notice to the soldiers as well as to the country at large that suffragism alone has the trademark of thoughtful and benevolent patriotism.'

But there is a new and rather daring patriotic movement afoot; a movement Mrs Humphry Ward is tempted to claim for her own. The 'White Feather Brigade' was the inspiration of Admiral Charles Penrose-Fitzgerald, and she has been quick to give the elderly military gentleman her fervent support. The movement started in the admiral's garrison hometown of Folkestone in October 1914, when he sent 30 young women out into the streets, each with a handful of white goose feathers. They were instructed to approach any idle, young, male pleasure seeker not in military uniform, and to push a feather through his buttonhole.

The white feather, the admiral has explained, symbolises cowardice. When a fighting cock turns tail, he is 'showing the white feather'. And the idea has simply taken off. Girls are handing out the ironic 'Order of the White Feather' to appalled men up and down the country.

Mrs Ward has a proven genius for enlisting female support, for networking and for stirring things up. She has put her name to this playful but incredibly powerful piece of patriotism, which sees young female Antis *and* suffragettes working together to shame Britain's men into signing up. It is the smarter type of young girl who has joined the White Feather Brigade, she notes; the sort confident enough to approach a strange man in the street – and to touch him. What woman would dare do such a thing, even a year ago?

Never mind that the girls so often seem to get it wrong. The newspaper stories – of feathers presented to legless veterans, or to soldiers on home leave, or men unfit for service who then go home and commit suicide – simply give the movement publicity. Lord Harmsworth at the *Daily Mail* hopes the gesture will 'shame every young slacker' into enlisting. Even *The Times* is giving it coverage now that Lord Kitchener is apparently in favour.

When Mrs Humphry Ward visits the trenches in 1916 – the first woman to do so – she will carry in her mind's eye that small, white feather. It serves as a reminder of human courage, and of its opposite, cowardice. Her reports, written at the request of former president Theodore Roosevelt, will be instrumental in bringing America into the war.

Black is the hardest colour of all to get right. The ostrich feathers have first to be placed in a cold water dye bath, then slowly heated until the water is very hot (but never boiling) so that the plume and its shaft will take the dye. Logwood dye is the best for black, mixed with chrome to set the colour, but it costs. The plumes are steeped in logwood for six days before a deep raven shade is achieved. Anything less, and they come out violet. The working women's arms are blackberry coloured and livid with rashes, their faces streaked grey, their aprons dark and damp.

Of course, it is strictly men's work, the dyeing of feathers. Skilled work. Women are used just for the preliminary washing. But since a man tried to claim exemption from the military for his two feather dyer sons and the press poured scorn on his court case, feather manufacturers have been under pressure to release male hands. And now, since the March 1916 Military Service Act, all the men under 41 have been conscripted.

Feather washer Alice Battershall is now Mrs Chipchase, 55 years old and a mother of three. She lives in a tightly packed household at 8 Europa Place, Lever Street, and her health is fading. Daughter Louisa has followed her into plumage, and together they are scraping through this precarious, final chapter in the ostrich feather trade. There are no extravagantly plumed hats seen on the crowded trams and motor omnibuses now. There isn't the room or the appetite. The ostrich feather industry has crashed, so they say, as no woman will touch those blowsy, old-style plumes. From a peak of 20,000 pre-war workers, by the end of the war just 2,000 will remain. Will Alice and Louisa be among those who survive?

For now, mass mourning has saved them from penury. Human death has, ironically, also taken a heavy toll on the birds. By 1916, almost all the material sold for coats, dresses and hats in London is black. Black osprey, black paradise, black albatross, black marabou. But black is a difficult colour to work with. Try willowing black ostrich fronds by gaslight when you can't afford spectacles.

Like so many of the women in their neighbourhood, Alice and Louisa are in mourning. In October 1916, the dreaded telegram boy calls at Europa Place with an envelope that nobody wishes to open. 'Deeply regret to inform you . . .' Alice's second born, 24-year-old Alfred, is 'killed or missing in action' at the Battle of the Somme, 15 September 1916. 'Lord Kitchener expresses his sympathy.' On a single day, the Royal Fusiliers lost 300 officers and men. Alfred Chipchase was one of them.

Alice and Louisa affix bedraggled ebony ostrich feathers to their hats. The black-market trade in black feathers is, no doubt, brisk on Lever Street at this time.

Mrs Lemon's war is spent as one might expect, alleviating the suffering of others. As quartermaster for the Reigate Red Cross, member of the workhouse Board of Guardians, treasurer for the Children's Care Association, prime mover on the Reigate Distress Committee, and former lady mayoress, she was the obvious choice to run Redhill War Hospital. When the army requisitioned the Redhill Workhouse infirmary in May 1917, Mrs Lemon was installed as commandant. A military name for a military woman: the 57-year-old daughter of a musketry captain, and a force of compassionate energy.

Etta walks briskly down Whitepost Hill towards Earslwood Common. She is dressed for work in a long, navy serge skirt and masculine jacket with three silver stripes on each sleeve, a navy cravat over a crisp white blouse and the St John Ambulance brassard on her left arm. In her pocket is a letter. Her dear old friend and RSPB co-founder, the inspirational Eliza Phillips, has died at her home in Croydon aged 92. With news of this loss come memories from the past, and a sense of profound dislocation. What world is this today, with such senseless slaughter in it? The suffering she sought to end for the birds is now eclipsed by human suffering.

Quarterly, the RSPB prints in its magazine a list of the birdwatchers and ornithologists who will not return from battle. Daily, Etta Lemon oversees the logistics of caring for men stretchered in straight from the Front; louse-ridden, maimed and shell-shocked young men, half-mad and half-dead.

Redhill has been taken over by the military, its margins of hedge and woodland destroyed. Soldiers are camping on every piece of open land. And yet – the goldfinch has returned to the common since the men went to war. In the Home Counties, timid species once in retreat are being seen again: cirl bunting and hobby, Dartford warbler and red-backed shrike. Mrs Lemon can only conclude that Britain's trappers have been sent off to war, and that the camping soldiers are feeding the birds their crumbs. Winifred, Duchess of Portland (busy running Welbeck Abbey as a supremely comfortable war hospital), has reported increased bird and wildlife on the estates, now that game shooting has ceased.

Strangely, perversely, the war is helping British birdlife. But the most perverse irony of all is that the international market in wild bird feathers has been temporarily quenched – not thanks to the efforts of the RSPB, but due to wartime trade restrictions. Luxury feathers are among the imports banned by the war office from February 1917. Here is the government enforcing what the RSPB has been calling for all these years – but only as long as this war endures. As for debating the Plumage Importation Bill again in parliament, this is a hollow hope with a war going on. Once again, the bill has been shelved.

Mrs Lemon pushes through the heavy front door of Redhill War Hospital and is hit by the tarry smell of carbolic lotion. The amputees of the Somme are a sobering daily ordeal; the chaplain a regular visitor. She has tried to introduce homely touches for her hospital of 80 patients: there is a recreation shed with a billiard table, a smoking room and indoor games. She has personally raised money for rest chairs and 100 feeding cups for men too weak to lift their heads to drink. Mrs Lemon, reports the *Surrey Mirror*, is 'simply loved by the patients for the maternal care she bestows on them'. Under her watch, nothing is overlooked.

Miss Madeleine Nutt, Matron, briefs her commandant. Etta nods, takes notes, tuts sympathetically. They manage between them a staff of 50 women, nurses and VADs (Voluntary Aid Detachment) who know each other of old. They have run local committees, raised funds, attended lectures, marched for their politics shoulder to shoulder. Some are known to be Antis, some suffragists. But all this is irrelevant now: what matters is doing one's bit. Which is why the posturing of self-styled 'ardent patriot', Emmeline Pankhurst, is particularly hard to stomach.

'I'm not nursing soldiers,' Mrs Pankhurst has announced to the press (and she is much in the papers during this war). 'There are so many others to do that . . . it's no more to be expected that our organisers should now necessarily take to knitting and nursing than that Mr. Asquith should set his Ministers to making Army boots and uniforms.'

While Mrs Pankhurst persuades the new prime minister David Lloyd George to send her to Russia on a morale-raising, anti-communism lecture tour, Mrs Lemon sits at her desk in the old workhouse infirmary, keeping pace with the ceaseless flow of casualties from this war. Her sheer competence for public office – her own, and that of thousands of women like her – does not go unnoted.

38

The Ballot Box

1918

Of the two women, Mrs Pankhurst was first to claim victory for her personal battle. 'Women's New Privilege' ran the *Daily Mail*'s momentous headline on Saturday 14 December 1918. As the country went to the polls in the aftermath of war, reporters were sent to investigate this strange new species, 'The Woman Voter'. Under the 1918 Representation of the People Act, around 8.4 million women over the age of 30 had been granted the vote: a 40 per cent stake in a newly increased electorate of 21 million.

What sort of women were they? Garrulous, undisciplined and unpredictable, came back the reporters' verdicts. For a start, it seemed that the secrecy of the ballot box had 'gone for ever'. The new women voters were incapable of keeping their voting decision to themselves – either they showed their paper to the polling booth officials, seeking approval, or they discussed their choice of candidate loudly with friends as they queued outside.

They were physically inadequate, too. The pack of journalists homed in on bent old ladies, voting for the first 'and probably last' time. Or else they were swarming with children, flustered, distracted. At one polling station, a total of eight perambulators were counted parked outside the town hall. Other women were so preoccupied with the housework that they couldn't be coaxed out. Many had no idea of the politicians involved. Mrs 'Granny' Lambert of Edmonton, north London, was '105 years of age, and says she has never heard of Mr Lloyd George', reported the *Sunday Pictorial*. All, noted the reporters, were 'ignorant of the procedure'.

Of course they were! They had not expected to cast a vote in their lifetime. But mid-way through the war the government's mood had begun to change. Women were showing the nation their worth. 'It was almost ridiculous to watch the amazement of the ordinary man when he saw how rapidly women learned men's jobs,' observed Millicent Fawcett archly. Whitehall alone took on 162,000 women in new ministries, while over a million young women were recruited to work in high-risk munitions factories (thanks, in large part, to Emmeline Pankhurst's lobbying). They had done the men's work, and for substantially less pay – stoking furnaces and building ships, ploughing and milking, plumbing and van driving. As window cleaners, porters and signalmen, bus conductors, shepherds and electricians, they had kept Britain going. They were due a reward.

'It was wildly illogical to be converted to women's suffrage because a girl who had been a good milliner could also be a good life attendant,' wrote suffragist Ray Strachey, 'but so it was.' In May 1916, Prime Minister Asquith had written to Mrs Fawcett that he recognised the magnificent contribution women were making to the war and that, in due course, he would 'impartially' consider the women's franchise. While Mrs Pankhurst toured the United States and Canada giving patriotic speeches, Millicent Fawcett's NUWSS quietly resumed lobbying for the vote.

On 19 June 1917, suffragists young and old had thronged the cramped Ladies' Gallery at the Commons to witness MPs voting on the women's suffrage clause in the Representation of the People Bill. Would they deny it yet again? In New Zealand, women had been able to vote since 1893; in parts of Australia, since 1895. Women in Finland, Norway, Demark, Iceland and Canada were now enfranchised. As the British MPs cast their votes, the Ladies' Gallery held its collective breath.

The bill was passed by 385 votes to 55. Under the consequent act, all men over 21 were now enfranchised; 19 if they'd seen active service. Of women, an estimated 8.4 million over 30 would now be able to vote:

householders, the wives of householders, occupiers of property with an annual rent of £5 and graduates. Yet this left almost a quarter of women over 30 still excluded through complicated property qualifications – restrictions that had now been abolished for men. It was undeniably a great leap forward – the electorate increased from eight to 21 million – but the act still enshrined inequality between the sexes.

The country went to the polls on 14 December 1918, a dull, unseasonably mild day of persistent rain. Once the novelty of the ballot box had worn off for Britain's first women voters, there was a sense of anticlimax. Was *this* all there was to it? A cross on a piece of paper? After all that fuss and fury – the smashing of shop windows, force-feeding, arson and monster demonstrations. 'Don't be frightened,' a Battersea housewife was overheard saying to a nervous friend she met at the polling station. 'I've just voted, and it's the easiest work I've done for many a day.'

Alice Chipchase (née Battershall) walked with her carter husband, Robert, from Lever Street to the nearest polling booth in St Luke's, Finsbury. Her 22-year-old daughter Louisa stayed at home, unable to vote under the Act's age restrictions. The couple made their way slowly, for Alice had the wheezing lungs of a plumage worker. She had nothing to celebrate: a son lost to war and a profession being slowly killed off by the anti-plumage fanatics – people determined to do women like her out of a job.

But perhaps Alice did not bother to make the journey. The candidates – Sir Martin Archer-Shee, a lieutenant-colonel from Berkshire, and Sir Harry Cotton, an old Calcutta hand – might as well have been from another planet. Despite Sylvia Pankhurst's best efforts in the East End, working-class women had not, in general, been awakened by the women's movement. If Mrs Alice Chipchase now had a vote, did it really mean anything to her? The election turnout in Finsbury was just 39 per cent.

Working-class wives were more easily coaxed out of their homes if there was a woman candidate to vote for. Margery Corbett Ashby, 36, Liberal candidate for the inner-city Birmingham district of Ladywood, zipped 'early round the constituency with her husband and little son in a motorcar driven by her mother', trying to drum up interest. 'I want to vote for Mrs Ashby,' announced the women as they entered the booth in twos and threes. 'I want to vote for the lady before I start on the housework.' Women in this hard-up district polled 'better and earlier' than the men, reporters noted. 'Dark horse' Ashby was a committed suffragist, secretary of Millicent Fawcett's NUWSS and founder of the Younger Suffragists at the age of 18.

Also campaigning in Birmingham (but garnering rather more press attention) was 38-year-old Christabel Pankhurst, motoring around in furs and a capacious mink muff. Hers was the newly formed Women's Party ('equal pay for equal work'), contesting Labour for the new constituency of Smethwick. The WSPU had undergone a metamorphosis in 1917, but Mrs Pankhurst still pulled the strings. The Women's Party was 'in no way based on sex antagonism', she wrote in the manifesto – and yet, addressing a male audience in Birmingham just before the election, Mrs Pankhurst couldn't help returning to her pre-war persona. 'The Women's Party is much needed, gentlemen, because you haven't made much of a success of things in the past, have you?' Christabel was the 'woman of the hour', proclaimed her mother, now aged 60. 'I am her most ardent disciple.'

Prime Minister Lloyd George was also an admirer, praising the Women's Party's 'splendid work during the war' in getting female workers into the munitions factories, but ultimately it was Christabel's feminine charms that won the men over. Press baron Lord Northcliffe gave her campaign special coverage in the *Daily Mail*, urging Lloyd George: 'The best possible seat should be got for Miss Pankhurst, who has more brains than the rest of the women put together, and is a lady into the bargain, and also pleasant to look upon – and will therefore have power over the men in the House.' As for the Smethwick electorate, Christabel and her team at best aroused curiosity, at worst sharp hostility. She made her election address wearing an academic cap and gown, and appeared to have completely lost her old, saucy command of working-class audiences. Her put-downs were ill judged, her 'Union

Jack versus Red Flag' sloganeering fell flat. She was, thought one woman, like a 'glorified governess'.

For Etta Lemon of Redhill, Saturday 14 December was just another working day. Her hospital was still full of the war's wounded, and she was still its commandant. It is fair to assume that she voted; she took her political responsibilities seriously. But how did Mrs Lemon feel as a woman voter? This committed anti-suffragist was required to do what she had so vehemently and publicly argued against doing. She was going to have to take part in the women's 'triumph'.

When the Representation of the People Act was given royal assent in February 1918, the Antis were aghast. Curzon had done *nothing* to lead the Lords against it – but he felt he could not vote against the Commons, which was overwhelmingly in favour. The last days of the Antis were spent in recrimination and disappointment. When Mrs Humphry Ward complained to Millicent Fawcett of Curzon's double-dealing conduct, Mrs Fawcett replied: 'That's what comes of trusting to your men friends.' Fawcett saw it as a 'very great victory' – though it was not quite the victory the head of the NUWSS had hoped for. 'A law which gives a boy the vote and withholds it from a woman until she is thirty cannot be said to be a fair one,' she told reporters crisply. Fawcett's enemies took solace from the glaring fact that this was no equal franchise.

Former virulent Anti Violet Markham had undergone a conversion to the cause during the war and was running as a Liberal candidate in Mansfield. Whatever the ironies, the Antis – so many of them strong and talented women – had undoubtedly earned their stake in this election. The National League for Opposing Woman Suffrage quietly handed over its reserve fund of £5,000 to the Royal National Pension Fund for Nurses.

Mrs Lemon might have taken some consolation from the common belief that it *wasn't* the suffragettes and their stunts that had won a proportion of women the vote (as Emmeline and Christabel Pankhurst maintained so exultantly). Nor was it due just to fear of renewed militancy if it hadn't been granted (as many others seemed to believe). It had surely been won because of women like her, competently doing the men's work.

Perhaps, to Mrs Lemon, the vote was insignificant. Far more exciting things were just around the corner. In March 1920, she would be singled out for the Most Excellent Order of the British Empire, a new range of honours designed to acknowledge the thousands involved in war work. A crowned silver cross ('For God And The Empire'), suspended from a purple ribbon, was earmarked for Etta's bosom. Aged 60, she would be adding MBE to her name. The following year she would be sworn in as a Justice of the Peace, becoming one of Reigate's first two women magistrates. 'JP' would join her swelling list of acronyms – initials that *mattered*.

On that unseasonably mild Saturday in December, she and Frank walked together down Whitepost Hill to cast their votes. Husband and wife, unanimous in their views, presumably kept no political secrets. They were conservative by instinct. Yet Frank's younger sister, Annie, who lived at Hillcrest with the Lemons, did not get to vote. She was 56 and a spinster without property. Annie was one of the 60 per cent of British women who remained disenfranchised – including the thousands of educated, white-collar workers living in bedsits who had fought for the vote, and the thousands of young 'munitionettes' the act was thought to be rewarding.

In Richmond, Surrey, 36-year-old writer Virginia Woolf made her way to the polling booth along with her husband, Leonard. This should have been a celebratory day for Woolf, who had done her bit with suffrage demonstrations, suffrage bazaars and pamphleteering. But like so many, she felt unequal to hoofing up the 'triumph'. There had been so much loss. 'I don't feel much more important,' she wrote in her diary, ' – perhaps slightly so. It's like a knighthood; might be useful to impress people one despises . . . But there are other aspects of it naturally.'

What she noticed, as she walked, were the shop windows. The war had wiped 11 million soldiers off the face of the earth, but the windows reflected nothing of this human tragedy. The hats might have shrunk, but the colours were, if anything, more intense; the displays more lavish. There was a frantic need to negate the loss; to alleviate grief with fantasy. Despite the import restrictions, Britain's hoard of stockpiled plumes had not been dented – and the Plumage Bill, shelved by the war, still hung unresolved in the air.

39

But What Do Women Care?

1919

Mrs Lemon bustled into Whitehall in a deputation. She and the Duchess of Portland – lone females in a posse of naturalists – were there to plead with the president of the Board of Trade to keep up the wartime ban on plumage imports until proper legislation could be introduced. It was July 1919, and the RSPB was losing patience. Eleven years had now passed since the original Plumage Bill had been introduced to parliament. Eleven years of obfuscation, foot dragging and deference to trade interests.

To make matters worse, the plumage trade was enjoying a post-war boom. 'Feather merchants are exchanging congratulations on the most prosperous year the feather trade has known,' reported *The Globe* that year. The 'osprey' quivered above every modish, close-fitting toque, while birds-of-paradise were 'the fancy of the moment', according to a feather dealer. 'In spite of their price we have hardly been able to keep up with the demand.'

Hundreds of bird species now risked extinction; it was as brutal as that. The plumed paradise birds – greater, lesser, Raggiana, ribbon-tailed; the snowy egret was nearly decimated, as were blue-throated and amethyst hummingbirds, the bright green Carolina parakeet, the Toco toucan, the lyre bird, the silver pheasant, the velvet bird, the tanager, the resplendent trogan … the list went on. Mrs Lemon's deputation handed a succinct letter to Sir Auckland Geddes and his re-elected Prime Minister David

Lloyd George, urging immediate action. They also handed over a list of 150 signatories – from earls to authors, editors to ornithologists. The celebrities of the day had put their names to the cause: H. G. Wells, Thomas Hardy, George Bernard Shaw, Joseph Conrad, Sir Arthur Conan Doyle, G. K. Chesterton. As a roll call of the moral, intellectual and scientific heavyweights of post-war Britain, it was impressively comprehensive. Yet there was not a single woman on the list.

Lord Geddes, former professor of anatomy at the University of Edinburgh, was suave, sympathetic and vague. He told them the import restrictions would be continued for 'as long as possible', but he would not give a definite promise. He 'hoped' that legislation would be successful at the beginning of 1920.

Britain was late in granting women the vote – and now it lagged behind the rest of the world in bird protection. The United States had long ago prohibited the import and export of wild bird plumage: first with the Lacey Act of 1900, and, more recently, with the far tougher Migratory Bird Treaty Act of 1918. British India forbade the export of plumage in 1902; Australia passed legislation in 1912, followed by the Dutch East Indies (Indonesia) in 1913. Yet in Britain, where the RSPB ladies had been trying to change the law since 1889, inertia ruled. 'To take a walk in the West End today is to be bowed down by a sense of the impotence of good to save the remnants of a wonderful life from universal pillage,' wrote the young ruralist Harold (H. J.) Massingham in *The Spectator* in October 1919. Three things were needed for the movement to be more effective, he declared. 'Impetus, cohesion, and direction.' Adding his voice to the RSPB's protest, he founded the Plumage Bill Group with the express goal of pushing legislation through parliament.

Massingham was fortunate to have an influential father, Henry (H. W.) Massingham, editor of *The Nation*, Britain's leading radical weekly. Henry stepped quickly in to help his son's cause. Under his usual pseudonym of 'Wayfarer', he wrote a column on the failed Plumage Bill in July 1920, condemning not the hunters but the heartless wearers of the snowy egret plumes. As everyone knew, the plumes were at their most beautiful during the nesting season – so the birds had to be 'shot in parenthood for child-begetting women to flaunt the symbols of it . . . But what do women care? Look at Regent Street this morning!'

Wayfarer's column was read by Virginia Woolf, breakfasting at the dining table of Hogarth House on Paradise Road, Richmond, home of the nascent Hogarth Press. Woolf was by instinct a non-participant, an outsider, conscious of the excesses and absurdities of the organisations she nevertheless supported. She wasn't a paid up member of the RSPB, but she *did* abide by its rule to wear no feathers – and not just because she wasn't interested in fashion. ('I don't like buying hats,' she confessed in her diary, 'though I've conquered some part of the horror by learning how to look into the eyes of milliners, & make my demands boldly.')

Woolf was a professional writer and public figure, able to influence public opinion if she cared to. Wayfarer's article piqued her. She took up her pen and wrote a reply. It was published in the *Woman's Leader*, a magazine edited by her suffragist friend Ray Strachey. She opened defiantly: 'If I had the money and the time I should, after reading "Wayfarer" in the *Nation* of 10 July, go to Regent Street, buy an egret plume, and stick it – is it in the back or the front of the hat? – and this in spite of a vow taken in childhood and hitherto religiously observed.'

Woolf couldn't have written a more provocative first sentence on a more contentious subject. Here, in a nutshell, were the two burning issues of the day: the woman question, and the bird question. Readers were gripped and confounded in equal measure. Why would she do such a thing? They read on.

She took them by the hand down Regent Street, conjuring up the treasures behind plate glass: 'Dressing bags, silver baskets, boots, guns, flowers, dresses, bracelets and fur coats.' Men and women 'pass incessantly this way and that'; few can do more than look and hurry on. And then comes a lady of a different class altogether. 'A silver bag swings from her wrist. Her gloves are white. Her shoes lustrous. She holds herself upright.' She is beautiful but her face is stupid, 'and the look she sweeps over the shop windows has something of the greedy petulance of a pug-dog's face at tea-time'.

The lady of the stupid pug-dog face pauses at the display of egret plumes. 'So do many women. For after all, what can be more ethereally and fantastically lovely? The plumes seem to be the natural adornment of spirited and fastidious life, the very symbols of pride and distinction.' Since she is going to the opera that night, 'a lemon-coloured egret is precisely what she wants to complete her toilet. In she goes; the silver bag disgorges I know not how many notes; and the fashion writers next day say that Lady So-and-So was "looking lovely with a lemon-coloured egret in her hair".'

Here was a picture of precisely that unthinking, heartless female consumer that Mrs Lemon and her RSPB local branch secretaries had been attacking over the decades. Here was the selfish buyer of plumes in 'egregious bad taste', in Etta's tart words. Was this really a woman worth defending – or indeed emulating?

Virginia Woolf was an impressionistic painter of pictures, and she offered the reader another: 'A blazing South American landscape. In the foreground a bird with a beautiful plume circles round and round as if lost or giddy. There are red holes in its head where there should be eyes. Another bird, tied to a stake, writhes incessantly, for red ants devour it. Both are decoys.' Woolf showed the reader 'innumerable mouths opening and shutting, opening and shutting, until – as no parent bird comes to feed them – the young birds rot where they sit.'

So much had been written about the plight of the egrets and those cruel ladies of fashion – reams and reams of articles in *The Spectator*, letters to *The Times*, editorials in the RSPB's magazine, *Bird Notes and News*. But no one had yet nailed it so shockingly or so viscerally, and in such a modern voice. Woolf seems in this essay to paint it anew, and we recoil with genuine horror. Yet her point was not the usual one.

'But these hands,' she continues '– are they the hands of men or of women? The birds are killed by men, starved by men, and tortured by men – not vicariously, but with their own hands.' Who, Woolf asked, was ultimately responsible for squashing the Plumage Bill in the House of Commons? Not women. 'The Plumage Bill was sent to Standing Committee C. With one exception each of its sixty-seven members was a man. And on five occasions it was impossible to get a quorum of twenty to attend. The Plumage Bill is for all practical purposes dead. But what do men care?'

There was an outcry. Bird lovers, men and women, did not appreciate playful irony or rhetorical whimsy. It baffled and infuriated them. 'Does it matter in the least to the birds so foully slain whether the blame rests most with men or women?' asked Mrs Meta Bradley in *The Woman's Leader*. Woolf's essay was castigated in the press.

'I am not writing as a bird, or even as a champion of birds; but as a woman,' she wrote in self-defence. 'It seems to me more necessary to resent such an insult to women as Wayfarer casually lets fall than to protect egrets from extinction.' Back-pedalling, but still defiant, she promised to donate her fee for the article to the Plumage Bill Group.

Woolf had, inadvertently, done the bill an immense favour. By evoking both Regent Street and the egrets' slaughter so vividly, she had provoked a mass reaction. This was her skill. And it was a skill far greater than that possessed by the monotonous, conservative and indignant voices of the RSPB. Woolf's voice was modern – in a way that Etta Lemon's was not.

Why could this bill not be passed? Virginia Woolf had shone a spotlight on the shambles of the Commons; the ineffectual 'male apparatus' of parliament as Mrs Pankhurst called it. Had women entering the political sphere made any difference? Christabel Pankhurst had not won a seat, losing in Smethwick by a narrow 775 votes. The Women's Party was quietly disbanded in 1919. Out of the 17 other female candidates for the 1918 election, only one won a seat, in Dublin – and the Irish Republican Constance Markievicz refused to take it because of their abstentionist policy.

But in 1919, a woman did scale the citadel. Nancy, Lady Astor, was a wealthy socialite, a temperance fanatic and a conservative. She stepped neatly into her husband's constituency at a by-election for Plymouth Sutton, in Devon, when he inherited his father's viscountcy. Nancy Astor's place in history as the first woman to take a seat in the House of Commons was galling in the extreme to Emmeline Pankhurst, since she had played no part in the cause.

It was also galling to MPs such as Winston Churchill, Secretary of State for War and Air, and former foe of the suffragists. Churchill was discomfited by the intrusion of a female into the men's club. He reportedly complained to her face that having a woman in parliament was like having a woman intrude on him in the bathroom, when he had nothing to defend himself with but a sponge. 'Nonsense, Winston,' came Nancy's quick riposte. 'You're not good-looking enough to have fears of this sort.'

The appointment of Viscountess Astor was cause for optimism at the RSPB. She moved in the same elite circles as the Duchess of Portland (lavish house parties at Cliveden, the Astors' country house in Buckinghamshire; shooting weekends; Royal Ascot). While Nancy might be a feisty American divorcée with a reputation for outspokenness, she was also devout, old-fashioned in her ideas and sober in her dress. She wore no feathers. She took her seat in December 1919, aged 40, and immediately started probing as to why the Plumage Bill kept being blocked. With characteristic astringency, she pronounced it 'astonishing' that a bill could have failed for so many years, when it had found favour with so many.

And so, after all that masculine 'impetus, cohesion, and direction' of H. J. Massingham's Plumage Bill Group, not to mention the RSPB's petition from 150 men of influence, it took a woman to finally make things happen. Under Lady Astor's 'formidable' aegis, a parliamentary group was galvanised into action.

The date the Plumage Bill gained royal assent, on 1 July 1921, the RSPB responded with strangely muted jubilation. Here was the culmination of their original *raison d'être* – the victory Mrs Lemon and her original band of ladies had campaigned for so determinedly ever since 1891, a long battle of 30 years. Yet there had been much wrangling over its terms.

Closing the English market for feathers, while the continental markets remained open, wouldn't stop the industry or save a single bird, argued some. Others felt that Britain had to lead by example, and the continent would soon follow. 'The privilege of leadership in humane affairs relating to animals is ours,' the author Holbrook Jackson wrote to *The Times*, 'and national pride alone should urge us not to forgo it.'

Mrs Lemon knew, in her heart of hearts, that the bill lacked teeth. To make it a crime to import exotic plumage, and yet perfectly legal to sell and wear it, seemed a travesty. 'It is impossible to say that the Act is a wholly satisfactory one,' she wrote wearily in the annual report for 1921 – for it would be up to women, as before, to choose whether to 'understand and support the spirit as well as the letter of the law'. Would women of fashion care where their feathers came from? The American campaigners had been less compromising and gained more. Their Migratory Bird Treaty Act of 1918 had made it a crime to deal in feathers; milliners and feather foundries were ordered to burn their plumage stocks or face a fine. Whole warehouses went up in smoke.

The Duchess of Portland, RSPB President now for 30 years, closed the 1922 AGM that March on a trenchant note. 'In America they do some things better than we do here. When a lady wears an osprey they tear it off her head, hat and all.'

40

Etta and Emmeline:
Two Portraits
1927

In the National Portrait Gallery in London, an oil painting hangs in the space reserved for distinguished political figures of the Edwardian period. It shows an elderly, twinkly lady with lorgnette and furs. Nothing in the painting suggests what this woman was famous for, but today she needs little introduction. Emmeline Pankhurst did not sit for her portrait during the giddy height of her pre-war fame, but in 1927, when her hair was silver, her eyes sunken and her star waning.

The portrait was painted by the suffragette artist Georgina 'Ina' Brackenbury, and commissioned by another stalwart from the glory days – Viscountess Rhondda, Margaret Haig Thomas. Like so many other political women of her generation, Lady Rhondda was, at 44, nostalgic for that intense earlier chapter of her life – the comradeship, the sense of purpose, the high drama of it all. Life after the war never quite lived up to those years of parliament storming, window smashing and hunger striking. She arranged to commemorate their great leader before that chapter had receded from memory entirely.

The decade between gaining the vote and sitting for her portrait was a strange, faltering time for Emmeline Pankhurst. In 1920 she moved to Canada and went on the celebrity speaking circuit, stirring up audiences on the Bolshevik terror, the might of imperialism and the threat of venereal disease. Then she appeared to lose her way. How could it be that the leader of the WSPU – that bulldozing political force of the pre-war years – could be found by 1925 running the English Tea Shop of Good Hope in Juan-les-Pins on the Côte D'Azur, eking out her pennies? And who would have thought that the crop-haired generation, who had gained from Mrs Pankhurst's fearless campaign, would turn and bite her hand, dismissing 'old-style feminism' as old hat – embarrassing, even?

Cigarettes, jazz, latchkeys and casual sex eclipsed politics. The 'bright young things' of the 1920s appeared irresponsible to the older suffragettes; too silly, even, to merit the vote. Their nickname – 'flappers' – was said to invoke a fledgling bird learning to fly, frantically flapping its wings. Others said it came from the modern fashion for girls to leave their overcoats unbuttoned, flapping to and fro when they walked (none of that tight, prudish clothing for *them*). Yet 'flap' was also a Victorian term for a teenage prostitute – and it came to mean, at its broadest, any independent, pleasure-seeking woman.

Flappers wanted to do what men did. To go smoking and drinking, motorcar driving and gambling. As such, they expected to be able to vote on the same terms as men as a *right*. *Punch* magazine enlightened its readers in November 1927: '"Flapper" is the popular press catch-word for an adult woman worker, aged 21 to 30, when it is a question of giving her the vote under the same conditions as men of the same age.'

Emmeline didn't wear the WSPU colours to sit for her portrait in Brackenbury's Kensington studio. If she had, who would even remember that purple had once stood for dignity, white for purity and green for hope?

Some years earlier, Etta Lemon had also sat for her portrait. She and Frank were to be commemorated as Mayor and Lady Mayoress of Reigate; a pair of oil paintings, commissioned by the borough, was the ultimate honour.

Many decades later, the two portraits were somehow bequeathed to the RSPB. Perhaps when Frank and Etta died, childless, the society was thought to be the closest to family that they had. Perhaps some well-intentioned councillors had them packaged up and sent over to the headquarters. Here they hung for years on the library walls – and so, when a former RSPB employee set about writing Mrs Lemon's entry for the *Oxford Dictionary of Biography* in 2004, he was able to scrutinise them.

'Descriptions of the Lemons show two very different personalities,' Nick Hammond wrote. 'The existing oil portraits and photographs confirm these differences: it is easy to see in Frank's features his genial, kindly manner, unfailing tact and good temper, and ready humour, no less than his knowledge of men and things, and his tolerant and equitable judgment, particularly in times when difficulties had to be confronted or differences of opinion blended into harmony.'

He then turned his attention – reluctantly, it seemed – to Margaretta Lemon. 'His wife's portrait and photographs, on the other hand, show a direct gaze and a determined mouth.' Mrs Lemon's brown-eyed gaze *is* direct: she squares up to the artist, alert to the importance of the occasion. It is true that her mouth looks determined: she is not simpering for posterity. It's also possible to glimpse, if you look for it, a quiet integrity, intelligence and compassion in Etta Lemon's face. No flashy furs or hand gestures, but a composed, clear-eyed stoicism.

The paintings of Pankhurst and Lemon seem to capture the defining difference between the two women: one is overtly feminine, the other rather masculine. It was a dichotomy that went deeper than surface appearance. Emmeline Pankhurst was one of the girls, a champion of women, a believer in female ascendancy. Etta Lemon, on the other hand, was an honorary man. She deferred instinctively to men, and she channelled a certain masculine energy. She was also, at some level, anti-women – as Mrs Pankhurst was, broadly, anti-men. They were, however, both more complex and contradictory than these portraits suggest.

Emmeline's feminine force field was always her greatest weapon – but put her in a prison cell and she was a 'wild animal'. Faced with hecklers, she was 'deadly in her methods'. Etta's portrait could not be more different in mood: her direct stare is discomfiting. Men found her abrasive. 'There was no point in fighting Mrs Lemon,' remembered one ornithologist. 'She would defeat you sooner or later.' Yet she was also a devoted and submissive wife, an affectionate aunt and a quiet lover of 'dumb creation'. She was soft at her core.

What both shared was compassion – and tenacity. Back in the mid-1890s, before her husband's death, Emmeline had served a five-year spell on the Board of Guardians for Chorlton Poor Law Union Workhouse. Here, in the heart of deprived Manchester, with charming determination, she had made the long-serving guardians' lives hell as she pressed for imaginative, caring change.

Her chief enemy was a diehard called Mainwaring – a boot merchant whose offensiveness only helped win Emmeline support during board meetings. (He took to scribbling 'Keep your temper!' on his blotting paper.) Within six months, his female opponent had introduced high-backed Windsor chairs for the elderly instead of benches, unlimited bread and butter, and new dresses and bonnets for the women, chosen by Emmeline herself. She changed the rule that workhouse uniform should be worn on outings, a stigma much hated by inmates. Within five years – and despite the apoplectic Mr Mainwaring – she had country cottages built for the workhouse children, with a modern school, trained teachers, a gymnasium and a swimming bath.

Etta's stint on Redhill's Board of Guardians was longer, from 1913 right up to the abolition of workhouses in 1930. The Reigate Poor Law Union minute books record her attendance, year after year, debating issues ranging from overnight heating to mental health, absconding children to the bread allowance. While Mrs Lemon was certainly tougher than Mrs Pankhurst in her administration of charity (she argued, for example, against giving vagrants bread and cheese 'for the road', as it simply 'encouraged vagrancy'; she also argued strongly for the resettlement of workhouse orphans in the Dominions), she had the same instinct for imaginative and compassionate change. In the institution's last year, 1929, the minute book records her proposal that chairs and tables be provided for the 'old ladies' room' instead of long tables and benches – exactly the same plea that Mrs Pankhurst had made in the 1890s. They voted against it. Mrs Lemon tried again. The vote came out even. She tried again – and got what she wanted. She usually did.

Etta's experience on the board helped confirm her belief that women did *not* need a vote, as they had real influence in the civic sphere. Emmeline's had the reverse effect – it served to radicalise her further. She looked back on her encounters with the workhouse girls as 'potent factors in my education as a militant'.

Both Etta and Emmeline's portraits were commissioned when the exciting early momentum of those two parallel movements – animal rights and women's rights – had receded. They are presented as women who might have had a rather interesting past, reflecting on their achievements. Yet there was so much work still to do. Emmeline Pankhurst and Etta Lemon were acutely conscious of this.

In 1927, a pioneering book on bird behaviour was published in Britain. Max Nicholson, the 23-year-old author of *How Birds Live*, was robustly critical of the current state of ornithology. The RSPB was a feeble joke, he thought, 'a monster of contradictory ideals'; an elderly and passive group of amateurs who 'say too much and do too little'. The society needed to be far more uncompromising, not least with the wealthy egg and bird skin collectors among its members.

The female founders of the RSPB, with their early policy of women-only membership, had unfortunately had the effect (so he thought) of sharply separating the growing bird protection movement from its 'natural scientific base'. Professional management was needed to bridge the gap between 'sentiment' and 'informed judgment'. Nicholson wasn't trained in science; he had read History at Oxford – but he wasn't afraid of kicking up a storm.

Sentiment. Accusations of sentimentality had dogged Mrs Lemon from the start, and she was well aware of the slur. 'The fatuous notion that a bird is merely a "dicky-bird," to be caged as a pet, stuffed for the hat, or served on toast, as occasion requires, is rapidly being relegated to the mental rubbish-heap,' she wrote crisply in 1912. Yet it is interesting to learn, from 21st-century experiments, that birds evidently do have personalities. It is interesting because women's 'unscientific' observations about birds and their characters earned Mrs Lemon and her local secretaries no end of contempt as the new era of ornithology dawned.

Emboldened by Max Nicholson's criticisms, the younger males began muttering about the elderly and staid core of the RSPB; those ladies with their 'amateurish methods'. Yet these women had, in their day, been extraordinarily bold. Raised by Victorian fathers to be modest and docile, they had dared to poke their nose into the masculine world of politics and antagonise the plumage trade. Had they kept their gaze politely averted, lamenting the plight of the birds over teacups and saucers, they would have got nowhere.

The same tension between 'masculine' and 'feminine' behaviour warred within Millicent Fawcett's constitutional suffragists, women who had cringed at the boldness of their first mass march through the West End. It was felt, too, by the militant suffragettes – women driven by frustration to antisocial extremes. The tension was even more excruciating for the anti-suffragists – conservative ladies full of indignation, yet unable to take to the podium and speak out. These were all women who had to dig deep to find their braver, more masculine selves; who had to become a little unnatural for the times.

In February 1927, Emmeline Pankhurst was adopted as the Conservative candidate for Whitechapel and St George's in the East End. She was back in the fray. Sylvia was mortified that her mother had chosen to take her crusade against communism into the heart of the working classes, yet Emmeline did not fit the Conservative Central Office mould at all. 'Our idea is to make friends with everybody and replace class hatred & suspicion by Friendliness and Cooperation,' she wrote to a friend.

She visited every narrow shop, tenement building and public house. She held open-air meetings, exhausting as this was. Buzzing with purpose, she felt as if she were reliving the early days of the suffragette movement – but Mrs Pankhurst was now 68 years old, and her body was weak. Before giving a speech, she would sit slumped in a chair, eyes blank, conserving her energies for the platform. And then . . . 'Radiant, inspired, she was as magnificent in attack, as irresistible in persuasion, as deadly in her methods with rowdies and hecklers as ever,' wrote her ever-admiring friend, the composer Ethel Smyth. 'Opposition had always called forth her full powers.'

The East Enders 'adored' Mrs Pankhurst, possibly simply because she showed an interest in them. But Central Office treated her 'like a poor and unwanted step-relation', according to her female secretary. Without money, property, aristocratic connections or even a motorcar, she simply wasn't one of the boys. If physically worn out, Mrs Pankhurst remained alert, perceptive and critical – and just as intolerant of sexism among Conservatives as she had been of it among Labour Party members and trade unionists many years before. It was one of the many grievances that compelled her to try and win a seat in parliament.

On Friday 9 March 1928, Mrs Pankhurst visited the House of Commons, sliding herself onto a polished wooden bench in the Ladies' Gallery. Viscountess Astor was holding the floor, batting down objections to the second reading of the Representation of the People (Equal Franchise) Act – an act that would finally remove the age bar and property qualifications for female voters. There were now seven women MPs in parliament, and Emmeline Pankhurst hoped very much to join them. The general election was one year away. 'She looked very old and frail,' commented a reporter, 'not even the shadow of an Amazon.'

She was living, by now, on a pittance, in rooms over a hairdresser's shop in Whitechapel, at the heart of her constituency. 'If only I could get back my strength,' she kept saying, 'I know I've got five years of good work in me yet!' Then she was dealt a paralysing blow from within her own family. Emmeline discovered that her ostracised daughter, Sylvia, whose communist politics she had always hated, had, three months previously, given birth to a son *out of wedlock*. She was living with an Italian anarchist in the east London suburb of Woodford Green. The news was whispered in Emmeline's ear as she was about to speak before an East End audience who had read the tabloid headlines. When a woman coarsely raised the question of Sylvia's illegitimate child, Emmeline briskly replied that it was not her custom to discuss private matters in public. Trembling inside, she went on with her speech.

Emmeline never spoke in public again: she never recovered from the shame. Sylvia wrote to her mother about the birth of her son, Richard Keir Pethick Pankhurst (she had even chosen to give him her own surname), but she received no reply. Emmeline had sunk into a deep depression. That one of her daughters should disgrace the Pankhurst name in such a vulgar way! That Sylvia should so publicly flout the moral standards that she, her mother, had promoted around the world – it was too much to bear. Her spirit was irreparably broken. A month before her 70th birthday, in June 1928, Emmeline Pankhurst died of influenza.

A dead Mrs Pankhurst was an easier proposition than a diminished one. Her death was mourned extravagantly in the global press, while her body lay in state on a purple catafalque in a West End chapel. All day long, women famous and obscure queued to pay homage. Her funeral was a return to the glory days of the WSPU ceremonial: 1,000 women honouring 'a dead general in the midst of a mourning army'. The congregation at St John's Smith Square, Westminster, bristled with purple, white and green flags, WSPU medals and broad-arrow prison badges. The little woman in the coffin, whose estate amounted to just £85 5s 6d, represented their finest hour.

The Brackenbury portrait was donated to the National Portrait Gallery in London and the Pankhurst memorial industry took off. Nostalgic memoirs were written. Emmeline Pankhurst had been tenacious, and she had paid the price with her health – but she would be remembered for her boldness. Two weeks after her funeral, the Equal Franchise Act became law. Women of 21 could now vote on the same terms as men.

Perhaps, if Mrs Lemon had taken more visibly personal risks, her portrait would have been presented to the National Portrait Gallery, too. Perhaps there would have been a Memorial Committee, as there was for

Mrs Pankhurst. But her careful, conservative nature both denied her notoriety and earned her remarkable longevity. By the time Etta Lemon died in 1953, aged 92, she was a faint, folkloric memory to RSPB staff. She was remembered simply as 'The Dragon'. Her portrait ended up stored in a remote cupboard of The Lodge in Sandy, Bedfordshire – final headquarters of the charity.

41

The Coup

1935–9

Etta Lemon pushed open the heavy entrance door to 82 Victoria Street, nodded at the porter and creaked up the carpeted stairs to the RSPB offices. Her dark, pleated skirt was a respectable mid-calf length, her beige stockings thick and her feet sensibly shod. She paused at the full-size portrait of W. H. Hudson – a sight that had once filled her with pride. She had put such energy into soliciting funds for it after the great naturalist's death in 1922. The painting, by a Royal Academician, was a fitting tribute to one of the society's best friends: a bird lover who had bequeathed them the bulk of his fortune. Rather than herself – a mere foot soldier – it was *Hudson* that Etta wished to commemorate as the figurehead of the RSPB.

But now Hudson's portrait prompted a feeling of melancholy. What would their patron saint make of his charity today? The 1930s had been riven with infighting. Every day brought a new malicious rumour to her in-tray, mostly of an unpleasantly personal nature.

She poked her head into the secretary's office. Her colleague Linda Gardiner, champion of bird education for the young and tireless editor of *Bird Notes and News*, had lately been making noises about retirement. Linda felt too old for all these newcomers and their radical ideas. She was 74, one year younger than Etta, and had been with the society since 1900. The two women jointly held the administrative reins, and Etta could not imagine how she would operate without her.

As for Etta – she was officially honorary secretary of the Watchers' Committee, those on-the-ground eyes and ears of bird protection; some 60 individuals spread the length of Britain. Her 'boys' were far more important to her than the young men creating waves at 82 Victoria Street. Now, however, she had a new, far weightier role.

She hung up her coat and hat, and sat down at her leather-topped desk. The office and the work it contained had become her solace; a distraction from grief. In April 1935, Mrs Lemon had been forced unexpectedly to assume her husband's role as honorary secretary for the RSPB.

The memory of Frank's last trip up to London in March still haunted her. Together, they had caught the train from Redhill to Victoria for the RSPB's annual meeting. He had not been at all well these past few years, but had become adept at disguising his pain. Frank was not one to shirk his responsibilities and he had continued to push himself well into his 70s – alderman, county magistrate, chairman of the Surrey County Council Education Committee, sage presence on dozens of boards and societies. Perhaps he had pushed himself too hard.

Halfway through the journey Frank had turned grey and started gasping for breath – and in the time it took Etta to yank at the leather window strap for air, he was slumped, unconscious, on the carriage seat. Husband and wife knew the drill by now. When the train pulled in to Victoria station, he was upright, recomposed and determined to attend both the RSPB meeting *and* a freemasonry ceremony at the Grand Lodge that afternoon. As Senior Grand Warden, he felt obliged to do so. And although it was clearly too much, Etta supported his wishes as she always had done. She put her arm through his, and the two walked slowly up Victoria Street.

Frank Lemon died at home three weeks later, on Easter Monday, 1935, aged 76. The curtains of Hillcrest remained closed, and the *Surrey Mirror* was fulsome in its obituary of a man who had devoted his life to public service. In Reigate's Council Chamber, Alderman Lemon's chair was wreathed in black crêpe and three minutes' silence observed. Mr Lemon's death had, said the Mayor, 'snapped a link' with an earlier era. Frank, who served as mayor between 1911 and 1913, was a typical product of the Victorian age – 'the embodiment of what we know as the Victorian spirit'. The same could be said for Etta Lemon – the devoted wife who 'ably assisted' her husband in all his work. But she was more than that. 'Mrs Lemon was a partner of his in a very real sense,' said the Mayor. Theirs had been a rare union.

Now it was just Etta and Annie at home, a widow and her spinster sister-in-law. Etta's small signature on a solicitors' document after her husband's death is firm, but almost unbearably poignant in its isolation. All her adult life she had been Mrs F. E. Lemon. Like an aged albatross, she had lost her mate, and she was vulnerable.

The first sally at the RSPB was fired shortly after Frank's death, and the timing cannot have been coincidental. Certain new council members started questioning exactly what went *on* in head office. Just how efficiently was this great charity being run? There were now 4,000 members to answer to – and answers were needed, for the Scottish question in particular. An ugly spat over aristocratic landowners and persecuted birds of prey was threatening to split the society in half: two lady ornithologists, Evelyn Baxter and Leonora Rintoul, were proposing to start their own Scottish society and take members with them.

Under scrutiny were Linda Gardiner, her two assistant secretaries and their handful of clerical staff – none of whom were married and 'all of whom were female', it was noted. Linda was now firmly set on retiring after 35 years' service, and with her loss, the last of Mrs Lemon's original acolytes would be gone. Emily Williamson was in a nursing home in Kensington, shortly to die in obscurity, in 1936, aged 81. Winifred, Duchess of Portland was – hard as this was to imagine – a frail, stick-thin woman, still with magnificent bone structure, but without the energy to travel much up to town.

The young Turks of the RSPB's Council struck swiftly. Here was an excellent opportunity to shake up the moribund culture. The old guard had been radicals in their day, but their conservative attitudes were infecting the charity's working culture. As the young ornithologist Max Nicholson never tired of pointing out, the society was too passive and too deferential to the establishment. These methods had worked excellently before the war, but this was the modern, vigorous, socially subversive 1930s. It was time for a clean sweep.

Many felt that a man's hand was needed at the helm, a man with ornithological and scientific credentials. But they hadn't counted on the indignation of Linda Gardiner's assistant secretaries – intelligent, beret- and trouser-wearing women who had more than earned their birding stripes. Beatrice Solly, 40, the daughter of a distinguished surgeon and ethical campaigner, had been with the society for 14 years. Phyllis Barclay-Smith was Etta Lemon's niece, one of the Barclays of Blackheath, daughter of a Cambridge professor of anatomy, who had joined the RSPB aged 21. Now aged 33, Phyllis was expert in international bird protection and highly respected in ornithological circles. She had yet to acquire her aunt's nickname 'The Dragon', but she had Mrs Lemon's forthright manner. Both women had been led to believe that they would jointly succeed to Linda's post.

On hearing that the Council had already recruited a male secretary to take 'supreme charge' (just as the Anti-Suffrage League had done 25 years earlier, at the will of Lord Curzon), Miss Solly and Miss Barclay-Smith were incandescent. They demanded that they should be regarded as equals to Robert Donaldson (even if they tacitly understood that he would, inevitably, be their superior). Fuelling their indignation was the current agitation for equal pay in the civil service, an ultimately successful campaign led by former suffragists. They announced to the Council that if their requests were not met – well then, they would resign. The two women, for so long essential to the society, imagined they were indispensable. What happened next was shocking.

Instead of backing them up – sister workers in an increasingly male-dominated culture – Mrs Lemon sought to crush them. She would *not* have insurrection in her ranks. She would not support anyone getting above themselves. The RSPB had been born out of womanly collaboration; no single individual had put herself forward. It was never a place for egos; just look at her and Frank, working for nothing, year after year. Nor was it a place for feminism. If one started to pander to women's slighted egos, the birds would suffer, Mrs Lemon was convinced of it. She was at heart a conservationist – *not* a feminist.

From a modern perspective, it is hard to forgive Mrs Lemon for what she did to these women. Mrs Pankhurst had put her daughter Christabel forward as the next generation's best hope. Etta could have promoted her niece as an able female ornithologist; an exceedingly rare breed. Yet her apparent callousness was entirely consistent with what she was – a woman born in the Victorian age, schooled in public service, subservient to the greater good. She was ruled, willingly, by the authority of men. Her deference to 'the stronger sex' was hard-wired into her, as instinctive as her loyalty to Frank. Men knew best. When Etta read, in the *Surrey Mirror* obituary of her husband, that his 'devoted wife' had given him 'loyal help in his leadership of the ornithological society', she would not have baulked (as I do) at this skewed version of the truth. Perhaps this really was how she saw it.

And so, in her new role as acting honorary secretary, she called the two women's bluff and accepted their resignations. Beatrice Solly and Phyllis Barclay-Smith departed in mute fury and disbelief. The brief, caustic note that Mrs Lemon wrote about the affair in *Bird Notes and News* did not even mention the pair by name. They were just 'two women Assistant-Secretaries' who had, 'no doubt to their surprise', done themselves out of a job.

Etta Lemon had won the first round. But she was wrong to place her faith in the men.

The next shot was fired on 29 February 1936, in a leader in *The Field*. 'On Monday, March 9th, at 3pm, the Royal Society for the Protection of Birds will hold their forty-fifth annual meeting,' it began. 'Fellows and Members may ask themselves whether all is for the best, or has been lately for the best, in the management of the Society's affairs.'

It felt as if a hand grenade had been lobbed into the Caxton Hall, Westminster. To cries of 'Shut up!', 'Sit down!' and hoots of 'ironical laughter', an uninvited RSPB member, one Captain Adrian Hopkins, shouted a barrage of angry accusations at the society's 73-year-old president, the Duchess of Portland. Why, he demanded, was the RSPB leaving all prosecutions for cruelty to birds to the RSPCA? Why was it gambling in real estate? Why were its administration expenses so high? And why were the ages of the ladies involved so 'excessive'?

Reporters in the aisles scribbled furiously. How things had changed since those deferential Edwardian gatherings at the Westminster Palace Hotel. Britain had a new monarch, King Edward VIII – a 41-year-old playboy entangled with an American divorcée named Wallis Simpson. He and his fast set of friends seemed to epitomise the modern era – impatient with protocol, indifferent to convention.

Winnie drew herself up to her full height, fixed the heckler with her pale blue stare and announced, in cut-glass tones, that she would take questions only. 'But Captain Hopkins persisted in addressing the meeting,' reported the papers. 'In the past year,' Hopkins shouted (a pugnacious-looking man in his forties, with bristling moustache and receding hairline), 'this society has been full of dissatisfaction and unrest.' Uneasy laughter ran around the room.

Mrs Lemon sat very still in her seat. This was her first annual meeting without Frank at her side, and she felt naked. No doubt about it, these attacks were personal. Chairman Sir Montagu Sharpe stepped in to shield the ladies, stemming criticism with smooth facts and figures, but it was impossible to ignore the issue on everybody's minds. Since Frank Lemon's death the year before, an internal 'investigation committee' had been set up to scrutinise the RSPB.

Sir Montagu agreed with this committee that staff should, from now on, retire at 65, 'unless otherwise determined'. He did *not* agree that a proportion of the Council should retire annually, as this would shed too many 'valuable and active' members. He pointed out that there had been eight changes on the Council since 1930 (changes that Mrs Lemon had felt most bitterly), and now six new members were to be added. These included Julian Huxley, 49, bespectacled champion of modern ornithology and chief witch-hunter on the investigation committee. Huxley was to prove Mrs Lemon's nemesis.

Buried in a navy foolscap box, stored in a cupboard at the RSPB headquarters, is a small sheaf of documents that shines a light on the painful extraction of Etta Lemon. It is astonishing that these papers have survived at all, given their highly personal nature and the vicious vendetta against her. On the top of this pile are a dozen sheets of blue writing paper, dense with Etta's purposeful black ink. Here she has put down her side of the story before it is too late; before the early days are dismissed as irrelevant, and her contribution erased from history.

Of her part in the society's birth, she was typically, gruffly modest: 'I was roped in and induced many hundreds to join.' On the relationship that defined her life: 'Then I married and Mr Lemon, as a barrister, being legally minded said we must have a constitution which he drew up for us . . . and from then until he died in 1935 Mr Lemon & I did the administration work of the Society, [giving] entirely gratuitous service as honorary secretaries, [which] involved both of us from 1889 onwards in considerable expense for which we never asked or received repayment.'

'Since then,' she continued, burying wounded pride, 'I have tried to loosen my hold on the Society & confine my energies to the management of the work done under The Watchers' Committee.'

After the revolt at the AGM in 1936, Mrs Lemon – deeply wounded – dug in and sat tight. It was only a matter of time.

> November 25 1938
> Dear Madam, (wrote Mrs Lemon to the Duchess of Portland)
> You have been so kind as to express a wish to know my reasons for severing my official connection with the work of this Society, other than that of the Watchers Committee.

The society had, she felt, changed beyond all recognition. The position of Honorary Secretary had been abolished, depriving her of influence. Money was being showered on scientific experiments in the RSPB's name – identification rings being attached to nestlings, census taking, the 'intimate photographing' of birds, all practices which Mrs Lemon 'deplored'. And yet her request that a wireless be presented to one of her oldest 'Watchers', a man who lived on a remote croft on a salary of £2 a year, was refused. The Finance Committee's only interest appeared to be 'hoarding, in the way of piling up investments'.

'I hope that all this will not weary Your Grace,' apologised Mrs Lemon, reining in her fury; 'I refrain from mentioning in detail the humiliation to which I have been subjected through being relegated to a very inferior position in the Society's office …

'With much respect, your obedient servant, M. L. Lemon.'

She was now 79 years old.

Etta Lemon was not a natural delegator. It might have been easier for her colleagues if she were, but she found it impossible to step back from *her* birds. In her own patch of the English countryside, she still patrolled her territory with Porro Prism binoculars (an improvement on opera glasses) and stout walking shoes.

Did she identify with the birds? She watched them, she followed them and she fought for them. Their freedom was a kind of release for her: a freedom that could not be compromised. This led, inevitably, to conflict with her fellow men. Etta was, for example, a zealous protector of the rust-winged red kite, a near-extinct species prized by egg collectors. By the early twentieth century there were thought to be just three pairs left, in mid-Wales. Her fierce, maternal instinct was aroused, and when the RSPB became involved with the Kite Committee in 1922, she took an active interest. When Frank Lemon later handed over the role of secretary to his wife, she took a closer interest still.

Professor of Botany John Henry Salter, eminent presence on the Kite Committee, found the unscientific Mrs Lemon not just 'proprietorial' of the red kites, but 'aggressively dictatorial' (as he later told his biographer).

One day, as he roamed the kites' nesting ground in Carmarthenshire, she 'descended' on him, so he said, 'from nowhere, bawling like a fish wife', and gave him 'a real roasting for trespassing in the vicinity of the kites'.

Etta Lemon shrugged off such criticism. She was simply, diligently, doing her job. But her possessive, dictatorial streak was to grow ever stronger until, by the late 1930s, she had become a liability.

It is hard not to read vindictiveness into the way Mrs Lemon was forced out of her society, necessary as it was. The image of a bird comes to mind, driven off a nest full of eggs. 'Mother of the Birds' was one of Etta's soubriquets, used both at home in Surrey and among bird lovers nationwide. Her many admirers might not have believed that such a formidable woman could be so rapidly cast aside. If Frank had still been alive, her attackers might not have had the courage.

The *coup de grâce* came just after the society's 50th-anniversary celebrations, as the country moved inexorably towards a second world war. The postman delivered a letter to Hillcrest, sent from London SW1. On RSPB notepaper, Mrs Lemon was informed, in crisp type, that her services would no longer be required.

> May 24, 1939. Personal.
> Dear Mr Woodbridge (she wrote to one of her trusted Watchers),
> I think you had better see this. I am quite bewildered & do not know
> where I am . . . the way I was 'baited' (there's no other word for it) at
> Watchers' Committee yesterday has dazed me.

Mrs Lemon had been informed in public that this would be her last committee meeting. She had not taken the hint thus far, and now she had to be told. The news was 'incomprehensible' – and yet for months past she had felt herself to be in a 'network of malevolent intrigue'. Her 'enemies & detractors' would see to it that she was 'thoroughly discredited in the eyes of the Council – so I have no appeal!'. Her last remaining ally, the Duchess of Portland, was 'too old & *remote* to be troubled'.

But the Duchess was fully aware of what was going on, and was even perhaps complicit in the removal of her old, obdurate campaigning partner. Winnie and Etta, Etta and Winnie – an unequal, yet productive relationship and a shared history that stretched back to their glorious prime, half a century before. When Winnie whistled, Etta came running. That is how it had always worked. Winnie could not come to Etta's rescue in 1939 – but she felt her misery. 'Mrs Lemon is to be made a Vice President,' she wrote in confidence to Sir Montagu Sharpe, 'to soften all the unhappiness of her having no active share in things.' Of all the documents that lie in the blue box, this scrawled letter is somehow the most poignant of them all.

Etta Lemon was wrong about being unloved. Letters from her 'boys' poured in. 'I never have heard a word spoken against *our* Mrs Lemon at Dungeness,' wrote Mr Cawson from the isolated shingle headland, 15 miles south of Etta's birthplace at Hythe. From the other end of the country, old George Arthur in the Orkneys had this to say: 'One thing certain is that the RSPB will always be to everybody synonymous with the name of Lemon. It certainly will not be the same for me without you. No one has done quite as much for the RSPB as you have, no one could do more, dear friend.' In 1938, the year before her ejection, Mrs Lemon had personally visited all her Watchers north of the Tweed and listened compassionately to their concerns.

'I just feel like one of your boys,' wrote Henry Watson from Cumberland. 'It seems awful that it should have to end in this way. How I wish I could just drop in and have a little comforting talk with you. Ever remembering your many kindnesses.'

And from his East End workshop in Walthamstow, Arthur Moorton – the RSPB's own 'garden ornamental craftsman', in the modern tradition – wrote from his indignant heart: 'I was absolutely flabbergasted to hear from you that you are finishing up with the Society at the end of the month, for to me you seem to be part and parcel of the Society and the complete inspiration of it.'

This sheaf of letters brought me to the soul of Mrs Lemon. After so many blandly formal annual reports and so much Victorian rhetoric, here was the meat of the matter. Raw and emotional, bewildered and affectionate – these letters revealed the soft heart within her gruff facade. Reading them brought her fierce, difficult, passionate and prejudiced nature vividly alive. The so-called 'fulminator in chief', the 'redoubtable' woman behind Britain's bird protection movement, was all too human.

'For me life holds a great many things other than the RSPB,' Etta wrote back staunchly to Watcher Mr Woodbridge, 'which I brought into being 50 years ago & have nursed into maturity.' But in the end, for it to grow and evolve, she had to let it go.

Etta Lemon died in a nursing home 14 years later, in 1953, aged 92. She was buried next to Frank at St Mary's in Reigate. Two representatives from the RSPB attended her funeral, a man and a woman – but they were overshadowed by the many other well-wishers who packed the pews. All Etta's many and varied causes were represented: the Royal Earlswood Institution for the mentally handicapped, the Reigate Education Committee, the Tuberculosis Aftercare Committee . . . She was, said the Reverend John Bertram Phillips, a 'magnificent character and personality', for whom the 'root and spring' of all her causes was a love for God, and a rare understanding of fellow humans. She also had great love for her fellow creatures. Mrs Lemon had championed the cause of wild birds, but her feet were very much on the earth. He 'had no doubt' that she was now in heaven.

The Reverend Phillips then paused. Sometimes, he said, Mrs Lemon and he would talk about the afterlife. 'And with a mischievous twinkle in her eye, she would ask, "Is that really true?"'

Etta Lemon's headstone – a restrained, polished granite – now lurches drunkenly to the right in St Mary's cemetery. Her name is carved simply beneath Frank's. As she would have wished, her extraordinary contribution to the protection and preservation of birdlife goes unmentioned. She is just another Victorian nonentity in an old English graveyard. Today, few, if any, have any idea that Britain's largest nature conservation charity was once – as Watcher Mr Arthur wrote so indignantly from the Orkney Isles – 'synonymous with the name of Lemon'.

EPILOGUE

'It rests with women themselves to make it clear to all humanity that they are worthy of the vote. It rests with women themselves to make themselves intelligent, to make themselves needed, to make themselves humaner beings, so that men would rather die than do without them in the life political.'

– LIZZY LIND AF HAGEBY, FEMINIST AND ANIMAL RIGHTS CAMPAIGNER, 'WOMEN AS HUMANITARIANS' SPEECH, JUNE 1910

'What does it mean to say that scruples on behalf of animals are merely emotional, emotive or sentimental? What else ought they to be?'

– MARY MIDGLEY, MORAL PHILOSOPHER AND ANIMAL RIGHTS PIONEER, *ANIMALS AND WHY THEY MATTER*, 1983

One hundred years after the RSPB's birth, a woman bowled into the charity's headquarters at Sandy. She knew nothing about birds. She'd been recruited from a career in health service management to bring an outsider's perspective; a fresh pair of eyes to this venerable institution. 'Who runs the country?' John Betjeman had asked, back in the 1950s. 'The Royal Society for the Protection of Birds. Their members are behind every hedge.' Barbara Young was its first female chief executive. The year was 1991.

Since the reign of that 'holy terror' Mrs Lemon, no woman had regained control of the RSPB. No one had even come close. Husbands and wives were even forbidden from working together, to prevent a Lemon-like monopoly ever arising again. Photographs of the 1960s and 1970s show staff line-ups on the lawn almost farcical in their sexual divide. Two secretaries in blouses and miniskirts stand among a solid mass of hirsute men in polo necks and flares. But things changed.

'I've been in organisations where it felt like a male bastion', said Barbara Young. 'But in 1991 the RSPB didn't feel like that at all. There were women in marketing, women in human resources, women in fundraising and communications. There were even a fair number of women scientists. It wasn't all hairy male conservationists.' Yet it seemed to have taken 50 years for the society to recover from Etta Lemon, and to dare to put another woman at the helm.

'Barbara kicked ass,' remembered Mike Everett, who joined the RSPB in 1964. 'She came in like a rocket.' The men cowered, not knowing quite what to expect. 'She shot a few bolts up people's backsides. But she made a great difference. Barbara amazed everyone with the speed at which she learned. She was almost – dare I say it? – one of the boys.'

She was, he said emphatically, *not* an Etta Lemon. 'She was a socialist, for a start.' Nor did she do what she did for the love of birds; joining the RSPB was a career move for which she was criticised – the first non-birder at the high table. Barbara Young excelled in management technique, but she knew that if she didn't try to love the birds she'd be 'dead in the water', and so she showed herself willing to learn – just as those middle class Victorian women had boned up on ornithology, the plumage trade and the legislative process.

Young realised that she had 'got the bug', as she put it, the day she watched a minister on television proposing something that she violently disagreed with – something that would affect the birds. In her fury, she picked up her briefcase and smashed it on the floor. It broke. *Here* was the passion. Here was the fighting instinct. The difference was that nobody called her 'redoubtable'.

There is something about Baroness Young's forthright manner that puts me in mind of Etta Lemon. She has the same single-mindedness, the same absolute belief that the impossible is possible. When Young joined the RSPB, there were 525,000 members. 'I thought, Hmm, a million's got a nice ring to it . . . ' The society elders shook their heads sagely, but she hit her target in 1997. 'What I do is campaigning,' she says, matter-of-factly. But Young is a woman, not a machine, and her gender alone seemed to encourage a different sort of interaction with members. There was the time that a female high court judge 'came steaming over' to her at a reception party:

'I thought, oh golly, is she going to take me to task on some policy?'

'I've got a really important question,' said the judge. 'On really cold nights, can I let the robins come into my kitchen? Is that OK?'

Barbara was 'slightly taken aback', but also rather moved.

*

For me, this encounter between two powerful, modern women nimbly and unexpectedly captures the joint legacy of Etta Lemon and Emmeline Pankhurst. What would our heroines have said, had they been able to flit through the reception party as ghosts in hats and furs? Here, in the heart of the British establishment, a female High Court Judge (nothing so unusual there, the first was appointed in 1965) is chatting to the chief executive of Britain's largest conservation charity – a woman who is also a baroness and a Labour life peer. As the women talk birds over corporate glasses of champagne, the chasm between those two veteran campaigners is deftly bridged.

Pankhurst and Lemon had not wanted the same thing, and their priorities had been very different. But somehow, over time, the results of their two separate campaigns for women's rights and animal rights have melded and merged to become so much a part of us that we barely give them pause for thought.

Should you let a robin into your kitchen? 'Robin-strokers' is derisive twitching patois for sentimental bird-lovers, often women – but the ability to tap into feminine compassion gained Baroness Young her goal of a million members, and a certain awed respect in the lobbies of Parliament.

The historic women's movements of Pankhurst and Lemon, while working to different and often opposite ends, were united around compassion. Each campaigned for the alleviation of cruelty and injustice. For the suffragists, it was injustice to women that mattered: 'equal pay for equal work' is a battle cry that still resonates today. If Victorian feather manufacturer Abraham Botibol had paid his women what he paid the men, Alice Battershall might not have stolen those two ostrich plumes.

'Poverty,' Mrs Pankhurst insisted, was ultimately down to 'bad government'. The suffrage movement fought on behalf of those less assertive women who worked with their hands in poorly paid, traditional feminine trades – the feather curlers, the indentured milliners, the hat box makers – all women who needed, in her words, 'more comfort, more leisure and better pay'.

Among the many who gained from the campaign for the vote, it was particularly satisfying to discover that Alice Battershall's daughter Louisa, a feather worker like her mother, was also to benefit. Thanks to determined suffragist Clementina Black and her investigative team at the Women's Industrial Council, a government trade board was created in 1919 for the ostrich, fancy feather and artificial flower industry. A minimum wage was set, working hours monitored and basic comforts introduced. And in 1927, A. Botibol and Company, 'the biggest in the feather trade', was thoroughly investigated for employer abuses. Abraham's son, Cecil, was found guilty of underpaying 27 of his 50 female employees, and of keeping no wage records. Forced to pay £234 in arrears and £17 in fines (around £40,000 in today's money), he threw up his hands and admitted that he deserved 'to lose on all points'. How the women must have cheered!

Etta Lemon and her RSPB local secretaries had different priorities. For them, it was cruelty to God's creatures that inspired the most pity: the obscene destruction of birdlife for something as seemingly trivial as the decoration of women's hats. This small, genteel band of campaigners relentlessly exposed to the world the human capacity for cruelty – until the world was shamed, and ultimately transformed, by their lesson in compassion.

Both movements changed Britain, making it the modern country we recognise today – a place in which it is simply a given that women have the right to vote, home to a conservation charity so powerful that governments ignore it at their peril. Today, you are not dismissed as 'sentimental' for having scruples on behalf of animals. A hundred years ago it was a very different story.

And yet we have heard of only one of these women.

In bird-watching terms, Emmeline Pankhurst is the 'charismatic species': plumed, elegantly attired, silver-tongued. She was a genius at self-publicity, a theatrical revolutionary who grasped brilliantly how to use the media. Next to this splendid bird-of-paradise, Mrs Lemon fades into obscurity. She is the uncharismatic species: the quacking female mallard or scurrying grey-brown rock pipit. Teetotal, evangelical, conservative, anti-suffrage... I have, at times, found Etta Lemon a hard woman to love. But the absolute selflessness at her core redeems her. She believed in a campaign far greater than herself, and this fervent belief expressed itself in her keen delight in the natural world – a delight so many of us now share.

Etta Lemon sought no glory in the public sphere. She was the agent, not the subject. Her modesty is the most attractive thing about her – but, in the end, it has not served her. While the suffrage story has found its place in history, the tale of Mrs Lemon and her Royal Society for the Protection of Birds has been left largely untold, right to the present day.

You might not realise it, but you experience her legacy – a direct link between those 'redoubtable' Victorian ladies and you, now – whenever you see a bird twisting around frantically in a tiny cage, or a great, dusty stuffed eagle in a provincial museum, or even those sensual, extraordinary dresses made entirely of feathers at the Alexander McQueen exhibition at London's V&A in 2015. The shock you might feel, the horror, or even just a feeling of sadness, is ultimately down to the efforts of Mrs Lemon and her band of women.

When I started researching this story, I made an appointment to view a selection of feathered hats from the millinery archive stored at the V&A Clothworkers' Centre in Kensington, London. I was shown into the textiles department by a curator – and there they were, laid out on an oblong, white-clothed table, like dishes at a dinner party for a dozen guests. Each was startlingly different, and shockingly *animal*. The various hats were over a 100 years old, but their iridescent feathers had not faded. Slowly, I circled the table.

Here was a black straw cloche from 1920 – the year before the Plumage Act – made by milliners D. C. Jones & Son of Swansea. Protruding from just above the brim was the whole head of a sharp-billed Raggiana bird-of-paradise: velvety green and black with little, glassy, yellow eyes. On either side of this truncated head a mass of dyed black paradise plumage spilled over the brim, in all its fine-filamented, charcoal-smudged gossamer beauty.

As I bent over this voluptuous yet savage piece of millinery, a group of visitors on a 'behind the scenes' tour was ushered through the glass doors and into the textiles room. There were the hats – my hats – laid out invitingly on the large, white table. Before the curators could stop them, the visitors ran over excitedly, hands and mobile phones outstretched. Then, suddenly, they faltered.

What *was* this? Whole *dead birds*? On top of hats? Birds with beaks, and eyes, and scrabbling little claws? Was this really a fashion? One woman reached out her finger and compulsively touched the yellow, staring, taxidermist's glass eye of the bird-of-paradise – and shuddered. The white-coated conservationist led her away.

Her shudder was Mrs Lemon's.

Notes

Relative values have been worked out using the website measuringworth.com, which employs a range of different calculations depending on the sum concerned (price, wage, output, etc).

Prologue

p.ix 'One baby is a patient baby' – Emmeline Pankhurst, 'Freedom or Death' speech delivered at Hartford, Connecticut, 13 November 1913. Extracted from (ed.) Brian MacArthur, *The Penguin Book of Twentieth-Century Speeches* (Penguin Books, 1993).

p. xii 'Worth a staggering £20 million a year' . . . 'Twice as much as an ounce of gold' – Robin Doughty, *Feather Fashions and Bird Preservation* (University of California Press, 1975).

p.xv '£2.6 million a year' – Sarah Abrevaya Stein, *Plumes: Ostrich Feathers, Jews, and a Lost World of Global Commerce* (Yale University Press, 2008).

Part 1 – Feathers

1 Alice Battershall

p. 2 'Alice Battershall, 23' – Police Intelligence, *Morning Post*, 4 September 1885.

p. 3 'Sentenced to six weeks' – London Metropolitan Archives CLA/005/02/019 (Court Registers Guildhall Justice Room).

p. 5 'Nearly suffocated' – E. S. Turner, *All Heaven in a Rage* (Michael Joseph, 1964).

p. 6 'Ineffable feel for feathers' – Sarah Abrevaya Stein, *Plumes: Ostrich Feathers, Jews, and a Lost World of Global Commerce* (Yale University Press, 2008).

2 Inspector Lakeman

p. 9 Inspector Lakeman's report from *Chief Inspector of Factories and Workshops Report, 1886–7* (Command Papers; reports of Commissioners: House of Commons Parliamentary Papers, 1888).

p. 10 'A "poor" household at this time' – Charles Booth, *Descriptive Map of London Poverty 1889*.

p. 12 'Rotten and reeking tenements' – Rev. Andrew Mearns, *The Bitter Cry of Outcast London*, 1883.

p. 12 'It just took them about two weeks to brush up' – 'A Feather Worker Never Forgets', *Nottingham Evening Post*, 9 July 1935.

p. 12 'A lightness of touch . . . damage the whole' – as above.

p. 13 'Just to lengthen it throughout by 1 inch' – Stein, *Plumes*, as above.

3 97 Lever Street

p. 16 'The fashion for sensational slum literature' – such as *The Bitter Cry of Outcast London*, attributed to the Rev. Andrew Mearns, 1883; *Povertyopolis: How the Poor Live* by George Sims, 1883; *Savage London* by Henry King, 1888; 'Whitechapel' by Arthur Morrison, published in the *Palace Journal*, 24 April 1889.

p. 16 'Each district has its character' – Charles Booth, *Inquiry Into Life and Labour of the People in London, 1886–1903*. The 'Descriptive Map of London Poverty' can be found at www.booth.lse.ac.uk/map.

p. 17 Observations on Lever Street taken from 'Walk with Police Constable R. Machell, 7 June 1898', accessed via www.booth.lse.ac.uk/notebooks/police-notebooks BOOTH/B/353, pp. 42–65.

4 Women Undercover

p. 19 'Whitechapel has never thoroughly recovered' – 'Report of the Lancet Special Sanitary Commission on the Polish Colony of Jew Tailors', *The Lancet*, 3 May 1884.

p. 20 'Pocket money . . . consumer' – Clara Collet, quoted in Ellen Ross, *Slum Travelers: Ladies and London Poverty, 1860–1920* (Berkeley, 2007).

p. 20 'There is hardly one thing which the Girton or Newnham girl requires' – Clara Collet, 'Women's Work' for Charles Booth, *Life and Labour* (1889).

p. 21 'Three storey hat . . . wilderness of feathers' – Jane Addams, *Some Reflections of the Failure of the Modern City to Provide Recreation for Young Girls*, quoted in Nan Enstad, *Ladies of Labor, Girls of Adventure: Working Women, Popular Culture, and Labor Politics at the Turn of the Twentieth Century* (New York, Columbia University Press, 1999).

p. 21 'Unknown saints' – Beatrice Webb, *My Apprenticeship* (Longmans & Co, 1926).

p. 21 'Machinists and pressers, well-clothed' – as above.

p. 22 'Pages from a Work Girl's Diary'– Beatrice Webb, *Nineteenth Century*, September 1888.

5 'Crewe Factory Girl'

p. 24 'I have come to the conclusion, Sir' – Ada Nield Chew, *The Life and Writings of a Working Woman* (Virago Press, 1982).

6 The Skylark

p. 26 'It seemed to us the world was upside down' – Emmeline Pethick-Lawrence, *My Part in a Changing World* (Hyperion Press, 1938).

p. 27 'A friend "in a class above her own"' – Agnes Louisa Money, *History of the Girls' Friendly Society* (Wells Gardner & Co, 1911).

p. 28 'The girls were wild and rude' – Alys Pearsall Smith (who later married Bertrand Russell), quoted in Charlotte Moore, *Hancox: A House and a Family* (Viking, 2010).

Part 2 – Birds

7 Young Etta

p. 32 'Simply an excuse for a feather' – Charles Blanc, *Art and Ornament in Dress* (1877), quoted in Michael Carter, *Putting a Face on Things: Studies in Imaginary Materials* (Education Enterprises, 1997).

p. 35 'A director of the Natural History Museum' – anecdote from H. G. Alexander, *Seventy Years of Birdwatching* (Poyser, 1974).

p. 35 'A mouth like a rat trap . . . might not have known how to do it' – former long-time RSPB staff member, interview with author, 2016.

p. 38 'He is fitting up my mansion/Which eternally shall stand' – anecdote from old girl Constance Maynard, who went on to found Westfield College, Hampstead, in 1882: one of Britain's first higher education institutions for women. Quoted in Naomi Lloyd: *The Life and Writings of Constance Maynard (1849–1935)* (University of British Columbia, Vancouver, 2011).

p. 38 'A band of admirably trained daughters' – Rev. Samuel Charlesworth, *Memorials of a Blessed Life*, 1882.

p. 38 'Finishing school in Lausanne' – Mrs Lemon's obituary, the *Surrey Mirror*, 17 July 1953.

p. 39 'A priestess of the genial day' – Henry James letter, date unknown, RSPB archives.

8 Young Emmeline

p. 40 'What a pity she wasn't born a lad' – E. [Emmeline] Pankhurst, *My Own Story* (Eveleigh Nash, 1914).

p. 40 'One of her favourite pastimes' – Ethel Smyth, *Female Pipings in Eden* (Peter Davies, 1934).

p. 41 'A graceful, elegant young lady' – E. S. [Sylvia] Pankhurst, *The Life of Emmeline Pankhurst* (T. Werner Laurie, 1935).

p. 41 'Beautiful hand' – E. S. Pankhurst, *The Suffragette Movement: An Intimate Account of Persons and Ideals* (Longmans & Co., 1931). Quoted in June Purvis, *Emmeline Pankhurst, A Biography* (Routledge, 2002).

p. 41 'Some great thing' – C. [Christabel] Pankhurst, *Unshackled: The Story of How We Won The* Vote (Hutchinson, 1959).

p. 41 'Dr Pankhurst did not desire' – E. Pankhurst, *My Own Story*, as above.

9 The Train Carriage

p. 43 'The Evangelicals ran three out of every four voluntary societies' – Frank Prochaska, *Christianity and Social Service in Modern Britain – The Disinherited Spirit* (Oxford University Press, 2006).

p. 44 'Begin low . . . When you can stand on a platform' – *The Story of the Evangelization Society, Briefly Told by the Honorary Secretary, John Wood* (Evangelization Society, 1907).

p. 44 'Discriminating advocacy . . . passionate and headlong declamation' – from 'Our Obligations to Wild Animals', *Blackwood's Edinburgh Magazine*, Volume 166, 1899. Reproduced in Martin Polley (ed.), *The History of Sport in Britain, 1880–1914: Field Sport, Volume 3*.

p. 45 'Feather bedecked women' – Etta Lemon's own term for plumage wearers.

p. 45 'First imperial wildlife measure' – British India, Straits Settlement 1884: the Ordinance was drafted by Arthur H. Lemon, C. M. G. 'The Story of the RSPB' by Mrs Frank E. Lemon, *Bird Notes and News* (early magazine of the RSPB), Autumn 1943.

p. 45 'Muff with a bird-of-paradise' – 'An Anti-Vivisectionist Reproved', *North Devon Journal*, 23 March 1882. 'Three points were observable in Miss Cobbe's outward presentment – namely, she had an ostrich feather in her bonnet, a bird of paradise on or near her muff, and she carried an ivory-handled umbrella.'

p. 45 When the RSPCA opened a Blackheath, Greenwich and New Cross branch in 1891, Frank Lemon was a prominent member.

p. 45 'Please Give the Horse His Head'– sign used by the RSPCA. Turner, *All Heaven in a Rage*, as above.

10 Of Bird-Wearing Age

p. 47 Frank Chapman, 'Birds and Bonnets' (Letter to the Editor), *Forest and Stream* 26, 25 February 1886. He went on to become Curator of Birds at the American Museum of Natural History.

p. 48 'Around *five million* birds were killed annually' – 'The Destruction of Birds for Millinery Purposes', *Ornithologist and Oologist* 11 (1886).

p. 48 'Taking almost anything with feathers . . . bird-wearing age' – Supplement to the American magazine *Science*, 16 February 1886.

p. 49 'The headgear of women' – George Bird Grinnell, *Forest and Stream*, December 1888.

p. 49 'On Wednesday 21 March 1888, a historic plumage sale was held' – *The Auk*, 1888, pp.334–5. Cited in Doughty, *Feather Fashions*, as above.

p. 49 The American Ornithologists' Union (AOU) was established in 1883; *The Auk*, its peer-reviewed scientific journal, in 1884.

p. 50 'Bird plumage could be worked into eight basic forms' – Charlotte R. Aiken, *Millinery* (New York, 1922), and Anna Ben Yusuf, *The Art of Millinery* (New York, 1909).

p. 50 '*The Dressmaker and Milliner* trade quarterly' – descriptions taken from Spring 1895.

p. 52 'Threatened 61 bird species' – Doughty, *Feather Fashions*, as above.

11 The Tea Party

p. 53 'Like many great British institutions' – Stephen Moss, *A Bird in the Bush* (Aurum Press, 2004).

p. 56 'All grass roots activism' – Alison Light, interview with author, 2015.

p. 57 'A living flame, active as a bit of quicksilver' – Mrs Stanton Blatch, quoted in C. Pankhurst, *Unshackled*, as above.

p. 58 'I swear that *cannibals* had more respect' – W. H. Hudson, letter to *The Times*, 17 October 1893.

p. 60 *The Evolution of Sex* by Patrick Geddes and J. Arthur Thomson, quoted in Barbara T. Gates, *Kindred Nature: Victorian and Edwardian Women Embrace the Living World* (University of Chicago Press, 1998).

p. 60 'It is our vanity . . . cruel work . . . keeper's gibbets' – Eliza Phillips, 'Destruction of Ornamental-Plumaged Birds', Society for the Protection of Birds (SPB) pamphlet, 1891.

p. 60 'Something 'masculine' about Mrs Phillips' – according to her obituary, she had 'a bent of mind perhaps somewhat masculine, and a deep sincerity of purpose', *Bird Notes and News*, 7, 1916.

p. 60 'Literally waded' – account by W. H. Hudson of visit to warehouse, quoted in Eliza Phillips pamphlet, as above.

p. 61 'The humming-bird exceeds all creatures' – W. H. Hudson, *The Naturalist in La Plata* (Chapman and Hall, 1892).

12 Emily Williamson

p. 63 'Stout Victorian woman' – Nick Towle, *Manchester Evening Press*, 17 February 1989.

p. 65 'People like birds for three reasons – ' Henry Stacy Marks, *Punch*, 26 October 1889.

p. 65 'Lessen, as by annual inches . . . Not a *very* severe self-denying ordinance that, Ladies?' – *Punch*, 26 October 1889.

p. 65 'Bessy heard the birds' – quoted in H. E. Litchfield, *A Century of Family Letters* (John Murray, 2015).

13 A Very Ambitious Title

p. 67 'The heart of fashionable London' – details on shops from Charles Eyre Pascoe, *London of To-day: An Illustrated Handbook for the Season* (1892).

p. 68 '"Vigogne cashmere" cloak . . . "Magicienne" fur bag muff' – catalogue of the Cavendish House, Cheltenham, 1886, cited in Alison Adburgham, *Shops and Shopping, 1880–1914: Where and in What Matter the Well-Dressed Englishwoman Bought Her Clothes* (George Allen & Unwin, 1964).

p. 68 'She wears a sealskin coat/Its grace and shape I note' – 'A Valentine' by American poet Oscar Fay Adams (1855–1919).

p. 68 'The waspish novelist Ouida' – 'The New Woman', *North American Review*, May 1894.

p. 69 'In 1891, there were 548 milliners' – Kelly's Directory.

p. 70 'Quiet dignity . . . lovable disposition' – obituary for Emily Williamson, *The Times* 13 January 1936.

14 Flight

p. 72 'Smiles of amusement . . . a sparrow's housekeeping book' – 'History of the Society', Mrs F. E. Lemon, *Bird Notes and News*, April 1903.

p. 72 'One is always glad to hear or read' – Rev. Francis Orpen Morris, *Nature Notes*, 1891 (the magazine of the Selborne Society).

p. 73 'Own fledgling' – Richard Clarke, *Pioneers of Conservation: The Selborne Society and the Royal SPB* (University of London, 2004).

p. 74 'Like a list from Debretts' – Tony Samstag, *For Love of Birds* (RSPB, 1989).

15 Impracticable Dreamers

p. 76 'About midway between the civilised man of our era' – Herbert Spencer's arguments were paraphrased by W. H. Hudson in a letter to *The Times*, 17 October 1893.

p. 76 Quotes from Samuel Smith, Millicent Fawcett and William Gladstone from excepts in Jane Lewis (ed.), *Volume V: Before The Vote Was Won: Arguments For and Against Women's Suffrage, 1864–1896* (Routledge & Kegan Paul, Ltd, 1987).

p. 78 '*The Spectator* swiftly congratulated Gladstone ' – *The Spectator*, 23 April 1892.

p. 78 'Half a loaf is better than none' – David Mitchell, *Queen Christabel* (Macdonald & Jane's Publishers Ltd., 1977).

p. 79 'He lighted a smouldering fire of indignation' – E. S. Pankhurst, *The Suffragette Movement* (as above).

p. 79 'So languid' – Mitchell, *Queen Christabel*, as above.

p. 80 'Can you imagine anything more ridiculous?' – *American Ornithology for the Home and School*, 1905. Quoted in Moss, *A Bird in the Bush*, as above.

p. 80 'Women of little education and possibly depraved minds' – Sir Harold Johnston, writing in *The Times*, 22 April 1911.

p. 80 'American plumage campaigner Harriet Hemenway' – Oliver Orr, *Saving American Birds* (University Press of Florida, 1992).

p. 81 'Darwin's latest ideas' – *The Descent of Man, and Selection in Relation to Sex* (John Murray, 1871).

16 Courting the Men

p. 83 'May perhaps reach the eyes of clergymen' – Eliza Phillips, referring to 'Letter to Clergymen, Ministers, and others', W. H. Hudson, *The Times*, November 1895.

p. 84 'Sentimentality . . . embarrassing accretions' – the Rev. Orpen Morris quoted in Clarke, *Pioneers*, as above.

p. 85 'The Scottish artist Jemima Blackburn' – Charles Darwin refers to her observations on the cuckoo in the sixth edition of *The Origin of Species* (1872). Blackburn died in 1909.

p. 85 'The little tender, loving mothers' – Eliza Brightwen, *The Life and Thoughts of a Naturalist* (T. F. Unwin, 1909).

p. 86 'A professional wildfowler' – anonymously writing to *The Times* in September 1891, quoted in the *SPB First Annual Report*, 1891.

p. 87 'Wings' – satirist George Du Maurier, *Punch*, 17 October 1893.

17 Winifred, Duchess of Portland

p. 88 'Dear Mrs Lemon' – RSPB archives, correspondence from the Duchess of Portland, 26 February 1903.

p. 91 'This is beyond doubt a woman's question' – Eliza Phillips, *Destruction of Ornamental-Plumaged Birds*, 1891.

p. 93 'Exactly like the sort of brush servants use to clean lamp-chimneys' – Eliza Phillips, *Mixed Plumes*, 1895.

p. 94 'They died from exposure' – Stein, *Plumes*, as above.

p. 95 'As painless as cutting human hair' – 'Is Ostrich Farming Cruel?', *The Times*, 17 August 1886.

p. 95 Ostrich farming: SPB Second Annual Report, 1892.

p. 95 Ostrich plucking: *Bird Notes and News*, No. 7, October 1904.

p. 95 'Spoiling other people's pleasure' – the Humanitarian League was founded by Henry Salt in 1891. Quoted in Henry Salt (ed.), *Killing for Sport – essays*, preface by George Bernard Shaw (Bell & Sons, 1914).

18 The Crème de la Crème

p. 98 'It is not ladylike to kill animals' – *Advice to a Grand-daughter: Letters from Queen Victoria to Princess Victoria of Hesse*, quoted in Jane Ridley, *Bertie: A Life of Edward VII* (Chatto & Windus, 2012).

p. 98 'She hunts the hare' – Ouida, 'The New Woman' (1894).

p. 98 'Impossible for a woman to do a long day's walking' – Jonathan Garnier Ruffer, *The Big Shots: Edwardian Shooting Parties* (Debrett's Peerage Ltd, 1977).

p. 99 'On 4 November 1896, a record 3,113 pheasants were killed' – Jane Ridley, 'The Sport of Kings': Shooting and the Court of Edward VII, published in *The Court Historian*, December 2013.

p. 99 'Very earnestly I ask you' – John Ruskin, *The Eagle's Nest: ten lectures on the relation of natural science to art*, 1872. Quoted in Turner, *All Heaven in a Rage*, as above.

p. 99 'As though they were dogs' – Turner, *All Heaven in a Rage*, as above.

p. 99 'John Sly'– *Bird Notes and News*, April 1904. The Wild Birds Protection Act came into effect on 15 March that year, prohibiting the 'killing and taking' of wild birds. It proved impossible to enforce.

p. 99 'Rough-looking…instinctively avoid' – *Bird Notes and News*, July 1904.

p. 100 'Starlings' wings wanted' – Turner, *All Heaven in a Rage*, as above.

p. 100 'Advocated headwear' – 'Sir – So long as Royalty and the *elite* wear aigrettes, more especially in so-called toques – the advocated head-gear for the Jubilee – so long will the unfortunate birds be "slaughtered", until they may become extinct like the "dodo". Signed, English Ladies.' *The Times*, 28 December 1897.

p. 101 'No one . . . has ever met with such an ovation' – *Queen Victoria's Journal*, quoted in Ridley, *Bertie*, as above.

p. 101 'Robed for coronation or beheading' – *Illustrated London News*, 11 June 1897.

p. 101 'Freak orders . . . several girls' – Jean-Philippe Worth, *A Century of Fashion* (Boston, Little Brown and Cie, 1928).

p. 101 'A record year of pillage' – *SPB Sixth Annual Report*, 1896.

p. 102 'Crème de la crème of Society, from Royalty downwards' – *Illustrated London News*, 2 July 1897.

p. 103 'Human beings too dispirited' – Consuelo Vanderbilt Balsan, *The Glitter and the Gold* (William Heinemann, 1953).

p. 103 'ghastly and repulsive' – *The Times*, 25 December 1897.

p. 103 'I have been forced to the conclusion' – Eleanor Vere Boyle, *The Times*, 31 December 1897.

p. 103 'A Mother of a Daughter' – *The Times*, 28 December 1897.

Part 3 – Hats

19 Dying to Get Out

p. 106 'An extraordinary, ritualised promenade' – Frederick Willis, *A Book of London Yesterdays* (Phoenix House, 1960).

p. 106 '"Animal-like" scenes' – Charles Cavers Esq., *Hades! The Ladies! Being Extracts from the Diary of a Draper* (Gurney & Jackson, 1933).

p. 108 'In constitution at least ten years older' – Henry Mayhew, *London Labour and the London Poor: Milliners and Dressmakers* (1851).

p. 108 'An anonymous letter to *The Times*' – picked up by regional papers on 15, 16 and 17 July 1884.

p. 109 'This unnerving document' – London Metropolitan Archives, Mary Ann Green's apprenticeship indenture as milliner, LMA/4714/00/003.

20 The Millinery Detectives

p. 111 Mary Van Kleeck, *A Seasonal Industry: A Study of the Millinery Trade in New York* (Russell Sage Foundation, New York, 1917).

p. 111 'Wages remained stuck at 1880s levels' – James A Schmiechen, *Sweated Industries and Sweated Labor – The London Clothing Trades, 1860–1914* (Urbana: University of Illinois Press, 1983).

p. 113 'A similar impact' – thanks in part to Black's work, the Ostrich and Fancy Feather and Artificial Flower Trade Board was established in 1919, tracking and monitoring the industry until the late twentieth century.

p. 113 Clementina Black (ed.), *Married Women's Work: being the report of an enquiry undertaken by the Women's Industrial Council* (G. Bell & Sons, London, 1915).

p. 114 'What's the birds for, if they aint to be used?' – quoted in Moss, *A Bird in the Bush*, as above.

21 Queen Alix

p. 115 'Whooping, "Queen dead!"' – *The Times*, 24 January 1901.

p. 115 'Everything that could be dyed was used' – Dickins & Jones memoir, Mr J.B. Smith, quoted in Jane Ashelford, *The Art of Dress: Clothes and Society, 1500–1914* (Harry N. Abrams, 1996).

p. 115 'Why on earth do you want women to be like men' – Ridley, *Bertie*, as above.

p. 115 'The most that could be said for him' – Wilfrid Blunt's diary entry for 23 January 1901. Quoted in Ridley, *Bertie*, as above.

p. 116 'In point of fact, she says more original things' – Brett, *Journals and Letters*, vol. 1 (28 July 1902). Quoted in Ridley, *Bertie*, as above.

p. 117 'Despised his beautiful wife as bird-brained' – Ridley, *Bertie*, as above.

p. 118 'Somewhat tame and insipid' – W. H. Hudson to the Ranee of Sarawak, 23 Feb 1905. Edward Garnett (ed.), *Letters Vol II 1904–22* (Nonesuch Press, 1923).

p. 119 'The millinery question . . . ethics and aesthetics' – *SPB Twelfth Annual Report*, 1902.

p. 120 'Twenty years of experience has led me to the conclusion' – Mrs Phillips' speech reported in *Bird Notes and News*, September 1906.

22 'Egret' Bennett

p. 121 David 'Egret' Bennett – *The Sun*, New York, Sunday 7 June 1896. 'Skill required to get the wary birds. Extermination imminent' ran the headline.

p. 122 'The delicate snow-white plumes' – naturalist Mr Herbert K. Job in *Country Life in America*, April 1905, reproduced in *Bird Notes and News*, October 1905.

p. 122 'Three hundred may be killed in an afternoon' – 'The Biography of a Lie', *Bird Notes and News*, July 1903.

p. 122 'I wish that the ladies who encourage this cruel trade' – Paul Fountain, *The Great Mountains and Forests of America* (Longmans, Green and Co, 1902) quoted in *Bird Notes and News*, 1902.

p. 124 'So thoroughly democratic' – *Bird Notes and News*, October 1905. Dickens used the osprey as a shorthand for social transgression when worn in the bonnet of drunken night nurse Sairey Gamp, sidekick to day nurse Betsy Prigg in *Martin Chuzzlewit* (1843). Mrs Lemon misspells their names.

p. 124 'Could fetch $32' – Oliver Orr, *Saving American Birds* (University Press of Florida, 1992).

p. 125 'The original Operation Osprey' – in 1958 the RSPB set up a 24-hour protection watch named 'Operation Osprey' at Loch Garten in Strathspey to protect a pair of breeding osprey, presumed extinct in Britain since the 1920s.

p. 126 'Thoroughly into the matter' – *Millinery Record*, July 1896. The same issue quotes the *Draper's Record*.

p. 126 'Wings and feather ornaments can be so cleverly made' – *Home Chat*, September 1897.

23 Deeds Not Words

p. 128 'Stoical, tragic expression' – C. Pankhurst, *Unshackled*, as above.

p. 129 'We must have an independent women's movement!' – C. Pankhurst, *Unshackled*, as above.

p. 130 'Plumage Cranks . . . Frothy Fanatics' – *Draper's Organiser*, November 1920.

p. 130 'Sensational campaign' – E. Pankhurst, *My Own Story*, as above.

p. 130 'We threw away all our conventional notions' – as above.

24 The Frontal Attack

p. 133 'She has selected this store for her purchases . . ."go on telling that story"' – *Bird Notes and News*, 1903. Some descriptive asides not contained by speech marks are my own.

p. 135 'London Commercial Sale Rooms' – of 2,067 paradise birds, 113 were sold. Reported in *The Globe*, 28 October 1903.

p. 135 'While these foreign birds' – as above.

25 Mrs Pattinson

p. 137 Mrs Pattinson, milliner, Ulverston – BDB 38, Cumbria Archive and Local Studies Centre, Barrow.

p. 140 Letters from Hilda Howard and Bishop Thornton, 1904 – RSPB archives.

26 The Countess Fabbricotti

p. 142 Records of Countess Fabbricotti, milliner – 434/1–7 City of Westminster Archives Centre.

p. 142 'A drawing room reception in the height of the season' – *Chicago Tribune*, 18 June 1905.

p. 144 'We have been dreadfully hard up . . . everybody's sympathy' – *San Francisco Call*, 28 June 1905.

p. 144 'The old notion that there is anything discreditable' – *Hennessey Clipper*, 16 August 1906.

p. 144 'I have received more invitations' – *Hennessey Clipper*, as above.

p. 146 'A more ridiculous picture could scarcely be transmitted' – *RSPB Seventeenth Annual Report*, 1907.

p. 147 'For this lady, who had very black hair' – George Bernard Shaw, letter to *The Times*, 3 July 1905.

p. 148 'Ethics and aesthetics' – *RSPB Fifteenth Annual Report*, 1905.

p. 148 'No more irresistible magnet' – Smyth, *Female Pipings in Eden*, as above.

p. 148 'Clothes are the first thing that catch the eye' – quoted in Anne de Courcy, *Margot at War: Love and Betrayal in Downing Street, 1912–1916* (Weidenfeld & Nicolson, 2014).

p. 148 'The Official Wretch of the Woman Movement' – H.G. Wells, *The Freewoman*, 23 November 1911. Wells urged the WSPU to cure itself of its 'morbid infatuation' with Asquith.

27. Royal Approval

p. 151 'The trimming is the hat nowadays and the hat the trimming' – *Western Daily Press*, June 1906.

p. 151 'I am afraid it is no use asking the Queen about a petition' – Winnie Portland to Etta Lemon, 4 January 1905, RSPB archives.

p. 152 'It was very gratifying' – 'The Story of the RSPB' by Mrs Frank E. Lemon, *Bird Notes and News*, Autumn 1943.

28 The 'Suffragette'

p. 157 'Pay no attention to those cats mewing' – attributed to Lloyd George in E. S. Pankhurst, *The Suffragette Movement*, as above.

p. 157 'Heavy hat tipped well over the face' – according to Margaret Wynne Nevinson, *Life's Fitful Fever*, quoted in Joyce Marlow,

Votes for Women: The Virago Book of Suffragettes (Virago Press, 2000).

p. 157 'They come here asking us to treat them like men' – Winston Churchill, speaking at St John's School Gartside, Manchester, on being interrupted by Sylvia Pankhurst. Quoted in Randolph S. Churchill, *Winston Spencer Churchill, Volume II: Young Statesman* (Heinemann, 1969).

p. 158 'Nothing would induce me to vote' – Churchill speaking at a hustings in a school in Cheetham Hill, Manchester, October 1906.

p. 158 'If I might illustrate my meaning from football' – Mr E Richmond, Chair of the Reigate Branch of the Central Society for Women's Suffrage, at a meeting in Redhill, September 1907. Quoted in Marlow, *Votes for Women*, as above.

p. 158 'Found the place full of fashionable ladies' – Alice Milne's diary, 22 October 1906. Quoted in Melanie Phillips, *The Ascent of Woman* (Little, Brown, 2003).

p. 158 'Six stalwart policemen' – 'Amazing Scenes at the Opening of Parliament: Shrieking Women Ejected', *Daily Chronicle*, October 1906.

p. 159 'From a wide acquaintance with women suffragists' – *RSPB Sixteenth Annual Report*, 1906.

Part 4 – Votes

29 Onto the Street

p. 162 'Kate Frye's entire family' – Elizabeth Crawford, *Campaigning for the Vote, Kate Parry Frye's Suffrage Diary* (Francis Boutle, 2013).

p. 164 'Wot abart the ole man's tea this orternoon?' – 'Sarcasm for Suffragettes', *Sheffield Evening Telegraph*, 11 February 1907.

p. 165 'Like sardines in a box' – *Leeds Mercury*, 11 February 1907.

p. 165 'An evident sympathiser' – 'The Policeman and the "Suffragettes"', *Yorkshire Evening Post*, 11 February 1907.

p. 166 'Hated this appeal to the Mob' – Mitchell, *Queen Christabel*, as above.

p. 167 ' Writer Israel Zangwill' – his speech, 'One and One are Two', was reproduced in an appendix to Broughton Villiers (ed.), *The Case for Women's Suffrage* (T. Fisher Unwin, 1907).

p. 167 'Stick-in-the-mud dodos' – Marlow, *Votes for Women*, as above.

p. 168 'If you went to a dinner party' – Lady Ricardo interviewed in 1974 by Brian Harrison for *Separate Spheres: The Opposition to Women's Suffrage in Britain* (Croom Helm Ltd, 1978).

p. 169 'At a smart trot . . . quite indescribable for brutality and ruthlessness' – E. Pankhurst, *My Own Story*, as above.

p. 169 Alice Hawkins' story, and Ramsay MacDonald's letter – www.alicesuffragette.co.uk, edited by her great-grandson Peter Barratt.

p. 170 'Were more impressed' – C. Pankhurst, *Unshackled*, as above.

p. 171 'Never before given a thought to public questions . . . long to have been men' – Ray [Rachel] Strachey, *The Cause: A Short History of Women's Movement in Great Britain* (G. Bell & Sons Ltd, 1928).

p. 172 'Do-gooder' Sophia Lonsdale – letter to *The Times*, 15 January 1907, in response to a letter from the journalist Frances H. Low in December 1906, asserting that if women were directly involved in politics, the triviality which pervaded newspapers written by or for women might descend on Westminster. Quoted in Harrison, *Separate Spheres*, as above.

p. 172 'She was at her best' – *The Times* obituary of Sophia Lonsdale, 27 October 1936.

30 The Antis

p. 177 'A real feminist' – suffragist and NUWSS member Baroness Mary Stocks on Violet Markham, in an interview with Joan Bakewell on *Late Night Line-up*, BBC2, 1 February 1968.

p. 178 'Discriminating advocacy . . . passionate and headlong declamations' – Sir Herbert Maxwell, *Our Obligations to Wild Animals* (Blackwood's Edinburgh Magazine, 1899).

p. 178 'We believe that men and women are different' – Violet Markham, quoted in Julia Bush, 'British Women's Anti-Suffragism and the Forward Policy, 1908–14', *Women's History Review*, 2002.

p. 179 'A important bill' – prohibiting the importation of wild bird plumage. Put before the House of Lords by Lord Avebury on 5 May, it was read a second time and referred to a Select Committee on 19 May, then passed by the House without opposition on 21 July 1908. Introduced by the Conservative Lord Robert Cecil into the House of Commons on 22 July, time ran out before the second reading and 'no opportunity was afforded for further progress during the Autumn Session', *RSPB Eighteenth Annual Report*, 1908.

p. 179 'If you have an influential position' – Emmeline Pethick-Lawrence speaking on 30 May 1907, quoted in Mitchell, *Queen Christabel*, as above.

p. 181 'Stunned surprise . . . permanent "Commander-in-Chief"' – Teresa Billington-Greig, *The Militant Suffragette Movement: Emancipation in a Hurry* (Frank Palmer, 1911).

p. 181 'Worked off their feet . . . £5 and £10 notes' – Fawcett, *What I Remember* (Putnam, 1924).

p. 182 'Jabbing the sergeant-at-arms with a hatpin' – *The Times*, 30 October 1908.

p. 182 'Seven hundred MPs, clerics, constituents' – *The Times*, 19 June 1908.

p. 182 'Daintily clad suffragettes' – Fawcett, *What I Remember*, as above.

p. 182 'Far from having injured the movement' – Millicent Garrett Fawcett in *The Times*, 27 October 1906.

p. 182 'Somehow wandered into the wrong camp' – *Common Cause* (NUWSS magazine), 10 November 1910.

p. 182 'Future generations will probably mete out' – Millicent Garrett Fawcett, *Women's Suffrage: A Short History of a Great Movement* (Jack, 1912).

p. 184 'Sucks up my soul like a tide' – Constance Lytton, *Prisons and Prisoners: Some Personal Experiences* (William Heinemann, 1914).

p. 184 'If a bevy of dainty, beautiful, exquisitely dressed women' – Marie Corelli, *Woman, or Suffragette? A Question of National Choice* (C. Arthur Pearson, Ltd, 1907).

p. 184 'It cannot be denied' – Strachey, *The Cause*, as above.

p. 185 'Awfully strong-minded in walking dress' – Elizabeth Garrett Anderson (Britain's first female surgeon), writing to Emily Davies (co-founder of Girton College, Cambridge) in the late 1860s about a fellow medical student. Quoted in Strachey, *The Cause*, as above.

31 The Feminine Arts

p. 186 'Amazon drum and fife band' – *News of the World*, 14 May 1909.

p. 188 'Will members please remember' – *Votes for Women* (newspaper of the WSPU), 4 February 1909.

p. 188 'Obtain contributions to the millinery stall' – *Votes for Women*, 11 February 1909.

p. 188 'Typically measured around three feet high' – Jenna Weissman Joselit, *A Perfect Fit: Clothes, Character and the Promise of America* (Henry Holt and Company, New York, 2001).

p. 189 'I feel myself impelled to put in a plea for the birds' – letter from Clara Evelyn Mordan, *Votes for Women*, 18 February 1909.

p. 189 'Handed over a total of £759 of her fortune' – noted in Elizabeth Crawford, *The Women's Suffrage Movement: A Reference Guide, 1866–1928* (UCL Press, 1999). Mordan went on to fund the rebuilding of St Hughes College, Oxford in 1914–16.

p. 190 'I was for some years a Fellow of the Bird Protection Society' – Joan Baillie Guthrie, *Votes for Women*, 12 March 1909.

p. 192 'A diminutive woman with a camera' – Anna Sparham, *Soldiers & Suffragettes: The photography of Christina Broom* (Philip Wilson Publishers for the Museum of London, 2015).

p. 193 'A brilliant success' – *Votes for Women*, 28 May 1909.

p. 193 'It has gradually edged the working class element' – Teresa Billington-Greig, *The Militant Suffrage Movement* (as above).

32 The Advice of Men

p. 195 'You naughty dog . . . in spite of himself' – Charles William Stamper, *What I Know* (Mills & Boon, 1913).

p. 195 'That horrid Biarritz' – Queen Alexandra to Sir Frederick Ponsonby, from Ponsonby's *Recollections*, quoted in Christopher Hibbert, *Edward VII: The Last Victorian King* (St Martin's Press, 2007).

p. 195 'Literally besieged from morning to night' – *Illustrated London News*, 14 May 1910.

p. 195 'Disembarking passengers could pick up' – *Dundee Evening Telegraph*, 12 May 1910.

p. 196 'Critical Frenchwoman . . . how that poor "little milliner" worked' – *Linlithgow Gazette*, 13 May 1910.

p. 196 'The Crux of the whole toilette' – *The Evening Standard and St James Gazette*, 10 May 1910.

p. 196 'A cart-wheel headdress' – *Sheffield Telegraph*, 12 May 1910.

p. 201 Correspondence between Cromer and Curzon – taken from the Cromer Papers and the Curzon Papers, quoted in Harrison, *Separate Spheres*, as above, and in Julia Bush, *Women Against the Vote: Female Anti-Suffragism in Britain* (Oxford University Press, 2007).

p. 201 'It was our fate, as antis' – Janet Courtney, quoted in Harrison, *Separate Spheres*, as above.

p. 202 'Seven of these peers were vice presidents or fellows of the RSPB': Lords Cromer, Curzon, Jersey, Rothschild and Cawdor; Ladies Mount Stephen and Wantage.

p. 202 'A handsome £300 a year' – Miss Lewis's salary is not recorded, but a female clerk would typically earn £30 to £70 a year.

p. 203 'A most harsh, repellent and unpleasing woman' – Crawford, *Campaigning for the Vote* (as above).

p. 205 'The scene down there was terrible' – testimony of Mary Frances Earl and others, quoted in, J. Murray and H.N. Brailsford, *The Treatment of Women's deputations by the Metropolitan Police* (The Women's Press, 1911).

p. 205 'Well dressed, in furs' – *Derby Chronicle*, 19 November 1910.

p. 206 'The police are even accused of using their heavy helmets' – *Draft Memorandum by Edward Henry, Commissioner of the Metropolitan Police, on Allegations Contained in Mr Brailsford's Memorial.* Quoted in Marlow, *Votes for Women*, as above.

33 Maternal Weakness

p. 207 'Married women have all the plums of life!' – E. S. Pankhurst, *The Suffragette Movement*, as above.

p. 207 'Courtesy . . . impartial manner' – *Surrey Mirror*, 11 November 1911.

p. 208 'The official photographic portrait of Mrs Lemon' – Surrey History Centre, Woking, Ref. 6918/1/4/4, Photo album: 'Borough of Reigate Jubilee Year of Incorporation: some portraits', 1913.

p. 210 'Rather a nest of suffragettes' – Edgar Jones (ed.), *The Memoirs of Edwin Waterhouse* (Batsford, 1988).

p. 211 'A vision of pale blue chiffon and lace' – Constance Maud, *No Surrender* (Duckworth, 1911).

p. 213 'In Fairyland . . . "'The Children's Mayor . . ."' – *Dorking and Leatherhead Advertiser*, 5 December 1911.

p. 213 '£50-worth of "ospreys"' – *RSPB Twenty-First Annual Report*, 1911.

p. 214 'Like foot-and-mouth disease' – Lloyd George, reported in E. S. Pankhurst, *The Suffragette Movement*, as above.

p. 215 'Bearer of the most pathetic insignia of poverty and failure' – Gareth Stedman Jones, *Outcast London: A Study in the Relationship Between Classes in Victorian Society* (Oxford, Clarendon, 1971).

p. 216 'The Sweated Industries' Exhibition' – held at Queen's Hall, Bayswater, 2–29 May 1906: 30,000 visitors went to see real women at work, and a photographic exhibition. The National Anti-Sweating League was formed, that July, as a result.

p. 216 Mary Van Kleeck's report was illustrated with photographs by the pioneering social photographer Lewis Wickes Hine.

p. 216 A. H. E. Mattingley's photographs, taken in a heronry in Mathoura, New South Wales in 1906, were published in *Emu* magazine in 1907 and acquired by the RSPB in 1909. The RSPB made him an Honorary Life Member.

p. 216 '618 tonnes of bird skins and feathers' – letter to *The Spectator* from RSPB member Ella Fuller Maitland, 19 August 1911.

p. 217 'The only girl in the family' – Purvis, *Emmeline Pankhurst*, as above.

p. 217 'Necessity' – C. Pankhurst, *Unshackled*, as above.

p. 217 'So ruthless was the inner call to action' – E. S. Pankhurst, *The Suffragette Movement*, as above.

p. 217 'Of course, now all is settled' – Adela Pankhurst, *My Mother*, Pankhurst-Walsh papers, quoted in Martin Pugh, *The Pankhursts* (Allen Lane, 2001).

p. 217 'The German man is manly' – Cromer speaking at a November Anti rally, 1910. Quoted in Harrison, *Separate Spheres*, as above.

p. 217 'Race regenerators' – according to Dr Mary Scharlieb, surgeon and gynaecologist.

p. 218 'The absorption of women in politics' – Edward David (ed.), 'Inside Asquith's Cabinet', in *The Diaries of Charles Hobhouse* (John Murray, 1977).

p. 218 'Mayoresses' – *RSPB Twentieth Annual Report*, 1910.

p. 218 'Prophetic' – E. Pankhurst, *My Own Story*, as above.

34 Peak Rage

p. 219 'I am what you call a hooligan' – E. Pankhurst, *My Own Story*, as above.

p. 219 'As if she were ready to pour a cup of tea' – from *Challenging Years, The Memoirs of Harriot Stanton Blatch* (New York, 1940), quoted in Purvis, *Emmeline Pankhurst*, as above.

p. 219 'Bold, coarse, aggressive . . . of rare ability' – *Votes for Women*, 12 November 1909.

p. 219 'With absolutely no demand, no ghost of a demand' – *Saturday Review*, quoted in E. Pankhurst, *My Own Story*, as above.

p. 220 'Protest imperative' – quoted in George Dangerfield, *The Strange Death of Liberal England* (Capricorn Books, 1961).

p. 220 'On Friday there will be an unannounced affair' – a letter written but not sent to Ethel Smyth, found in a police raid on WSPU offices, used in the prosecution evidence presented on 20 March 1912. Quoted in Purvis, *Emmeline Pankhurst*, as above.

p. 221 'I walked down the Strand' – Charlotte (Charlie) Marsh, quoted in Marlow, *Votes for Women*, as above.

p. 221 'Brought the country to a state' – Press Association report in *Nelson Evening Mail*, New Zealand, 4 March 1912.

p. 221 'These wild women' – Curzon speaking at a National League for Opposing Woman Suffrage council meeting, June 1914, quoted in Harrison, *Separate Spheres*, as above.

p. 222 'Deplorable proceedings' – letter from NUWSS leader Millicent Fawcett to Liberal government minister David Lloyd George, National Archives, PRO ref: T 172/968b.

p. 222 *The Suffrage Annual and Women's Who's Who (sponsored by Selfridges)* (Stanley Paul, 1913).

p. 224 'Hundreds and even thousands relieved of their decorations' – Thomas Gilbert Pearson, *Adventures in Bird Protection* (D. Appleton-Century Company, 1937).

p. 224 'Hold up of Five Hats' – *New York Times*, 9 January 1914.

p. 226 'To *frustrate the efforts* being made by the Plumage merchants' (italics my own) – *RSPB Twenty-Second Annual Report*, 1912.

p. 226 'I incite this meeting to rebellion' – speech made in the Royal Albert Hall, 17 October 1912, quoted in E. Pankhurst, *My Own Story*, as above.

p. 226 'History will not listen to the plea' – Henry Oldys, quoted in Doughty, *Feather Fashions*, as above.

p. 227 'The acknowledged autocrat of the Union' – F. W. Pethick-Lawrence, *Fate Has Been Kind* (Hutchinson, 1942).

p. 227 'There was something quite ruthless' – Emmeline Pethick-Lawrence, *My Part in a Changing World* (as above).

p. 227 'Are you a Peth or a Pank?' – E. H. Shepard cartoon, *Punch*, 30 October 1912.

35 The Feeding Tube

p. 229 'The first published testimony of forcible feeding' – Mary Leigh was interviewed by her solicitor in prison: *Votes For Women*, 15 October 1909.

p. 230 'Mary Leigh, die-hard militant' – the drum major of the WSPU drum and fife band, Leigh threw a hatchet at Asquith and set fire to Dublin Theatre Royal, among other acts of militancy. Imprisoned and force-fed many times, she was a close friend of Emily Wilding Davidson.

p. 230 'Around 1,000 suffragettes' – Purvis, *Emmeline Pankhurst*, as above.

p. 231 'A human being in the process of being turned into a wild beast' – E. Pankhurst, *My Own Story*, as above.

p. 231 'They prize open my mouth with a steel gag' – letter contained in Home Office file on Sylvia Pankhurst's force-feeding, 18 March 1913.

p. 232 '42 days in 10 imprisonments' – E. S. Pankhurst (who herself that year served 65 days in 9 imprisonments), *The Life of Emmeline Pankhurst* (Laurie, 1935).

p. 232 'She was heartrending to look on' – Smyth, *Female Pipings in Eden*, as above.

36 Dumb Creation

p. 235 'O kind fate that cast me for this glorious role' – letter to Ethel Smyth from Emmeline Pankhurst, quoted in Smyth, *Female Pipings in Eden*, as above.

p. 236 'It's just like going to a lunatic asylum' – Lloyd George in conversation with C.P. Scott, Editor of the *Manchester Guardian*, 2 December 1911. T. Wilson (ed.), *The Political Diaries of C. P. Scott 1911–1928* (Collins, 1970).

p. 237 'Like a great octopus, stretching out its tentacles' – *The Times*, 2 June 1913.

p. 240 'The love of dumb creation' – *Surrey Mirror*, 15 August 1913.

Part 5 – Power

37 At War

p. 243 'The hatchet is buried' – quoted in Purvis, *Emmeline Pankhurst*, as above.

p. 243 'Brighton Dome two weeks' hence' – Emmeline spoke on 21 September 1914, Christabel on 8 September. They arrived back in London on 6 September, according to a French newspaper. Cited in Mitchell, *Queen Christabel*, as above; Purvis, *Emmeline Pankhurst*, as above.

p. 245 'Written at the request of former president Theodore Roosevelt' – Mrs Humphry Ward, *Six Letters to An American Friend* (Smith, Elder & Co, 1916).

p. 245 'From a peak of 20,000 pre-war workers' – Stein, *Plumes*, as above.

p. 247 'Market in wild bird feathers' – in 1915, 648,000lbs of wild bird feathers were imported (Hansard). The Board of Trade banned plumage imports from 1917.

p. 247 'Simply loved by the patients' – *Surrey Mirror*, 29 November 1918.

p. 248 'I'm not nursing soldiers' – *Daily Sketch*, 27 January 1915.

p. 248 Mrs Pankhurst's lecture tour of Russia ran June–October 1917. Purvis, *Emmeline Pankhurst*.

38 The Ballot Box

p. 249 'Gone for ever,' – *Aberdeen Daily Journal*, 16 December 1918.

p. 250 'It was almost ridiculous' – Millicent Garrett Fawcett, *The Women's Victory – and After: Personal Reminiscences, 1911–1918* (Sidgwick & Jackson, 1920).

p. 250 'It was wildly illogical' – Strachey, *The Cause*, as above.

p. 251 'Almost a quarter of women over 30' – 22 per cent were excluded. In total 8,400,000 women were enfranchised, representing 39.6 per cent of the electorate. Harold L. Smith, *The British Women's Suffrage Campaign 1866–1928*, (rev 2nd ed., Pearson Education Ltd, 2007).

p. 251 'Don't be frightened' – *Aberdeen Daily Journal*, 16 December 1918.

p. 252 'Early round the constituency . . . I want to vote for Mrs Ashby . . . the housework' – *Birmingham Gazette*, 15 December 1918.

p. 252 'Better and earlier' – *Aberdeen Daily Journal*, as above.

p. 252 'The newly formed Women's Party' – launched 1917, at the dissolution of the WSPU.

p. 252 'The Women's Party is much needed, gentlemen' – quoted in Mitchell, *Queen Christabel*, as above.

p. 252 'Splendid work during the war' – Lloyd George to Christabel Pankhurst, December 1918.

p. 252 'The best possible seat should be got' – Lord Northcliffe to William Sutherland, aide to Lloyd George, 31 October 1918. Both quoted in Mitchell, *Queen Christabel*, as above.

p. 253 'Glorified governess' – Mitchell, *Queen Christabel*, as above.

p. 253 'That's what comes of trusting to your men friends' – quoted in Harrison, *Separate Spheres*, as above.

p. 253 'Very great victory . . . cannot be said to be a fair one' – *National News*, 10 March 1918.

p. 254 'I don't feel much more important' – *The Diary of Virginia Woolf, Volume 1, 1915–1919*, entry on the passing of the Suffrage Bill, January 1918. Quoted in Naomi Black, *Virginia Woolf as Feminist* (Cornell University Press, 2004).

39 But What Do Women Care?

p. 256 'Feather merchants are exchanging congratulations' – *The Globe*, 31 December 1919.

p. 258 'I don't like buying hats' – *The Diary of Virginia Woolf, 1915–1919*, as above.

p. 258 'The Plumage Bill' by Virginia Woolf, *Woman's Leader*, 23 July 1920.

p. 258 'The woman question, and the bird question' – Reginal Abbott, 'Birds Don't Sing in Greek: Virginia Woolf and "The Plumage Bill"', in Carol J. Adams and Josephine Donovan (eds.), *Animals and Women: Feminist Theoretical Explorations* (Duke University Press, 1995).

p. 260 'Does it matter in the least to the birds' – Mrs Meta Bradley, letter to the *Woman's Leader*, 30 July 1920.

p. 260 'I am not writing as a bird' – Woolf's response to both H. W. Massingham and Mrs Meta Bradley, 'Letter to the Editor', the *Woman's Leader*, 6 August 1920.

p. 260 'Male apparatus' – E. Pankhurst, *My Own Story*, as above.

p. 261 'Nonsense, Winston' – quoted in introduction to J. P. Wearing (ed.) *Bernard Shaw and Nancy Astor: Selected correspondence of Bernard Shaw* (University of Toronto Press, 2005).

p. 261 'Immediately started probing' – letter to *The Times*, 26 October 1920.

p. 261 'Astonishing . . . formidable' – Alan Haynes, 'Murderous Millinery: the struggle for the plumage act, 1921', *History Today*, Vol. 3, 3 July 1983.

p. 262 'The privilege of leadership' – Holbrook Jackson, letter to *The Times*, 26 March 1920.

40 Etta and Emmeline: Two Portraits

p. 264 'The English Tea Shop of Good Hope' – Purvis, *Emmeline Pankhurst*, as above.

p. 264 '"Flapper" is the popular press catch-word' – *Punch*, 30 November 1927.

p. 265 'Genial, kindly manner' – Nick Hammond is quoting Frank Lemon's obituary from *Bird Notes and News*, July 1935.

p. 265 'There was no point in fighting Mrs Lemon' – Alexander, *Seventy Years of Birdwatching*, as above.

p. 266 'Keep your temper!' – Purvis, *Emmeline Pankhurst*, as above.

p. 266 'Encouraged vagrancy' – Surrey History Centre, Ref. BG9/11/26–29: minute book of Reigate Board of Guardians, Feb 1916–March 1930; various minute books for Reigate Poor Law Union committees.

p. 267 'Potent factors in my education as a militant' – E. Pankhurst, *My Own Story*, as above.

p. 267 Max Nicholson, *How Birds Live* (Williams & Norgate, 1927).

p. 267 'Monster of contradictory ideals' – Max Nicholson, *Birds in England: An account of the state of our bird-life, and a criticism of bird protection* (Chapman & Hall, 1926).

p. 267 'Group of amateurs . . . sharply separating . . . informed judgment' – Max Nicholson, *The Art of Bird-watching* (H. F. & G. Witherby, 1931), which led to the founding of the British Trust for Ornithology (BTO).

p. 267 'The fatuous notion that a bird is merely a "dicky-bird"' – *RSPB Twenty-Second Annual Report*, 1912.

p. 268 'Our idea is to make friends with everybody' – Emmeline Pankhurst to Margaret Bates, 5 February 1927, quoted in Purvis, *Emmeline Pankhurst*, as above.

p. 269 'Adored' – Smyth, *Female Pipings*.

p. 269 'Like a poor and unwanted step-relation' – secretary Nellie Hall-Humpherson to biographer David Mitchell, 12 June 1984, quoted in Purvis, *Emmeline Pankhurst*, as above.

p. 269 'The second reading' – the Representation of the People (Equal Franchise) Bill passed its second reading in the House of Commons by a majority of 387 to 10. On 2 July 1928 it became law: all women could now vote at 21.

p. 269 'Seven women MPs' – Nancy, Viscountess Astor; Mrs Mabel Philipson; Katharine, Duchess of Atholl; Rt Hon. Margaret Bondfield; Arabella Lawrence; Rt Hon Ellen Wilkinson; Gwendolen, Countess of Iveagh, CBE.

p. 269 'She looked very old and frail' – quoted in Purvis, *Emmeline Pankhurst*, as above.

p. 269 'If only I could get back my strength' – Smyth, *Female Pipings*, as above.

p. 269 'Given birth to a son out of wedlock' – Sylvia Pankhurst's lover was the Italian anarchist Silvio Corio.

p. 270 'Who had read the tabloid headlines'– '"Eugenic" Baby Sensation. Sylvia Pankhurst's Amazing Confession', *News of the World*, 10 April 1928.

p. 270 'A dead general in the midst of a mourning army' – *Daily Mail*, 19 June 1928.

p. 270 'Donated to the National Portrait Gallery' – in 1929 by the Emmeline Pankhurst Memorial Committee.

41 The Coup

p. 274 'Snapped a link . . . very real sense' – 'An Appreciation By Alderman', *Surrey Mirror*, Friday 26 April 1935.

p. 274 Baxter and Rintoul were involved in establishing the Scottish Ornithologists' Club in March 1936.

p. 274 'All of whom were female' – Nicholas Hammond on the RSPB in Ronald Hickling, *Enjoying Ornithology* (T & A. D. Poyser, 1983).

p. 275 'Dragon' – obituary in *Ibis* magazine, 1980. Phyllis Barclay-Smith went on to become editor of the *Avicultural* magazine and build up the International Council of Bird Preservation. In 1958, she became the first woman to receive an MBE for work in conservation, and in 1971 was made CBE.

p. 275 'Supreme charge' – letter to *The Field* from RSPB Council member Philip Gosse, 25 January 1936. Gosse calls for a 'keen, intelligent secretary, a young man for preference'.

p. 277 '"Shut up"... ironic laughter ..."Unless otherwise determined" . . . "valuable and active"' – *Bath Chronicle*, 13 March 1936.

p. 280 'Mother of the Birds' – *Surrey Mirror*, 17 February 1939.

p. 280 'Proprietorial . . . a real roasting' – Dr Gilbert Clark, *A Victorian Naturalist Odyssey: The Life and Times of Professor John Henry Salter DSc (London) 1862–1942* (Xlibris, 2013).

p. 282 'Fulminator in chief' – T. Samstag, *For Love of Birds*, as above.

Epilogue

p. 283 'It rests with women themselves' – Lizzy (Louise) Lind af Hageby, 'Women as Humanitarians': address given to the Humanitarian League's AGM, June 1910. Quoted in Hilda Kean, *Animal Rights, Political and Social Change in Britain since 1800* (Reaktion, 1998).

p. 283 'What does it mean' – Mary Midgley, *Animals and Why They Matter* (The University of Georgia Press, 1983).

p. 284 'Holy terror' – Mike Everett, RSPB staff member 1964–2003, author interview November 2015.

p. 284 'Husbands and wives were even forbidden' – Nick Hammond, interviewed November 2015. He recalled the rule was in place when he joined the RSPB in 1966.

p. 284 'I've been in organisations where it felt like a male bastion' – Baroness Young, Chief Executive of RSPB 1991–8; author interview November 1915.

p. 287 'Poverty . . . bad government' – *Britannia*, 1 March 1918. Edited by Christabel Pankhurst, *Britannia* was the old *Suffragette* magazine revamped as a patriotic war paper.

p. 287 'More comfort, more leisure and better pay' – *Britannia*, 8 February 1918.

p. 287 'The biggest in the feather trade . . . to lose on all points' – National Archives, LAB2/1630, 'Ostrich and Fancy Feather and Artificial Flower Trade Board, A. Botibol and Co.'

SELECT BIBLIOGRAPHY

ARCHIVES CONSULTED

British Library, London

RSPB, Sandy, Bedfordshire

Museum of London

London Metropolitan Archives

LSE: The Women's Library

Museum of Brighton

Worthing Museum

Wardown Park Museum, Luton

SELECT PRIMARY SOURCES

A. J. R. (ed.). *Suffrage Annual and Women's Who's Who* (London: Paul, 1913).

A MEMBER of the Aristocracy. *Manners and Rules of Good Society* (Frederick Warne, 1892).

BALLIN, Ada S. *The Science of Dress in Theory and Practice* (Sampson Low, Marston, Searle, & Rivington,1885).

BILLINGTON-GREIG, Teresa. *The Militant Suffrage Movement: Emancipation in a Hurry* (Frank Palmer, 1911).

BOOTH, Charles. *Life and Labour of the People in London*, 17 vols, 1889–1903. Especially: *First series, Poverty: Trades of East London Connected with Poverty* (London, 1902).

COURTNEY, W. L. *The Soul of a Suffragette & other stories* (Chapman and Hall, 1913).

ESCOTT T. H. S. *Society in the New Reign by 'A Foreign Resident'* (Fisher, Unwin, 1904).

FAWCETT, Millicent Garrett. *The Women's Victory – and After: Personal Reminiscences, 1911 –1918* (Sidgwick & Jackson, 1920).

FAWCETT, Millicent Garrett. *What I Remember* (Putnam, 1924).

FERGUSON, Rachel. *We Were Amused* (Jonathan Cape, 1958).

HAMILTON, Cicely. *Life Errant* (J. M. Dent, 1935).

HORNADAY, W. T. *Our Vanishing Wildlife: Its Extermination and Preservation* (C. Scribner's Sons, 1913).

HUDSON. W. H. *Osprey, or Egrets and Aigrettes* (Society for the Protection of Birds, 1891).

HUDSON, W. H. *Feathered Women* (Society for the Protection of Birds, 1893).

HUDSON, W. H. *Lost British Birds* (Society for the Protection of Birds, 1894).

HUDSON, W. H. *The Trade in Bird Feathers* (Society for the Protection of Birds, 1898).

MARTIN, Annie. *Home Life on an Ostrich Farm* (G. Philip & Son, 1890).

MEARNS, Andrew. *The Bitter Cry of Outcast London: an Inquiry in the Condition of the Abject Poor* (1883; this edition, Frank Cass & Co Ltd, 1970).

MUDIE-SMITH, Richard (ed.). *Handbook of the Daily News Sweated Industries' Exhibition* (Burt, 1906).

NEWTON, Alfred. 'The Zoological Aspect of Game Laws,' Report of the British Association for the Advancement of Science 1868, 108–9.

NICHOLSON, Max. *Birds in England: An Account of the State Of Our Bird-Life, and a Criticism of Bird Protection* (Chapman & Hall, 1926).

NICHOLSON, Max. *How Birds Live* (Williams & Norgate, 1927).

PANKHURST, Christabel. *Unshackled: The Story of How We Won the* Vote (Hutchinson, 1959).

PANKHURST, Emmeline. *My Own Story* (Eveleigh Nash, 1914).

PANKHURST, E. S. (Sylvia). *The Life of Emmeline Pankhurst* (Laurie, 1935).

PANKHURST, E. S. *The Suffragette Movement – An Intimate Account Of Persons And Ideals* (Longmans, Green and Co., 1931).

PEEL, Dorothy Constance. *The Hat Shop* (John Lane, 1914).

PEEL, Dorothy Constance. *Life's Enchanted Cup: An Autobiography 1872–1933* (John Lane, 1933).

PETHICK-LAWRENCE, Emmeline. *My Part in a Changing World* (Victor Gollancz, 1938).

PRICE, Julius Mendes. *Dame Fashion, Paris– London (1786–1912)* (Sampson Low, Marston & Co 1913).

RICHARDSON, Mary. *Laugh a Defiance* (George Weidenfeld & Nicolson, 1953).

SALT, Henry. *Animal's Rights* (G. Bell & Sons, 1892).

SALT, Henry (ed.). *The New Charter, a Discussion of the Rights of Man and the Rights of Animals: Humanitarian League* (G. Bell & Sons, 1896).

SALT, Henry (ed.). *Killing for Sport: Essays by Various Writers* (G. Bell & Sons, 1914).

SHAW, George Bernard, Salt, Henry and others. *Forecasts of the Coming Century by a Decade of Writers* (Labour Press, 1897).

SMYTH, Ethel. *Female Pipings in Eden* (Peter Davies, 1933).

STRACHEY, Ray. *The Cause: A Short History of Women's Movement in Great Britain* (G. Bell & Sons Ltd, 1928).

SWANWICK, Helena. *I Have Been Young* (Victor Gollancz Ltd, 1935).

SWIFT, Deborah. 'The Tyranny of Fashion.' *The Englishwoman*, 4.11, 135–43 (1909).

TUCKWELL, Gertrude (ed.). *Women in Industry from Seven Points of View* (Duckworth, 1908).

SECONDARY SOURCES
I: THE NATURAL WORLD

ADAMS, Carol J. and Donovan, Josephine (eds.). *Animals and Women: Feminist Theoretical Explorations* (Duke University Press, U.S., 1995).

BARBER, Lynn. *The Heyday of Victorian Natural History 1820–1870* (Cape, 1980).

BARCLAY-SMITH, Phyllis. 'The British Contribution to Bird Protection.' *Ibis*, Vol. 101, Issue 1, 115–22 (1959).

BOARDMAN, Robert. *The International Politics of Bird Conservation: Biodiversity, Regionalism and Global Governance* (Cheltenham, Edward Elgar, 2006).

CLARKE, Richard. *Pioneers of Conservation: The Selborne Society and the Royal SPB* (University of London, 2004).

DAVIS, Janet M. *The Gospel of Kindness: Animal Welfare and the Making of Modern America* (Oxford University Press, 2016).

DORSEY, Kurkpatric. *The Dawn of Conservation Diplomacy: U.S.–Canadian Wildlife Protection* (University of Washington Press, 1998).

DOUGHTY, Robin W. *Feather Fashions and Bird Preservation: a Study in Nature Protection* (Berkely, University of California Press, 1975).

EVANS, David. *A History of Nature Conservation in Britain* (2nd ed., Routledge, 1997).

GATES, Barbara T. *Kindred Nature: Victorian and Edwardian Women Embrace the Living World* (University of Chicago Press, 1998).

GREGORY, James. *Of Victorians and Vegetarians: The Vegetarian Movement in Nineteenth-Century Britain* (I. B. Tauris, 2007).

HAYNES, Alan. 'Murderous Millinery: the Struggle for the Plumage Act, 1921.' *History Today*, Vol. 33/7, 26–31 (July 1983).

KEAN, Hilda. *Animal Rights: Political and Social Change in Britain Since 1800* (Reaktion, 1998).

LANSBURY, Coral. *The Old Brown Dog: Women, Workers and Vivisection in Edwardian England* (University of Wisconsin Press, 1985).

MANNING, Aubrey and Serpell, James. *Animals and Human Society: Changing Perspectives* (Routledge, 1994).

MCIVER, Stuart B. *Death in the Everglades: The Murder of Guy Bradley, America's First Martyr to Environmentalism* (University Press of Florida, 2003).

MOORE-COLYER R. J. 'Feathered Women and Persecuted Birds; the Struggle Against the Plumage Trade c.1860–1922.' *Rural History*, 11/1, 57–73 (2000).

MOSS, Stephen. *A Bird in the Bush* (Aurum Press, 2004).

ORR, Oliver. *Saving American Birds* (University Press of Florida, 1992).

PREECE, Rod. *Animal Sensibility and Inclusive Justice in the Age of Bernard Shaw.* (UBC Press, 2011).

RITVO, Harriet. *The Animal Estate* (HUP, 1987).

RUFFER, Jonathan Garnier. *Big Shots* (Debrett's Peerage Ltd, 1977).

SAMSTAG, Tony. *For Love of Birds: the Story of the RSPB* (RSPB, 1988).

SHEAIL, J. *Nature in Trust: the History of Nature Conservation in Britain* (Blackie, 1976).

SHRUBSALL, Dennis (ed.). *The Unpublished Letters of W. H. Hudson, the First Literary Environmentalist, 1841–1922* (Edwin Mellen Press, 2006).

SPIEGEL, Marjorie. *The Dreaded Comparison: Human and Animal Slavery* (Mirror Books, 1996).

STEIN, Sarah Abrevaya. *Plumes: Ostrich Feathers, Jews, and a Lost World of Global Commerce* (Yale University Press, 2008).

TAYLOR, Antony. "Pig-Sticking Princes": Royal Hunting, Moral Outrage and the Republican Opposition to Animal Abuse in 19th and early 20th Century Britain.' *History*, Vol. 89, 44 (2004).

THOMAS, Keith. *Man and the Natural World: Changing Attitudes in England 1500–1800* (Allen Lane/Penguin Books, 1983).

TURNER, E. S. *All Heaven in a Rage* (Michael Joseph, 1964).

II: FASHION AND INDUSTRY

ADBURGHAM, Alison. *Shops and Shopping 1800–1914: Where and in What Manner the Well-Dressed Englishwoman Bought her Clothes* (George Allen & Unwin, 1964).

ASHELFORD, Jane. *The Art of Dress: Clothes and Society, 1500–1914* (National Trust, 1996).

ATKINSON, Diane. 'The Politics of Homework: with Special Reference to Spitalfields, 1880–1909'. (PhD Thesis). (University of London, 1994).

BEATON, Cecil. *The Glass of Fashion* (Weidenfeld & Nicolson, 1954).

BERMAN, Marshall. *All That is Solid Melts into Air* (Verso, 1983).

BUCKLEY, Cheryl and Fawcett, Hilary. *Fashioning the Feminine: Representation and Women's Fashion from the Fin de Siècle to the Present* (Tauris, 2002).

CANNADINE, David. *Ornamentalism: How the British Saw Their Empire* (OUP, 2001).

CARTER, Michael. *Putting a Face on Things: Studies in Imaginary Materials* (Education Enterprises, 1997).

CLARK, Fiona. *Hats* (Anchor Press, 1982).

COFFIN, Judith. *The Politics of Women's Work: The Paris Garment Trades, 1750–1915* (Princeton University Press, 1996).

COLLINS, Michael. *The Likes of Us: A Biography of the White Working Class* (Granta, 2004).

COURTAIS de, Georgine. *Women's Headdress and Hairstyles in England from AD 600 to the Present Day* (Batsford, 1986).

CRANE, Diana. *Fashion and Its Social Agendas: Class, Gender and Identity in Clothing* (University of Chicago Press, 2000).

CUNNINGTON, Cecil Willett. *The Perfect Lady* (M. Parrish, 1948).

CUNNINGTON, Cecil Willett. *Handbook of English Costume in the Nineteenth Century* (Faber & Faber, 1959).

DALY, Nicholas. 'The Demographic Imagination and the Nineteenth-Century City: Paris, London, New York.' *Local Government Studies*, Vol. 42 2, 351–2 (2016).

DAVIDOFF, Leonore. *The Best Circles: Society, Etiquette and the Season* (Croom Helm, 1973).

DAVIES-STRODDER, Cassie, Lister, Jenny and Taylor, Lou. *London Society Fashion 1905–1925: The Wardrobe of Heather Firbank* (V&A Publishing, 2015).

ENSTAD, Nan. *Ladies of Labor, Girls of Adventure: Working Women, Popular Culture, and Labor Politics at the Turn of the Twentieth Century* (Columbia University Press, 1999).

FRIED, Albert and Elman, Richard (eds.). *Charles Booth's London* (Hutchinson, 1969).

GERNSHEIM, Alison. *Fashion and Reality* (Faber & Faber, 1963).

GIBSON-BRYDON, Thomas R. C. *The Moral Mapping of Victorian and Edwardian London. Charles Booth, Christian Charity, and the Poor-but-Respectable* (McGill-Queen's University Press, 2016).

HALL, Peter Geoffrey. *The Industries of London Since 1861* (Hutchinson, 1962).

HOLCOMBE, Lee. *Victorian Ladies at Work: Middle Class Working Women in England and Wales 1850–1914* (Newton Abbot, David & Charles, 1973).

KAPLAN, Joel H. and Stowell, Sheila. *Theatre and Fashion: Oscar Wilde to the Suffragettes* (Cambridge University Press, 1994).

KOVEN, Seth. *Slumming: Sexual and Social Politics in Victorian London* (Princeton University Press, 2004).

KYNASTON, David. *The City of London: Golden Years, 1890–1914. Vol. 2* (Chatto & Windus, 1994).

LAVER, James. *Taste and Fashion: From the French Revolution to the Present Day* (G. G. Harrap & Co. Ltd, 1945).

LYSACK, Krista. *Come Buy, Come Buy: Shopping and the Culture of Consumption in Victorian Women's Writing* (Ohio University Press, 2008).

MCDOWELL, Colin. *The Literary Companion to Fashion* (Sinclair Stevenson, 1995).

MCCREESH, Carolyn. *Women in the Campaign to Organise Garment Workers, 1880–1917* (Garland, 1985).

MCDOWELL, Colin. *Hats: Status, Style and Glamour* (Rizzoli, 1992).

MICHIE, R. C. *The City of London: Continuity and Change, 1850–1990* (Macmillan, 1992).

NAVA, Mica. 'The Cosmopolitanism of Commerce and the Allure of Difference: Selfridges, the Russian Ballet and the Tango, 1911–1914.' *International Journal of Cultural Studies* 1, No. 2, 163–96 (1998).

NEFF, Wanda Fraiken. *Victorian Working Women: A Historical and Literary Study of Women in British Industries and Professions, 1832–1850* (G. Allen & Unwin, 1929).

PENRY JONES J. 'Feathers.' *Port of London Authority Monthly*, 33 (April 1958).

RAMAMURTHY, Priti. 'Why is Buying a "Madras" Cotton Shirt a Political Act? A Feminist Commodity Chain Analysis.' *Feminist Studies* 30, No. 1 734–70, (2004).

RAPPAPORT, Erika Diana. *Shopping for Pleasure: Women in the Making of London's West End* (Princeton University Press, 2000).

RICHARDS, Thomas. *The Commodity Culture of Victorian England: Advertising and Spectacle, 1851-1914* (Stanford University Press, 1990).

ROBERTS, Mary Louise. 'Gender, Consumption and Commodity Culture', *American Historical Review*, No. 203, 817–44 (1993).

SCHMIECHEN, James A. *Sweated Industries and Sweated Labor – The London Clothing Trades, 1860–1914* (University of Illinois Press, 1983).

SCHWEITZER, Marlis. *When Broadway was the Runway: Theater, Fashion and American Culture* (University of Pennsylvania Press, 2009).

SMITH, F.B. *The People's Health 1830–1910* (Weidenfeld and Nicolson, 1990).

STEDMAN JONES, Gareth. *Outcast London: A Study in the Relationship Between Classes in Victorian Society* (Clarendon Press, 1971).

WALKOWITZ, Judith R. *City of Dreadful Delight: Narratives of Sexual Danger in Late-Victorian London* (University of Chicago Press, 1992).

WHITAKER, Wilfred. *Victorian and Edwardian Shopworkers* (Newton Abbot, David & Charles, 1973).

WILLIS, Frederick. *A Book of London Yesterdays* (Phoenix House, 1960).

WILSON, Elizabeth. *Adorned in Dreams: Fashion and Modernity* (Virago, 1985).

III: WOMEN AND SUFFRAGE

BATTISCOMBE, Georgina. *Queen Alexandra* (Constable, 1969).

BUSH, Julia. 'British Women's Anti-Suffragism and the Forward Policy, 1908–14.' *Women's History Review*, 11:3, 431–454 (2002).

BUSH, Julia. *Women Against the Vote: Female Anti-Suffragism in Britain* (Oxford University Press, 2007).

CAINE, Barbara. *Victorian Feminists* (Clarendon, 1993).

CHRISTENSEN NELSON, Carolyn (ed.). *Literature of the Women's Suffrage Campaign in England* (Broadview Press, 2004).

CRAWFORD, Elizabeth. *The Women's Suffrage Movement: A Reference Guide 1866–1928* (University College London, 1999).

DANGERFIELD, George. *The Strange Death of Liberal England* (Capricorn Books, 1961).

ELLENBERGER, Nancy W. 'The Transformation of London "Society" at the End of Victoria's Reign.' *Albion*, Vol. 22, 640–1 (1990).

FARAUT, M. 'Women Resisting the Vote: A Case of Anti Feminism?' *Women's History Review*, 12/4, 605–21 (2003).

GULLACE, Nicoletta F. '"The White Feather Girls": Women's Militarism in the UK.' www.opendemocracy.net (published 30 June 2014).

HARRISON, Brian. *Separate Spheres: The Opposition to Women's Suffrage in Britain* (Croom Helm Ltd, 1978).

JOANNOU, M. 'Mary Augusta Ward (Mrs Humphry) and the Opposition to Women's Suffrage.' *Women's History Review*, 14/3&4, 561-80 (2005).

LEWIS, Jane. *Women and Social Action in Victorian and Edwardian England* (Stanford University Press, 1991).

LIDDINGTON, Jill. *Rebel Girls: How Votes for Women Changed Edwardian Lives* (Virago, 2006).

LIDDINGTON, Jill and Norris, Jill. *One Hand Tied Behind Us: The Rise of the Women's Suffrage Movement* (Rivers Oram, 2000).

MITCHELL, David. *Queen Christabel* (Macdonald & Jane's, 1977).

NIELD CHEW, Ada. *The Life and Writings of a Working Woman, Remembered and Collected by Doris Nield Chew* (Virago, 1982).

PUGH, Martin. *The March of the Women: A Revisionist Analysis of the Campaign for Women's Suffrage, 1866–1914* (Oxford University Press, 2000).

PUGH, Martin. *The Pankhursts* (Allen Lane, 2001).

PURVIS, June. *Emmeline Pankhurst: A Biography* (Routledge, 2002).

ROLLEY, Katrina. 'Fashion, Femininity and the Fight for the Vote.' *Art History*, Vol. 13, Issue 1, 47–71 (March 1990).

ROSS, Ellen. *Slum Travelers: Ladies and London Poverty, 1860–1920* (Berkeley, 2007).

SMITH Harold L. *The British Women's Suffrage Campaign 1866–1928*, Rev. 2nd ed. (Pearson Education Ltd, 2007).

TICKNER, Lisa. *The Spectacle of Women: Imagery of the Suffrage Campaign, 1907–14* (Chatto & Windus, 1987).

WHITE, Cynthia. *Women's Magazines 1693–1968: A Sociological Study* (Michael Joseph, 1970).

Acknowledgements

Much has changed since this book was first published as *Mrs Pankhurst's Purple Feather* in 2018, the year that Britain celebrated the centenary of women – some women – gaining the right to vote. It was a year of fresh story telling, of fresh challenges to the conventional narrative. Forgotten characters such as Etta Lemon began to nudge their way into the mainstream and, finally, onto the covers of books.

I'm delighted to report that Etta Lemon is also back on her perch at The Lodge, RSPB headquarters. That gimlet-eyed portrait in oils has been exhumed from the attic, restored, reframed and now hangs in pride of place opposite Etta's great champion, the naturalist W.H. Hudson. Etta Lemon now figures in the society's roll call of important figures. Her picture is on the website. She has begun to take her rightful place.

RSPB founder Emily Williamson has become a genuinely iconic figure since the discovery of that photograph. We live in an age of images. Emily's clear-eyed gaze, now shared on social media, has brought a more urgent focus to the story. In 2019, a crowd-funded plaque was unveiled at her house in Didsbury by her great great niece, the bird scientist Dr Melissa Bateson. A bronze statue of Emily is now intended for Fletcher Moss Park, her former garden, with the aim of inspiring the next generation to value nature and to understand the power of activism. My thanks to the RSPB's new CEO, Beccy Speight, for her enthusiasm and support for this campaign, also to Nic Scothern for recognizing the galvanising power of an Emily statue. For expertise and dynamism I'm grateful to have Andrew Simcock on board, the man responsible for bringing a statue of Emmeline Pankhurst to Manchester in 2018.

Emily founded her modest Society for the Protection of Birds by rallying her friends and asking for a simple pledge. I hope that this statue campaign will also prove a catalyst for change, with every small contribution counting. www.emilywilliamsonstatue.com

Researching this book of invisible heroines and vanished trades would have been impossible without the generosity of a great many specialists and enthusiasts. For help resurrecting Alice Battershall's world, thanks to archivist Julie Melrose at Islington Local History Centre. For letting me examine the feathers and hats: Martin Pel at the Museum of Brighton, Tim Long at the Museum of London, Mary Miah at Wardown Park Museum, the curators at the V&A Clothworkers' Centre and, in America, conservator and feather fanatic Carlos Benevides at New York Vintage. For fascinating thoughts on feathers and adornment, thanks to Edwina Ehrman, Curator of Textiles and Fashion for the V&A.

Now to the feather fight. I gained access to the RSPB archives at Sandy thanks to librarian Elizabeth George. Former chief Executive Mike Clarke put the society's history in context; his predecessor, Barbara Young, was refreshingly candid. Author and long-serving RSPB staffer Conor Mark Jameson has been a patient and interested sounding board. Former long-timers Mike Everett, Ian Dawson and Nicholas Hammond were frank and unguarded: I hope not too unguarded.

Looking for Etta Lemon led me first to Neil Rhind, President of the Blackheath Society, and then to Tim Lemon, a generous source of images and anecdotes on the family. In Redhill and Reigate, local historian Sean Hawkins was prompt and assiduous. Catherine Hutchison let me into Hillcrest, both her own and the Lemons' home. Rhona Elstone of Surrey History Centre combed the archives for Lemons, suffragists and Antis.

Eliza Phillips was traced with help from Paul Sowan of the Croydon Natural History & Scientific Society. We have yet to find a photograph, but Hugo Blomfield (RSPB South East) has since found her weathered gravestone in Brompton Cemetery, and John Davis (RSPB Croydon) has identified where her house once stood. A memorial is in discussion.

In Didsbury, Manchester, on the trail of Emily Williamson, Alan Hill – keen birdwatcher and Chair of the Friends of Fletcher Moss Park – has given his ongoing support. Nicola Schofield's play on Emily, *Flight*, made me see it all anew and in situ. And I am very grateful to the late Professor Patrick Bateson FRS and his family for sending me images of Emily: an exciting moment. I wish he could have read this book.

The bird fraternity showed interest, enthusiasm and not *too* much suspicion. My thanks to the venerable, late James Fergusson Lees, to Mark Avery, Stephen Moss and Robert Lambert. For the female birder's perspective, Lucy McRobert. Errol Fuller gave me information on exotic birds, dead and extinct; he also passed my book to Sir David Attenborough who, to my elation, wrote back.

A handful of academics have helped keep me on track. Mrs Pankhurst's biographer, June Purvis, was very generous, as was Diane Atkinson on suffragettes and home workers, and Hilda Kean on suffrage and animal rights. Beverley Cook, at the Museum of London, shed light on the purple feather; Elizabeth Crawford filled in gaps on all things suffragist. My thanks also to Alison Light, John Carey, Jane Ridley, Clair Hughes, Merle Patchett and Jane Whetnall.

For invaluable help with the book's structure, I'm grateful to Graham Coster (who first alerted me to the RSPB's origins), Joanna Swinnerton and my husband, Nick Glass. Most of the writing was done in the former home of suffragist Muriel Matters (1877–1969) – for which privilege, huge thanks to the team at St Mary in the Castle, Hastings.

At Aurum, many thanks to my paperback editor Katie Bond for instantly grasping that Etta Lemon was the revelation, and for encouraging a rethink on the cover. I imagine Etta would have tutted with gruff modesty, before taking issue with any mistakes – all my own.

Finally, a salute to the memory of my meticulous researcher Beryl Holt (1943-2019), keen birder and Chair of Berkswich History Society. Beryl always thought that Etta Lemon was the real heroine of these pages – and she was right.

Index

Picture Credits

p.1 Above: © Bateson family archive, below: © The Lemon family archive;

p.2 Above: © Granger Historical Picture Archive / Alamy Stock Photo from The National Child Labor Committee Collection by Lewis Hine. Below: © National Portrait Gallery, London;

p.3 Above: Courtesy of Luton Culture, © Luton Museums, centre: Gift of Susan Dwight Bliss, 1937, courtesy of The Met, below: © Chronicle / Alamy Stock Photo;

p.4 Above: © Mary Evans Picture Library, below: © Chronicle / Alamy Stock Photo;

p.5 Above: © National Portrait Gallery, London, centre: Photo by Hulton Archive/Getty Images, below: Photo by W. and D. Downey/Hulton Archive/Getty Images;

p.6 Above: © The Lemon family archive, below: Courtesy of Sean Hawkins;

p.7 Reproduced by permission of Surrey History Society;

p.8 Above: Courtesy of Hancox Archive, below: © Pictorial Press Ltd / Alamy Stock Photo;

p.9 Above: © Museum of London; below: Courtesy of Getty;

p.10 Above: © Chronicle / Alamy Stock Photo, below: © Heritage Image Partnership Ltd / Alamy Stock Photo;

p.11 Above: © PA/PA Archive/PA Images, below: © Heritage Image Partnership Ltd / Alamy Stock Photo;

p.12 Above: © GL Archive / Alamy Stock Photo, below: © RSPB (rspb-images.com);

p.13 Above: Courtesy of the State Library of Victoria, below: Courtesy of the Library of Congress, LC-DIG-ppmsca-27739;

p.14 Above: © Museum of London, centre: Photo by Hulton Archive/Getty Images, below: © Art Collection 3 / Alamy Stock Photo;

p.15 Above: © Heritage Image Partnership Ltd / Alamy Stock Photo, centre: © Illustrated London News Ltd/Mary Evans, below: Photo by © Hulton-Deutsch Collection/CORBIS/Corbis via Getty Images;

p.16 Above: Courtesy of Ian Dawson, below: Granger Historical Picture Archive / Alamy Stock Photo.